PEACE IN THE AGE OF *CHAOS*

THE BEST SOLUTION FOR A SUSTAINABLE FUTURE

INSTITUTE FOR
ECONOMICS
& PEACE

PEACE IN THE AGE OF CHAOS

THE BEST SOLUTION FOR A SUSTAINABLE FUTURE

STEVE KILLELEA

One man's journey to measure and understand a sustainable world

Hardie Grant

BOOKS

Published in 2020 by Hardie Grant Books,
an imprint of Hardie Grant Publishing

Hardie Grant Books (Melbourne)
Building 1, 658 Church Street Richmond,
Victoria 3121

Hardie Grant Books (London)
5th & 6th Floors
52–54 Southwark Street London SE1 1UN

hardiegrantbooks.com

A catalogue record for this book is available from the National Library of Australia

Peace in the Age of Chaos: The Best Solution for a Sustainable Future
ISBN 9781743796757

Publishing management by Courtney Nicholls
Edited by Bernadette Foley
Cover and text design by Kate Slattery
Typeset by Megan Ellis
Cover image by iStock/Jo Wing Ying
Printed and bound in Great Britain by Clays Ltd, Elcograf S.p.A.

About the author

Steve Killelea is the founder of the internationally renowned global think tank the Institute for Economics and Peace (IEP). He is regularly quoted in the media on subjects ranging from terrorism to conflict and is also a sought-after international speaker. His funding of the IEP was recognised as one of the 50 most impactful philanthropic gifts in Australia's history by a coalition of Australian Foundations in 2013. He has been recognised as one of the world's 100 most influential people on reducing armed violence. In acknowledgment of Steve's deep commitment to peace, he has twice been nominated for the Nobel Peace Prize.

Contents

INTRODUCTION

A journey begins

Like so many people, I look at the world and realise that our leaders and our institutions are out of step with the needs of our times. Many hold attitudes that are outdated or, worse, they are undoing what little positive action is being undertaken. We are all enmeshed in our ecological and societal systems and dependent on them for our very survival. Yet the rapid pace of change in the world is causing these systems to decay. It is estimated that the biomass of all mammals on the planet comprises of 60 per cent livestock, 36 per cent human and only four per cent is all other mammals. This is clearly unsustainable.[1]

Imagine that all of the life on the planet is a tapestry, beautifully woven, intricate and exquisite in detail. Now imagine your role in relation to the tapestry. Is it to continue to weave and enhance it with loving care, or to take to it with a pair of scissors, indiscriminately cutting it? Put simply, we would all hope that our lives have a positive impact, but our collective actions can hardly be seen that way. We are simply shredding the tapestry of our existence.

More through luck than anything else, my own personal journey has provided me with insights and a strategy that can offer a new and original approach to alleviating and helping to solve many of the intractable problems that humanity is facing.

I am what some people would call a 'self-made man', successful in business and other pursuits as well. But I do not necessarily feel self-made. Much of my success has come about by chance. Those chances could have easily fallen to others, but what really sets me apart are the circumstances

---

1 Olivia Rosane, 'Humans and Big Ag Livestock now account for 96 percent of Mammal Biomass', EcoWatch, 23 May 2018, accessed at www.ecowatch.com/biomass-humans-animals-2571413930.html

surrounding me. I have worked hard, but as far as I can see no harder than a subsistence farmer in northern Kenya. It is also true that I have spotted successful business openings, but who is to say that given the same opportunity a young Syrian entrepreneur wouldn't have been just as nimble? I've taken risks, but they are nothing compared to the risks that many Afghans take every day going to work.

I feel lucky because I was born in a prosperous country where I could take advantage of opportunities as they arose. I had loving parents who were always there for me, and I was fortunate to live in an environment where the conditions were right for me to flourish. This is not true for the majority of people in the world.

But most of all, I have been part of a peaceful society. Because without peace, all the hard work, vision and opportunity would most likely have been overwhelmed by the essential struggle to survive. Peace is the single most important factor in enabling people to reach their full potential.

My journey towards understanding peace started almost by accident with my family foundation, The Charitable Foundation, which works with the poorest of the poor. This took me to many war zones and near post war zones. It became obvious to me that violence and poverty were linked, but more importantly, I realised that understanding what creates peace is very different from understanding the causes of violence, or even how to stop it.

I quickly realised that these insights were not only relevant to the poor, but to all societies, including those in the most developed countries.

Given our global challenges we need new ways of thinking. The Institute for Economics and Peace, which I set up, became a vehicle to do this. What's more, the factors that create highly peaceful societies also create the necessary conditions for many other aspects of life that we think are important to flourish, including prosperity, happiness and sustainability. This is as applicable to developed countries as it is to fragile countries. It is as much needed in the advanced Western democracies, whose institutions are failing, as elsewhere.

For something so important, real peace has been studied surprisingly little. Humanity has spent a lot of time studying war, but mostly to amplify and refine its impact and on occasion to find out how to prevent it. Our leaders often speak about creating peace, but generally they do so through an act of aggression. When we think we are studying peace, generally we are studying how to stop conflict. Peace is not the inverse of war, just as having a healthy body involves more than stopping disease when it occurs.

This book is about my search for a way to study, measure and understand peace. It's also about the practical application of the work, which is gathering momentum at an ever-quickening pace. Our work is now used by the major multilaterals and many governments, and in conjunction with NGOs we have run programs on every continent. It is about the realisation that peace is at the heart of a sustainable future, because without peace we will never be able to obtain the levels of international trust, cooperation and inclusiveness necessary to solve our global challenges.

There has been little work done on understanding what creates a highly peaceful country. If we can't quantify peace, then how can we work out which factors and policies make some countries more peaceful than others? For peace to be sustainable societies need to be resilient to shocks, manage disputes and adapt to changes in their environments. Replicating these and other factors in all countries is vital; otherwise a sustainable future is but a dream. Just look at the national responses to the COVID-19 pandemic, some performed well, others collapsed.

Some of the facts about peace run contrary to what most people think. Peace has mainly been presented in emotional terms. However, it can be measured and through measurement it can be understood. This can drive new approaches to solving one of humanity's oldest challenges – the quest for peace.

Expanding our understanding of peace requires expanding our definition of it. There is an inherent contradiction in how we have traditionally thought of peace. We see it as something positive, but generally define it in negative terms: the absence of violence. This definition is useful, but it has its limitations. It implies that once the guns fall silent, peace has been achieved. This way of thinking doesn't describe what creates a resilient peace, one that will not lapse back into violence.

There is another form of peace, one that is positive, dynamic and inspirational – Positive Peace.

In this book, I hope to show that the elements that create peace can be understood through empirical research. Peace is an active and flourishing state, and what creates peace also creates the optimal conditions for other highly desirable things to flourish. They include stronger performing economies, better ecological performance, happier societies, more inclusion, including gender, and societies that are resilient and more capable of adapting to change.

Finally, I want to show how societies operate as systems. Thinking of societies as systems profoundly changes our conceptualisation of them and how they develop. This new approach or conceptualisation is much needed as it allows us to understand how humanity fits within the larger ecological systems upon which we depend. Our societies are simply one system within larger systems.

Throughout the chapters I have woven my personal journey. This is partly because it helps to explain an entrepreneur's approach to building peace but more importantly, many of my experiences, especially in the developing world, involved peace, sustainability and understanding the totality of our system.

Like many journeys this one was not done alone. There were many helpers along the way, first and foremost my wife, Debbie. Without the freedom and unwavering support Debbie gave me, my work would not have been possible. Often I would get on a plane, as I still do, and travel for three to five weeks at a time, building my thoughts, ideas and the Institute. Never once did she complain. But she was not a passive passenger: she is highly engaged with the family foundation and has accompanied me on many trips, sometimes to very dangerous places.

Tim Johnston, whose helpful hand and skill with words made this book much better than what I could have done alone.

Bobbi Dunphy was instrumental in getting the endorsement of over 100 eminent people for the first launch of the Global Peace Index, while Tim Wise filmed and edited our movie *Soldiers of Peace*, which helped with the development of the early thinking of why peace is important.

Some of the early supporters could see the value of the work well before it caught on, such as Kevin Clements and Scilla Elsworthy. Others who were instrumental in the early success of the work were Chic Dambach and Bill Vendley, both of whom became dear friends.

Like so many successful endeavours in life, our actions are interwoven with the actions of others. We are part of a vast system, not independent of it, and our ability to succeed and thrive is dependent on the actions of countless others who preceded us and those who live around us. We are enmeshed in a system from which we can never extract ourselves. For the few who see it, there are many more who do not.

The dynamics of international relationships, the ecology and politics are in a state of constant change. This is especially true for peace. While writing this book I have had to revise parts of it a number of times as the situation on the ground changed. Islamic State is a good example. In 2016, at the height of their power, it was hard to imagine that their state would be destroyed by the end of 2019. Another example is COVID-19.

Steve Killelea

CHAPTER 1

Finding a new approach

Driven mainly by overpopulation and increasingly impactful advancements in technology, humanity is facing a series of existential threats unlike anything it has experienced before in its short history. Mostly of our own making, the combination of these factors could be fatal for humanity. Countering environmental degradation, pandemics, species extinction, our increasingly scarce stock and overuse of natural resources, population growth, social discontent, and the proliferation of extraordinarily destructive weapons – to name but a few – will require a new way of conceptualising our relationships with each other and the ecosystems we depend upon.

We need to find a new approach that will allow us to adapt in the short term and reverse the decline in the longer term. Despite the diversity of the problems, they share one important characteristic: they cannot begin to be solved without collaboration. And neither collaboration nor adaptability are possible without peace.

To put it simply, without peace we will never achieve the level of trust, cooperation and inclusiveness necessary to solve these challenges. Therefore, peace is a prerequisite for the survival of society as we know it in the 21st century. In the past, peace may have been the domain of the altruistic, but in this century it is in everyone's self-interest. Peace is central to a safe and productive society.

For decades the concept of peace has suffered from association with the utopian anti-establishmentarianism of the 1960s. Critics point out that trying to put flowers down the barrels of the guns of groups such as the Islamic State is as effective as attempting to hold back a tsunami. Peace advocates, at best, were seen as being impractical and irrelevant to real-world issues and at worst as being socially destructive. Moderate advocates of peace, in their efforts to be relevant, shrivelled the concept of peace so that its meaning was little more than security, and it was epitomised by phases such as human or personal security. The concept of peace as something that is thriving, positive and fulfilling for the human spirit was all but lost. When I started working on peace I was counselled not to use the word 'peace', especially in Washington, as my work would not be taken seriously.

The desire to live in a safe, sustainable and prosperous world is universal. I believe it is achievable if we use a more expansive understanding of the concept of peace. It is a peace that is practical, one that recognises threats and believes a level of military action is needed. Many parts of the world are not safe, and therefore the military is a necessity; similarly, violent criminals do need to be locked up. However, it is possible to lessen the number of wars and reduce the number of criminals.

I believe peace, when properly defined, is the first fundamental human right that makes all other rights possible. The right to life, liberty and the pursuit of happiness, to use the examples enshrined as 'unalienable rights' in the US Constitution, will remain forever out of reach in the absence of peace.

The most common definition of peace is the absence of violence or conflict, which is also referred to as Negative Peace. The problem with this definition is not that it is wrong, but that it is incomplete and leads to many misconceptions of how peace can be achieved. Much of the work that has been done under the banner of Peace Studies has in reality been conflict studies. Trying to understand peace by studying war is like trying to understand what it is to be healthy by studying illness: it might help us to understand how to cure a particular sickness, but will tell us little about how to stay healthy and avoid illness in the first place.

For me, this conundrum became painfully clear on a visit to Goma, which lies on the northern shore of Lake Kivu in the Democratic Republic of the Congo (DRC), and is one of the most violent and geographically unstable places on earth. When faced with the sort of conflicts that wrack North East Kivu, the obvious line of inquiry is to ask what makes countries such as the DRC and its neighbours, Rwanda and Burundi, so violent. But it was a more opaque and potentially more interesting question that occurred to me:

Which are the most peaceful countries and what can be learnt from them to help those countries that are not?

This turned out to be a paradigm-changing question.

While it was a simple question to ask, it quickly became clear that there was no simple answer. The first problem was that there was no objective ranking of countries in terms of their peacefulness, thereby making informed comparisons impossible. I was dumbfounded. What struck me was that if a simple businessman, such as myself, could be walking through Africa and wonder which are the most peaceful nations in the world and the research hadn't been done, then how much do we know about peace? In any pursuit, if we can't measure something, how can we truly understand it? And if we can't measure something, then how do we know whether our actions are helping or hindering us in achieving our goals? We simply don't, and peace is not an exception. This realisation started a life-changing journey for me, one in which understanding the positive qualities that sustain and create highly peaceful societies became the central theme of my work life.

The Global Peace Index

In 2007 I launched a project called the Global Peace Index (GPI). It was the first study to rank the nations of the world by their levels of peacefulness, and it led to a plethora of other research. The launch of the Index was very successful, with news articles appearing in over 100 countries. People were particularly interested in their country's relative ranking, generating a lot of discussion about their position in the Index. More importantly, the Global Peace Index provided the base from which to analyse what factors are associated with highly peaceful societies and what sustains them. The result of this research became known as Positive Peace, a new and transformational approach to conceptualising societies.

To undertake further research, I established the Institute for Economics and Peace (IEP) in 2008. The goal of the Institute was to better understand the intersection of business, peace and economics. Also, to discover the factors most closely associated with highly peaceful societies and to ascribe an economic value to changes in peace. At the time of its founding most of the study of peace did not use quantitative techniques. It was more subjective and usually based on the insights of highly experienced individuals and their observations. The focus on the quantitative aspects of peace, mainly through statistics, made the Institute unique.

The starting point in developing the Global Peace Index was to determine what should be included in the Index, and we made the decision to take a broad approach and be as holistic as possible. We expanded the data net to include not just warfare but also internal factors, such as criminality, terrorism and violence perpetuated by the state against its citizens. This led to the inclusion of three domains within the Index – militarisation, conflict and societal safety – each of which could be studied individually but with a commonality between all three. A mother whose son was a homicide victim in Baja California, Mexico, cares little if he was killed for criminal or ideological reasons or as a by-product of civil war or a drug war. His death is still an assault on peace.

After much thought we used 'The absence of violence or fear of violence' as the definition of peace. This was a definition that most people could agree on. It is termed Negative Peace, as it measures the lack of violence, rather than measuring the positive factors that lead to the creation of peaceful societies.

The Global Peace Index ranks 163 countries, which comprehensively covers over 99.7 per cent of the world's population. We did not cover many of the smaller nations as it's too hard to get good data. Some examples of the indicators included in the Index are the number of homicides, the ease of access to small arms, political instability, the impact of terrorism, and military expenditure, to name a few.

What the Global Peace Index did was provide the raw materials to better understand and debate the differences between nations and shed light on their changing levels of peace. When the GPI was founded, I was struck by how important this initiative could be. One simple observation was that politicians became interested in their country's rankings as the publicity for the GPI's findings grew, which in turn affected the perception of their country and their political capital. When countries rose in the Index politicians would claim responsibility, and when they fell their political opponents would use it as a form of attack. As the data became more widely used by risk analysts, changes could also affect foreign investment and tourism, both positively and negatively.

Most pleasingly, the Index highlighted the countries that had improved. Peace is the absence of conflict, so it rarely gets media attention. We had now developed a way to shine a light on the positive, something the media usually does not do. Publishing their improvements helped to raise these countries' profiles, aiding with inbound investment and tourism, thereby further improving their prospects for greater peace.

In some ways the timing of the Global Peace Index was opportune. Because of the wars in Iraq and Afghanistan, their poor execution and in some instances the downright lies to rationalise them, there was growing public thirst for better approaches to international peace. That created an audience ready for our work.

Much of the debate on peace is muddied by misperceptions about both the nature of violence and how to create peace. This is partly because most politicians do not understand peace. They do understand aggressive responses to threats that are popular with their citizens and often confuse these with peace. This is simply because in most instances they are ignorant of what truly creates peace.

There is, for example, the idea that we live in an exceptionally violent era, epitomised by rampant terrorism and the huge refugee flows of recent years, both of which are true. However, the data uncovers a much more nuanced and complex situation. In the decade to 2019, 81 countries deteriorated in peace, while exactly the same number of countries improved, pointing to how finely balanced peace has actually been. If the Middle East were taken out of the list of countries, then the world would have increased in peace over the decade. Much of the lost peace of that decade has been due to the West's inability to solve some of the wars that it started. At the time of writing this book, the Afghanistan War had been running 18 years and the war in Iraq 16 years.

When viewed over millenniums, violence has been declining, almost since the dawn of time, as Steven Pinker pointed out in his book *The Better Angels of Our Nature.*

Establishing an empirical baseline helps build a solid argument to propagate a true understanding of what creates a peaceful society. Because without this how can we address the broader societal impulse to counter violence with more violence? It's a natural human reaction. While there are justified wars, and nations need to support a level of military spending and policing capacity to maintain security, all too often fighting for peace is exactly the oxymoron it sounds like. In part this is fuelled by our system. The media is driven by the negative, based on the assumption that negative news sells better than positive news. This creates a perception of rising crime and insecurity even when it is declining, often leading to unnecessary or even counter-productive responses.

Political leadership and peace

In the early part of the 5th century the Roman military strategist Vegetius wrote, 'The best way to prepare for peace is to prepare for war.' The irony is that this was written just before the collapse of the Roman Empire. How often has this slogan been repeated through the ages and yet it is as false today as it was then.

Our leaders, often ignorant of the long-term dynamics of peace, are, however, all too aware of the short-term electoral benefits of a robust and violent response to threats real or perceived. This leaves them more inclined to take a tough stance than to search for the underlying issues, which if solved would lead to higher levels of long-term peace. In this they are assisted by a deeply ingrained mythology of the heroic war. It tends to gloss over much of the human suffering and ignores the fact that so many wars are costly and in the worst cases self-defeating. The Iraq War springs to mind. There is no greater sacrifice for someone than to lay down their life for their country and it should be remembered and celebrated; however forgetting leaders who start wars on false premises or, worse, for their own gains, sleepwalks us into the next conflict and further human suffering.

These clashes between perception and reality are more frequent than is commonly realised. Policy debates that are not grounded in empirical data tend to degenerate into slanging matches: one perception, when divorced from reality, is as valid as another. We just need to look at the rise of fake news. The growth of fear-based political agendas depends in large part on a politician's ability to bend the facts to their will, if not ignore them entirely.

Incarceration is increasing globally; however, it comes at a high price, both in the direct cost of keeping someone in prison, and in the indirect cost of lost earnings and social disruption, especially to their families. The lost family income can create poverty traps, leading to further problems for society. Violent criminals do need to be locked up but all too often incarceration is counter productive. There are clear examples that other policies do work – in New York, crime, policing and incarceration levels have fallen together. This suggests that other more systemic approaches can reduce the causes of crime and be more effective and less socially damaging than trying to treat the symptoms with imprisonment.

The full facts and the data to back them up are the only effective antidote to poor political narratives, but at the heart of it is a lack of awareness of what actually creates peace. In some ways this is not the politicians' fault, it's simply that they do not understand peace.

The Global Peace Index answers the question: Which are the most peaceful countries? On its own, though, it cannot explain why some societies are more peaceful than others or the societal mechanisms that made them more peaceful. The Global Peace Index can tell us with a high degree of confidence that Norway is more peaceful than the Democratic Republic of the Congo because, in part, Norway had fewer homicides and no conflict compared to the Congo, but not why it had fewer homicides.

The meaning of Positive Peace

Enter the concept of Positive Peace. If Negative Peace represents the *absence of violence* or *the fear of violence*, Positive Peace represents the *attitudes, institutions and structures that create and sustain peaceful societies.* It's a positive expression of an active peace, one that allows humanity to flourish, providing more avenues for more people to achieve their full potential.

The modern origins of Positive Peace go back to Martin Luther King, Jr, who pointed out in a letter from Birmingham City Jail that: 'True peace is not merely the absence of tension; it is the presence of justice.' His comments build on an ancient tradition that understands peace is more than the passive absence of violence. The Old English word *frith* not only denoted an absence of war, but crucially also the nature of social relationships conducive to peace. Pax Romana was less about Rome's ability to suppress revolts within its territory than about creating the conditions for the citizens of the empire to flourish through trade, philosophy and art, among other things.

There are many parallels between physical health and social health. Just as exercise and a healthy diet build physical resilience against the onset of disease, Positive Peace builds social resilience against the onset of violence: it is preventative. Importantly, just as we can measure the healthiness of apparently healthy people by looking at markers such as cholesterol levels or testing their performance on a treadmill, we can measure Positive Peace by measuring aspects such as the levels of governance, the flow of information and the acceptance of the rights of others. Positive Peace, like healthiness, is a measurable phenomenon.

To do this we started by taking the countries at the top of the Global Peace Index to find the factors that are most statistically associated with these countries, by analysing tens of thousands of datasets, indexes and attitudinal surveys against the Global Peace Index. The results were further analysed using statistical techniques to cluster them together, resulting in eight groups that became known as the Pillars of Positive Peace:

Well-Functioning Government
Sound Business Environment
Equitable Distribution of Resources
Acceptance of the Rights of Others
Good Relations with Neighbours
Free Flow of Information
High Levels of Human Capital
Low Levels of Corruption.

These are intentionally broad categories. For the model to work, it needs to be spacious enough to accommodate the cultural, moral, social and political specifics of different peoples, cultures and countries. The formulation of the Pillar *Acceptance of the Rights of Others*, for example, recognises that different cultures have different conceptions of what those rights might be, and avoids making moral judgements based on those differences. What is important is that the social contract is acceptable and inclusive within the moral bounds of that society.

Another example is the *Free Flow of Information*, which is underpinned by a free press but it is more than that. It's also related to the quality of information, the availability of the internet, and the ability to have access to information to accurately price a financial transaction.

One of the important qualities of Positive Peace is that it creates societies that are more resilient. In other words, better capable of adapting to their changing environments. This is especially needed in the 21st century as the planet's ecosystems are stretched by the sheer number of people inhabiting it, pandemics, such as COVID-19, or because of the technological changes reshaping work and the way people interact.

The stronger the Positive Peace the more likely the systems are to adjust to change. These adaptive qualities are not only expressed in avoiding violence, they are the very processes by which societies adjust to new technologies, cultural practices, immigration flows and new-found wealth. For example, countries that are high in Positive Peace have fewer civil resistance movements, these movements last for a shorter period of time, are much more moderate in their aims and are also more likely to achieve them, and are far less violent. On the other hand, low Positive Peace countries have weaker mechanisms, they find it harder to adapt to change, and when challenged by shocks are more likely to violently suppress them, and if they are not suppressed, are more likely to descend into violence.

Since Positive Peace can be used as a measure of resilience and adaptability it can also be used as a predictor of which nations are most likely to adjust to or absorb shocks, whether financial, ecological or societal. It can also be used as a measure of the likelihood of a country descending into violence. Research suggests that countries that performed the most tests for COVID-19 were highly correlated with Positive Peace. There have been numerous attempts to try to create models to predict outbreaks of violence or conflict, but they all suffer from the impossibility of predicting black swan events like terrorist attacks, pandemics or economic collapses. The IEP's conception of Positive Peace largely avoids this problem by assuming that shocks of one sort or another are inevitable. What is important is the ability of the country's formal and informal institutions to withstand those shocks, recover from them and prepare for future shocks. This is the key to understanding risk. When using this approach, it is possible to predict with roughly a 60 per cent accuracy rate the countries that will have the largest falls in peace, up to seven years prior to the falls.

Through understanding the levels of Positive Peace, it is possible to identify and assist fragile states so they do not descend into violence. In 2018, the global cost of violent conflict was well over $600 billion. In that same year only $7 billion was spent on what can be termed peace-building – just one per cent of the cost of conflict. It's hard to create peace without the appropriate investment.

When there are references to money in this book and the currency is not denoted then it will always be US dollars.

The world has a lamentable record of preventing state failure. This is partly because it is difficult to identify fragile states and because expensive interventions are hard to justify to a domestic political audience before there is incontrovertible evidence of failure, by which time it is often too late. Positive Peace gives governments the ability to spot weakness before states descend into collapse. Educating voters about the value of Positive Peace would make timely international interventions more politically acceptable, while the Pillars provide a framework to more effectively deploy scarce international resources.

We are all immersed in a system

As we fleshed out the thinking behind the Pillars, it quickly became apparent that they do not function in isolation. All eight of these Pillars interact with each other, providing a complex set of interactions that cannot be explained through simple concepts of cause and effect. A well-functioning government, for example, will contribute to a sound business environment, leading to increased tax revenues, which then improve the functioning of government. The additional tax revenue could be used to invest in improving human capital, which in turn improves the business environment. This example highlights what can be termed a virtuous cycle, where the interdependency and reciprocal relations reinforce and strengthen each other. This illustrates how it operates as a system.

Similarly, separating the interactions between the free flow of information, corruption and the functioning of government is difficult if not impossible. Each of these factors affect the others to varying degrees. Governments can control corruption and the media, but corruption can influence both, while media affects society's perceptions of the government and perceptions of corruption. Any attempt to untangle the narrow causal chains involved in these actions and inter-reactions quickly fails in the face of extreme complexity. The solution is to apply systems thinking to the problem.

Systems thinking circumvents the complexity by focusing on the flows and relationships within the system, rather than individual actions or events. The application of systems thinking to societies is a recognition that the whole is greater than the sum of its parts, and that emergent phenomena like peace are irreducible.

Systems display a number of traits that help explain why it can be so hard to create change within society. Systems favour the status quo – this is called homeostasis; societies try to maintain a steady state. Think of the human body: when we are hot, we sweat and when we are cold, we shiver. Both are aimed at helping to maintain a steady body temperature. Societies also seek to self-regulate towards a set of patterns. These patterns can be seen through the laws of the country or the moral codes of its citizens. It can be as simple as people understanding they need to queue at a bus stop.

One example can be explained through crime. In an ideal world, if the balance of society is thrown out by a violent crime, it triggers the intervention of law enforcement, which captures, tries and imprisons the criminal. But the reaction does not stop there. The act of apprehending the criminal creates a feedback loop that deters future crime, restoring balance. However, if this feedback loop is dysfunctional then people are jailed who do not need to be jailed, and then other negative outcomes will occur. Their families might be negatively impacted by increased levels of poverty through the loss of the wage or higher levels of stress, creating another set of feedback loops that create further dysfunctionality. Similarly, if criminals are not apprehended then this will lead to more crime, as the feedback loop says crime pays.

The societal tendency to try to re-establish homeostasis is in itself neither good nor bad. But just as it can help prevent negative change, it can also hinder positive change. For example, when vested interests fight attempts to curb the pollution that drives climate change.

The dynamic of homeostasis also indicates that nudging the system in the right direction is more successful in the long run than radical change, which tends to provoke more resistance. Simply put, evolution is more effective than revolution.

The fundamentals of Positive Peace should appeal to both elected and unelected leaders because it makes it more likely that they will be able to fulfil the mutual desires to maintain power and to deliver economic growth. That is because one of the key benefits of Positive Peace is that it promotes the necessary conditions for social and economic progress. We compared the Gross Domestic Product (GDP) growth rates in the 50 countries that had the largest improvements in Positive Peace between 1994 and 2016 with the 50 countries with the largest deteriorations: the improvers had over two per cent per annum higher GDP growth rates on average every year. Extrapolated over decades this creates a substantial difference in wealth. This substantial difference is because Positive Peace creates not only high levels of peace, it also creates an optimal environment for many other things that we think are important to flourish, including business.

Measurement lies at the heart of understanding peace

Unless we have accurate measurements, can we really say that we understand the dynamics of peace, or whether our attempts to steer it in the right direction are working or not?

An example of the value of measurement can be seen in the inclusion of peace in the United Nations Sustainable Development Goals (SDG).

The Goals are designed to 'end poverty, protect the planet and ensure prosperity for all'. The SDGs succeeded the Millennium Development Goals (MDG), which had been in place for the prior 15 years to 2015. The MDGs were successful, even beyond their creators' best expectations. They provided a clear focus for many of the more important aspects of developmental aid. However, many considered the goals too narrow. For example, the MDGs didn't contain anything on disabilities; nor did they contain any mention of peace, which is a prerequisite for achieving the other goals. This was mainly because agreement couldn't be reached on what peace is. At the time the MDGs were developed, peace was generally seen as the absence of conflict. Inclusion was not possible as most nations did not want other nations involved in their internal conflicts or interfering in their internal affairs.

Another benefit of the IEP's work is that we can put a financial price on the real cost of violence, by country and globally. If this was classified as an industry it would be the largest in the world. There are long-standing indexes of military expenditure and the cost of crime, but no one had before attempted to combine these costs and to do it for most of the countries in the world. Since the Global Peace Index had measures of violence for 163 countries, it was possible to develop a model that calculated the cost of violence to the global economy from the bottom up. This model includes not just military spending or the costs of policing, for example, but also the lost lifetime income of the victims of homicide, judicial and incarceration costs, and crucially the lost opportunities if that money had been redirected into more productive avenues of expenditure.

The numbers were staggering. We estimate that in 2018, violence cost the global economy $14.1 trillion, equivalent to over 11.2 per cent of Gross World Product or $1,853 for every man, woman and child on the planet. Even in an ideal world this number would never fall to zero, but it does not have to. As little as a ten per cent saving would be equivalent to the size of the combined economies of Switzerland, Belgium and Ireland every year, or the size of all foreign direct investment in 2019. This would be a substantial boost to the global economy. Even one per cent would be equivalent to all the Official Development Assistance spent in 2019. A 20 per cent reduction in the cost of violence in the United States would more than cover the country's annual budget deficit.

According to figures released by the US Department of Defense's Special Investigator General for Afghanistan Reconstruction, the current Afghanistan War cost the American taxpayer in excess of $104 billion between 2002 and 2014. After adjusting for inflation, this is more than the entire cost of the Marshall Plan, which rebuilt Europe after World War II. Other independent estimates are much higher, Nobel laureate Joseph Stiglitz and Linda Bilmes estimate the total impact of all of the US's wars in the Middle East in that period to be over $5 trillion. It should be noted that these costs do not factor in the cost to the Iraq or Afghan economies, the lost earnings of casualties on either side, or the lost opportunity cost if the money had been spent elsewhere.

There is a myth that the money spent on the military is good for the economy. Its supporters point to the spin-off benefits of military research, such as GPS and microwave ovens, and argue that government spending on the military spurs on economic growth. Numerous researchers have pointed out the obvious fallacies in these arguments. Money spent on civilian research programs will produce larger economic gains because that is what they are designed to do, whereas with military research it can only be a by-product.

Most wars are financed using a combination of debt and higher taxes, which can in the short term mimic an economic stimulus but in the longer term economic growth almost always slows as civilian investment and consumption are squeezed out to fund the war effort. For most wars, including World War II, the Vietnam and Korean wars, GDP growth increased. This has given rise to the argument that war is good for the economy. However, both investment and consumption stalled or declined and were accompanied by higher taxes or higher debt. The benefits were illusionary because using GDP as the single yardstick of success misses many other important points. It counts that which is destructive for society in the same way as what is good. Polluting industries, sickness, gambling, tobacco, dealing with the consequences of crime: all add to GDP. However, even with its shortfalls, it's the standard way of measuring the size of a country's economy and for convenience we use it in the work of the IEP.

For countries in conflict, the economic costs are devastating and long-lasting. We estimate that the economic impact of violence in 2016 was equivalent to 67 per cent of Syria's GDP, 58 per cent of Iraq's GDP and 52 per cent in Afghanistan. The effect lingers: the civil war in Sierra Leone formally ended in 2001, but we estimate that nine years later, annual GDP was 31 per cent lower than if there hadn't been a war.

Enumerating the costs of conflict can be a powerful tool to educate people about the positive benefits of peace, making them more receptive to the policy shifts that will be necessary to create a more peaceful world.

For millennia, the survival of humanity was predicated on its ability to conquer or adapt to natural systems. Historically our natural environment was considered limitless, unpredictable, dangerous and needed to be controlled or tamed, but things have changed. Today we have the power to create or destroy our environment. For the first time in the history of the planet, substances are being found in the geological records that have not occurred naturally, rather they are the products of human activity, such as plastics or radioactivity. It is no longer a boundless world and in many ways it is a sick world. This is a new era and it has ushered in a new age some are calling the Anthropocene. It is less about human versus nature than about competing visions of humanity's relationship with nature. Is the natural world merely a resource to be exploited, or the foundation on which all human existence and its systems are built? For humanity to thrive it must become the sculptor of its habitat, making it sustainable, not just for humanity but for the ecosystems upon which we depend for our survival.

It is encouraging that the latter view is gaining ground but depressing that there has been so little collective action. Environmental challenges, such as global warming, air pollution, eco extinction, ocean acidification and depletion of vital natural resources, cannot be solved by individual action, or even the actions of individual nations. They require global cooperation on a scale unmatched in human history. This will only be possible in a world that is basically peaceful; otherwise the levels of international trust and cooperation necessary to solve these problems will remain beyond our reach.

Terrorism is an excellent example of one of these global problems and it has recently dominated much of the global security debate, but the discussion is plagued with emotionally charged assumptions and high levels of fear. The IEP started producing its annual Global Terrorism Index in 2013 to quantify and clarify some of the issues, with the aim of providing insights through the use of mathematical and statistical analysis. One of the more striking findings was that over 99 per cent of terrorist acts occurred in countries with high levels of state-sponsored terror or that were embroiled in conflict. Of all terrorist attacks, 75 per cent were carried out by four groups, all of which followed a form of Sunni Salafist teachings. Therefore, the link was strong, but there are also many countries with mixed Sunni and Shia communities that were not in conflict. Other factors needed to be present.

As part of this work we produced a short report in 2014 looking specifically at the connections between religious belief and peace and therefore broader than terrorism. We found that factors such as corruption, political terror, group grievances, economic inequality, and political instability are all more significant in determining the levels of peace than the level of religious belief. In fact, the data suggests the opposite might be true: only two of the ten most peaceful countries in 2013, when we did the analysis, had more than ten per cent of their population as self-described atheists.

This is not to say that there isn't a link between religious ideology and terrorism: Salafi Jihadism, the violent ideology that informs groups including Islamic State, Boko Haram and al-Qaeda, has become a lightning rod for other grievances.

Although locking up violent radicals and mounting military action against the larger terrorist groups are essential, they need to be seen within a broader counter terrorism policy. Systems thinking would suggest that unless the underlying causes of terrorist recruitment are addressed, the problem will persist. For example, research by the Combating Terrorism Center at the West Point Military Academy on foreigners who have joined Islamic State shows a significant mismatch between levels of education and occupational status. This indicates that employment discrimination, a symptom of group discrimination or unmet expectations, plays a significant role in driving radicalisation.

Part of the problem is the West's willingness to support despots who produce an illusion of stability through repression. These regimes may be militarily strong, but their repression creates a system that has little adaptive capacity. Once they weaken due to internal fighting or are faced with a major shock, they break and descend into conflict. The repression means that in many cases violent insurrection is the only vector of change that is available. We can see this in Libya, Syria, Iraq and Yemen.

The data also destroys a number of commonly held myths about terrorism. Terrorism is in decline: it peaked in 2014 at almost 33,000 deaths, with the vast majority of them being Muslims. Since then the number of deaths has declined by 75 per cent to roughly 8,000 in 2019 and is expected to fall further since Islamic State has been pushed out of its strongholds in the Middle East and Boko Haram is in decline.

Our research also found no significant correlation between inward migration and terrorism. Nationalist political movements, particularly in Europe and the United States, have consistently opposed resettling migrants and refugees on the grounds that they present a terrorist risk, but the data shows this argument to be flawed: the number of refugees involved in terrorism incidents are minimal. When looking at mass killings in the United States, most are performed by Americans with access to military-grade weapons and with a grudge against some part of society. There is no better example than the mass killings in schools.

Even without the element of terrorism, the displacement and mass movement of people is one of the most pressing issues of our time. In 2018, the UN estimated that almost 70 million people – one in every 115 people on the planet – had been forcibly displaced by violence or persecution.

In the United States and Western Europe, the debate about migration has been dominated not by the suffering of the displaced, the tragedy of war or even how to stop it, but about the threat the migrants may pose. The German government's decision in 2015 to allow a million refugees to settle in the country provoked a strong nationalist backlash and boosted the fortunes of nationalist political parties. Again, the data provides a different perspective. A million immigrants represent approximately one per cent of the German population; Australia has successfully absorbed the equivalent of one per cent of its population in immigrants every year for the past 50 years.

Climate change is likely to increase the risk of mass migration as populations flee prolonged droughts and rising sea levels: think of the impact on the water tables in China or India becoming dry. This would result in hundreds of millions of people on the move, dwarfing recent immigration flows and further stressing ecological and societal systems. Unless we can strengthen our systems, many countries will be overwhelmed, leading to social collapse and possible conflict.

The good news is that the measures of Positive Peace have been improving in more countries than they have been deteriorating. From 2007 to 2018 roughly two out of every three countries improved. However, that was not true for the Attitudes domain of Positive Peace, with roughly two-thirds of the countries deteriorating. Some of the measures used in the Attitudes domain are *Exclusion of Socio-economic Groups*, *Quality of Information*, *Fractionalised Elites*, *Hostilities to Foreigners*, and more. On this domain only two countries improved in Europe, and neither the United States or Canada improved.

These decreases in Attitudes provide the backdrop for the rising fortunes of anti-establishment movements. Notably, falls in working conditions, rising perceptions of corruption in government and reductions in press freedoms have led to these falls in Positive Peace. The biggest fall occurred for the *Acceptance of the Rights of Others* when many European countries were confronted with large flows of refugees.

From a systems perspective, relationships and flows are far more important than events. The Trump effect is not so much about the man but the background systemic conditions that made it possible for him to be elected President. It's the system attempting to adapt to the mismatch between expectations and outcomes. The American dream is vanishing, the idea that anyone can rise to the top through hard work and that prosperity is shared by all is dying. Highlighting this, *Group Grievances* deteriorated by 38 per cent in the United States between 2009 and 2018. *Group Grievances* measures the intensity of the grievances between different groups within society. This can be seen with the African American community and the Black Lives Matter movement, or in the increasing number of both Republicans and Democrats who see the other as being destructive to society. President Trump appears to be the tipping point, ushering in a new set of dynamics both nationally and in international relations.

A new theory of change

Positive Peace, when combined with systems thinking, provides a new and exciting theory of change. It's a new way to conceptualise how societies function and a new approach to solving our most intractable problems. It not only creates peace but also creates an optimal environment for human potential to flourish. Humanity is facing a vast array of challenges, many of which are posing existential threats to our shared future. New problems seemingly appear from nowhere. Who in 2019 would have thought of COVID-19, and its impact on heath systems, supply chains and the economy and how it is straining the resilience of many nations to breaking point?

We have an obligation to pass on a more peaceful world to the next generation. This is not just because they deserve the chance to reach their full potential, but also because unless we can improve our cooperation and collaboration, they will not be able to survive the challenges of environmental change, resource exhaustion, the threat posed by nuclear annihilation or another more deadly pandemic.

We need to build societies that can withstand the inevitable shocks of the future.

This will take a new way of thinking. We need to build the institutional frameworks that allow disagreements within and between societies to be resolved before they become dysfunctional. I believe that if we can achieve this, we will create the optimal conditions for the next generation to thrive, both economically and socially.

CHAPTER 2

Personal experiences in peace

It has been my good fortune to live a life imbued with a wide variety of experiences, adventure and success. I grew up in Beacon Hill, a leafy suburb that overlooks many of the beautiful northern beaches of Sydney. My father, a successful and intelligent man, was an engineer who eventually ended up second-in-charge of the Electricity Authority in Sydney, managing the northern side of the city. He was small, somewhat overweight, but had great personal skills and an extensive repertoire of jokes, none of which I can remember now. My mother was a housewife and dedicated to her kids. My memory of her when I was a child was of a slim, beautiful woman who loved sports and tennis in particular. I like to think I inherited my father's love of problem-solving and interest in people and my mother's competitiveness. They were loving parents and deeply bonded.

My own family life has been equally as good. My wife, Debbie, and I have been together for over 30 years. We have four kids – three girls and a boy – and 11 grandchildren. The marriage has been good for both of us and we have grown throughout it. I think we are better people for it. Although there are many areas where we share interests, such as the family foundation, there has also been a lot of latitude, allowing both of us to pursue our own interests. Without this it would have been difficult for me to build global businesses or create and grow the Institute for Economics and Peace. There have been disagreements, but also considerable accommodation. We have learnt to give each other space to pursue our own needs.

I left school early and set out to explore life. I would put a surfboard and a mattress in the back of my panel van and take off up the east coast of Australia, surfing with friends, sometimes for months at a time. My first overseas trip was to surf Bali. Today it is a major tourist destination with hundreds of thousands of visitors a year, but at that time it was still largely unexplored. In Kuta, now the epicentre of the island's tourist industry, there was only one electric light and that was on a street corner. I would stay with local families for 40 cents a day and ride underpowered motorbikes along dusty roads to unspoiled surf breaks. I remember the feeling of freedom, but also a dawning realisation of how lucky I was.

My time in Indonesia also gave me my first lesson in understanding poverty: how the sick die for lack of a pittance to buy medicine; how a young boy's future is mortgaged by taking him out of school because the family needs his wage to survive; about the daily compromises that stunt ambition and kill hope. I will never forget the fear on the faces of the people I stayed with when someone got sick, even with a simple cold.

When I reached 25, I realised that surfing was great but I couldn't do it forever. At the time I was working as a clerk and felt that I needed to do something more fulfilling. One idea was to take people on adventure travel trips around the world, such as trekking to Mount Everest base camp or white water canoeing down the Zambezi River. I discarded this option, believing that I would have to stop when I was 35 because I would be too old. In retrospect I realise I was wrong; I can see now that I would have created some type of business around it.

My second choice was to be a social worker. I had done some work as a psychiatric nurse and enjoyed helping people, but I worried I would not earn enough money for the lifestyle I wanted. The third choice, inspired by simple curiosity rather than experience, was to learn how to program computers. It was very much an intuitive decision, just something that I wanted to do. I had never seen a computer, let alone programmed one, but I was good at maths. In those days the simplest of computers cost many millions of dollars. Sometimes our best decisions come from within, beyond our conscious mind and knowledge. They are simply intuitive.

When I began, computing was in its early stages. This was well before Microsoft or even mini-computers, for that matter. My first job was with an Australian bank where programmers would only be allowed one punch-card run a day. We would write our code out on a form and send it to the punch-card department, where it would be converted into machine-readable format. We would then check it again to make sure there were no mistakes. The cards would be run through the computer once and we would attempt to work out what, if anything, had gone wrong. It was not until the next day that we would get another try.

It sounds cumbersome now but at the time it was exhilarating. I was working on the frontier of technology alongside some of the brightest minds in that generation. It called for an incredible level of focus, thoroughness and attention to detail. It was a great training ground.

From these rudimentary beginnings I went on to develop a computer program called Enlighten, which became a world-class product. It gave users the ability to look inside some of the most complex computer systems available to see what was actually happening, so that if there was a problem it could be solved quickly before the problem impacted the services. The company eventually ended up listing on NASDAQ in 1990, one of the Exchange's very early entrants. This funded my next venture, Integrated Research, which is now listed on the Australian Stock Exchange. Integrated Research developed highly technical products that worked very close to the operating systems. These programs are called systems management products. The company's success was based on developing code that would be used many times over to solve multiple problems. This allowed the rapid development of products that were faster to market and cheaper to produce than those of the competitors. These products were purchased by organisations such as the New York, London and Hong Kong stock exchanges and managed the switching networks for Visa, American Express and Mastercard, as well as most of the major point-of-sale and ATM networks in the world. The company now has received revenue from roughly 80 countries.

The critical point of difference in both of these ventures was my ability to discover what I call the 'white space' on the canvas: to identify a problem or a need that didn't have an adequate solution. Even if I could not compete in scale with the emerging behemoths such as IBM, HP or Apple, I could identify niche challenges the market had missed and write innovative, user-friendly solutions that gave me an almost unbeatable first-mover advantage. Now, nearly 30 years after its foundation, Integrated Research is still a market leader in its field.

What I derived from my business success was a skill set that included an understanding of the value of listening to customers; managing sophisticated research; communicating the value of its outputs simply; and developing the management skills necessary to run a global operation. These skills are invaluable in my work with peace.

After Integrated Research became successful and having made a considerable amount of money, I decided I should use my skills and resources to help others. I quickly realised that my money would have a much more significant impact overseas than in Australia. Huge sums of money were already being spent on Australia's big issues, most notably the plight of Aboriginal communities, and not necessarily to good effect. My contribution would have been a drop in this vast sea of funds. So I decided to work with the world's neediest.

Debbie and I set up The Charitable Foundation in 2001, although we had been funding projects for six years prior to this. The goal was to work with the poorest of the poor, performing interventions that could be described as substantial and reaching as many beneficiaries as possible.

I was introduced to the world of international development aid by Kevin Gray, the former Treasurer of World Vision Australia. He joined the organisation when it had only ten employees, helping to build it up into one of the country's major charities. Kevin is an extremely good person and one of the most charitable people I have met. A tall, skinny man with a love for marathons, he is also a veteran of the Vietnam War. He has strong Christian values and is dedicated to trying to make the world a better place.

In the mid-1990s, Kevin took me on my first visit to Laos, which at the time was still a closed country. It was communist, totally rural, and it felt like life had changed little in a millennium. Today much has changed and it's a popular tourist destination, but then access required special permits and there were almost no other Westerners there. The first project we undertook together was to provide clean water. We supplied pumps that gave more than 30,000 people access to drinkable water for the first time. It was a transformative experience for all. We reduced the mortality rate for children under five, one of the worst in Asia, from 18 per cent to 12 per cent. Also, we were able to knock out about a third of the diseases, because they were water-borne. It was all done for under $20 a head. I was hooked. It is hard to describe how motivational it was to see the benefits.

When I look back on the charity Debbie and I founded all those years ago, I am struck by the number of people it has helped. One of the practices that we set up right from the beginning was to record the number of direct beneficiaries helped by each of the projects, adopting a cautious approach to counting so that we would not overestimate. At the time of writing the figure is over 3.8 million people. It is a truly staggering number.

Gulu

My involvement in development aid through the charity's work in many ways exposed me to the horrors of war, setting in motion a deep questioning of why such brutality exists. These experiences and questions were instrumental in forming my approach and motivation in helping to create a more peaceful world.

One of the most moving and impactful events on my journey towards peace occurred in Gulu, in northern Uganda. This experience left an indelible mark on my consciousness and became a reference point for how indiscriminate brutality can be. The area had been devastated by the Lord's Resistance Army (LRA), the most brutal guerilla group I have ever come across in more than 25 years of development aid. It's worse than Islamic State. The LRA liked to capture boys between the ages of seven and ten. They would often kill as many as one in five before they got back to the camp. If any of the boys were slow or complained, they would be killed. Often the newly captured kids would be forced to beat them to death. If they refused, they too would be beaten to death. This was their initiation into the death cult that is the LRA. The girls they captured were generally aged between 14 and 16, but the vast majority, probably 80 per cent, were boys.

Usually, within 12 months they would be made to raid their home villages and forced to kill someone, sometimes their own parents. That way they would be given no escape route, no home to go back to; their only choice was to fight with the LRA. They were outcast: the LRA was the only 'family' they had left. The boys were used as fighters while the girls and young women had a different value. They became wives, cooks and porters to the commanders. On one of my trips I met an LRA commander who had six wives, who were still with him. He had done a deal with the Ugandan army so that he, along with his troops, would surrender, providing they found him employment. They were taken into the Ugandan army.

During that time, Debbie and I were to have an experience that will stay with us for the rest of our lives. It was so unsettling we could not talk publicly about it for almost a decade. It was a graphic illustration of just how difficult the circumstances are in violent societies, the impossible choices they involve, and how deep the emotional trauma can be.

We had decided to fund a project rehabilitating child soldiers who had escaped from the LRA or been captured by the Ugandan army. One of the aspects of the rehabilitation process was to find a mentor who would help them overcome their trauma by listening to their stories, offering practical advice and assisting their re-integration into society. Mentoring was risky; given the chance, the LRA would kill mentors if they could. We admired their courage. None of them were paid; they did it out of compassion for the children.

Part of our project review consisted of meeting one of these counsellors. We were taken to a village that, over time, would become one of the sprawling, squalid camps for the internally displaced which, at the conflict's peak, were home to nearly two million people.

The first time we met Michael, a former schoolteacher who had counselled a dozen or so young survivors, I was struck by his intelligence. Under different circumstances he could have been one of the research developers that I had working for me back in Sydney. We were sitting talking outside Michael's traditional earthen-floor round hut. He suddenly looked up and saw a young woman walking by and called her over. She had arrived in the camp about two weeks earlier, but he had not heard her story. He asked her to share it with us.

Her face was like no other I had seen before. In a soft, subdued voice she started to retrace the last eight years of her life. She had been captured at the age of 16 by the LRA, taken into southern Sudan and given to one of the commanders. She had a child with him, but the child died before the age of one. One day, while the guerilla group was on a raiding trip into Uganda, they were ambushed by the Ugandan army. Caught in the crossfire, she ran for her life but dropped her commander's goods, which it was her job to carry. Her punishment for losing the commander's property was to have her nose and lips cut off. That was what accounted for her disfigured face.

She longed to escape but opportunities were few and far between, and the LRA kills anyone who tries, or is even suspected of trying, to flee. Eventually she saw her chance and managed to escape, but although she was free of the LRA and her tormentors, she was broke, hungry and stranded hundreds of kilometres from home, somewhere in the lawless lands of southern Sudan – an area with a bloody history and a fiefdom of competing militias. While struggling to find a way out, she was captured by a Sudanese man who enslaved her. She spent another 18 months with this man, bearing him a child. That child also died within the first year of life.

Eventually, she managed to escape again, this time finding her way back into northern Uganda. Yet again, she was captured by a man; however, because she was in Uganda she did have some options. After a while, she was able to get a letter in the post that eventually found its way to her sister's house. The sister had some meagre resources and she set out to find her. She did not know exactly where her sister was, only the general area, but after three months she found her and arranged her release.

Eight horrible years had elapsed. I tentatively asked her if there was anything she wanted and she immediately responded that she just wanted to go back to school. It dawned on me that all she really desired was to return to the life that she had known before her abduction. But she was 24, and the cut-off age for our assistance program was 21. That is one of the hard lessons of aid. There is only a limited amount of money available and profoundly difficult decisions often have to be made.

We were so moved by the tragedy of her situation that we decided to design an intervention especially for her. The first thing was to help her recover her health, so we arranged for her to undergo a number of health checks. What we found was a young woman whose body was ravaged with multiple diseases. She was suffering from an STD (sexually transmitted disease), tuberculosis, a urinary tract infection and AIDS. We cured what diseases we could and gave her some money to live, but the AIDS was well advanced and ultimately she was beyond our reach. She died some months later from an AIDS-related infection.

It is impossible not to be affected by such experiences; the plight of a single young woman we met for a few short hours amid the dusty squalor of a refugee camp halfway across the world would mould my actions for years to come. It brought home the limitless suffering of the victims of violence, how random violence can be, and the great courage of those people who have nothing to gain from helping but help anyway. Such suffering and heroism usually go unrecorded.

External peace and the mythology of war

The story of the young woman in Gulu shows all too clearly the extreme brutality of civil war, and for that matter all kinds of war. Yet the unfortunate truth is that most cultures have developed a mythology around war, which has in turn become a mythology of violence. Our stories of war often represent a small set of narratives of selfless sacrifice and glorious bravery, rather than a complete picture including other narratives of pain and loss, and seemingly senseless horror. This sanitisation of the real nature of war represents a great challenge to creating a more peaceful world because it hides the true human costs of violence.

In Australia, the prevailing war legend is based around the ANZACs (Australian and New Zealand Army Corps). In World War I, young men – making up a significant portion of Australia's male population – laid down their lives for a cause in which they believed. The first engagement was at Gallipoli in Turkey. This was the first time Australia had gone to war as a nation, having only become a country upon Federation in 1901. This was to become Australia's national day of remembering. Every year on the day of the Gallipoli landing, 25 April, Australia remembers those who have died fighting for their country. We can learn from their stalwart heroism. There is no greater sacrifice than to lay down your life for a cause that you believe in and their bravery should be remembered, but it represents an incomplete account. What is missing is their suffering, the post-traumatic stress of most of the survivors and the way it played out in their lives and those of their loved ones. However, the most glaring oversight is ignoring the mistakes, the bloody mindlessness and at times the stupidity of some of their leaders. By whitewashing key elements of the narrative we risk falling into the trap of repeating the mistakes of the past because we fail to remember it properly. To quote George Santayana, 'Those who cannot remember the past are condemned to repeat it.'

The lessons from Gallipoli are instructive. The Allied powers did not need to make an enemy of Turkey. The Turks had overthrown the Sultan in 1908 and reinstated their constitution; their economy was weak and there was a lot of unrest. They found the Germans too militaristic and they didn't trust the Russians; they felt more aligned with Britain and France. The American ambassador got on well with them, but the British felt differently. A slightly different set of circumstances and an enemy could have been instead an ally. However, Australia, being under the command of the British, followed their orders.

World War I was the first war in which the weapons escalated the scale of the violence in ways that were hitherto unimaginable. Two and a half million soldiers were killed in the first three months. Yet even this was not enough to bring the European leaders to their senses. It was the first unmistakable sign of the power of industrial machinery to kill in a manner that had never been seen before.

What World War I showed is that in the face of such carnage, the habit of leaders is to pursue even more violent options. The Allies, realising that they were fast approaching a stalemate, decided to attack on a new front. They resolved to take Istanbul, sending out an armada to conquer it, and failed. The Turks had limited defences but managed to plant mines in the Aegean Sea. The Allies had gunships that could detect these mines, but in the early stages of the fighting decided to retreat. As a result, a French battleship was torpedoed and sank, and the Turks won the day. The Allies decided to open a new front along the Dardanelles, instructing the Australians and New Zealanders to land at Gallipoli.

The outcome is well enough known. It became one of Australia's greatest military disasters.

Once violence and war take hold, leaders show little capacity to see a route to peace that does not involve more violence. This was even the case when the warring parties were suing for peace at the end of the war, when the killing was supposedly coming to an end. Some of the worst slaughter of World War I occurred in the last two months, when both sides were negotiating the Armistice – 11,000 men were killed or wounded on the last day of the war alone.[1]

There is great self-sacrifice and heroism in war. The level of courage required to take up arms and risk death rarely has any parallel in civilian life. But it is also true that there is no greater waste of life if it doesn't need to occur. I am not a pacifist: I believe some wars must be fought. The Gulf War, the Korean War and the Timor-Leste peacekeeping operation are good examples, but if wars can be avoided then they should be.

Many wars are avoidable or entered into because of a flawed premise, such as the Iraq War, the initial responses in Syria and the violence in Libya. Although these countries were ruled by despots, what has followed is human suffering far beyond what these tyrants inflicted. The cure has proved worse than the disease.

From my perspective it's important to honour those who have laid down their lives for their country, but we must also focus on the mistakes and bloody mindedness of these encounters. Otherwise our war mythologies can never be complete and we will continue to sleep walk into conflicts like Vietnam and the Iraq War. While some wars do need to be fought and appropriate military resources need to be maintained – there are aggressive nations and there are aggressive leaders – too many wars are avoidable.

Why do so many leaders make so many decisions that tend to escalate violence in the name of peace? The answer is simple: they do not know what else to do. This highlights the need for modern leaders to be better equipped to understand what creates peace, rather than relying on violence to create their version of peace.

---

1 Joseph E. Persico, *Eleventh Month, Eleventh Day, Eleventh Hour: Armistice Day 1918*, Penguin Random House, 2007.

Nevertheless, the idea of the heroic warrior lies embedded deep within our subconscious. Soldiers have provided protection through most of human history, but given the challenges facing humanity in the 21st century, and the destructive power of modern weaponry, a new way of avoiding conflict is needed. That new way is Positive Peace.

We need to develop an antidote to the mythology of glorious violence. This is not to argue for pacifism because there will always be violent people prepared to dominate. But we need to develop ways to proclaim the heroism of not only those who fight but also those who seek ways to reduce or avoid violence and seek peace.

Improvements in peace over time

While violence between states retains the potential to be cataclysmic, the level of violence within states is moving in a more positive direction when looked at on a millennial scale, although there has been a worrying escalation over the past decade.

For the past 200 years, there has been a well-documented, long-term gradual improvement in internal violence across the world. Despite the headlines, many countries are now at historically high levels of peace, with military expenditure as a percentage of GDP 30 to 40 per cent lower than during the 1950s and 1960s, and homicide rates in countries such as Japan, Singapore, Austria, Switzerland and Australia are now lower than in any time in the last 50 years.

This is in part because of a change in the perception of violence. Violence that would now be regarded in many societies as abhorrent was once considered everyday. In the 16th century, visitors to Elizabethan London would be greeted by rows of heads on stakes as they sailed up the Thames, something that would be considered barbaric today.

The impact of the Enlightenment movement in the 18th century had a beneficial effect on peace because it established the principle that people have inalienable rights, eventually leading to the abolition of slavery, judicial torture, superstitious killings and other forms of sadistic punishment. The Age of Reason led to many changes in our attitudes, including a revulsion towards the persecution of minorities and the idea that basic human rights should be observed to protect all people against violence. Most countries today would subscribe to this.

Steven Pinker argues in his book *The Better Angels of Our Nature* that although the reduction in violence has been slow and uneven, it has been inexorable.[2] The first stage was the transition from hunter-gatherer or horticultural societies to agricultural civilisations, which brought with them cities and governments. This led to an 80 per cent reduction in the rate of violent death. Next came what Pinker calls the 'civilising process', a 500-year evolution starting in the late Middle Ages that saw a further 90 per cent reduction in the rate of violent death as feudal territories were consolidated into large kingdoms with centralised authority. Progress continued as the development of the infrastructure of modern commerce made trade a more effective means of obtaining resources than war.

There is considerable debate about whether Pinker is right about the long-term reduction in violence when it comes to war, but when looking at interpersonal violence, such as homicides, muggings or state-sponsored torture of its citizens, the improvement is indisputable. It is reasonable to say that, at least in terms of internal peace – that is, peace within a country – there has been a long cycle of improvement, albeit uneven.

Sarajevo and Kasulu

The problem with statistics is that they are just that: statistics. They lack emotional resonance and the personal narratives that allow people to relate to the human suffering they record. Too often, people ignore suffering simply because they cannot or will not emotionally engage. Personal narratives can fill that void. The statistic that 3,700 people died crossing the Mediterranean in 2016[3] has little effect compared to the photo of a weeping father cradling his drowned child, whose body was washed up on a cold pebbly beach after their boat sank fleeing the violence in their homeland.

---

2 Steven Pinker, *The Better Angels of Our Nature: Why Violence Has Declined*, Viking Adult, 2011.

3 UNHCR Staff, 'Mediterranean death toll soars, 2016 is the deadliest year yet', 25 October 2016, accessed at www.unhcr.org/en-au/news/latest/2016/10/580f3e684/mediterranean-death-toll-soars-2016-deadliest-year.html

Beneath all the statistics that we gather at the Institute of Economics and Peace lie a multitude of deeply affecting and powerful stories. For the individuals drawn into these situations, these stories are their world.

There are some experiences that in hindsight I would prefer not to have had, but these experiences have been fundamental in developing my approach to peace, and therefore they are worth recounting.

Debbie and I took a trip down the Adriatic coast of Croatia in 1995. Just before we arrived in Dubrovnik, we ran into someone who said the road to Sarajevo had recently re-opened. It was only a short time after the United Nations had negotiated a ceasefire. We thought we would go there as tourists, and it turned out we were the only tourists in the country. As we were driving to Sarajevo, we passed UN military convoys, travelling in 20 to 100 cars at a time. There were machine-gun emplacements, tanks and sentries guarding all the bridges.

We saw the desolation of the civil war everywhere. For about 80 kilometres every farmhouse and every village along the road had been destroyed, part of the Serbian attempts to cleanse the country of Bosnians. Each one of these tens of thousands of households represented multiple accounts of personal tragedy, a trail of cumulative suffering that brought to mind Robert Burns: 'Man's inhumanity to Man / Makes countless thousands mourn.' Many of the farmhouses were surrounded by landmines, so there was no way back for those who had for generations called these villages home. We couldn't help but wonder what had become of all these people.

We arrived at Mostar, where some of the heaviest violence had occurred. Spotting a highway that provided a very good vantage point over the city, we decided to drive up it. I started to take photos of the blown-out city, especially a historic 12th-century bridge that had been destroyed. Seeing me with my camera, the Muslim civil militia unfortunately mistook me for a Croatian spy. Evidently the vantage point where I was taking photos was the same place from which the city had been shelled.

They did not speak any English and I did not speak any Serbo-Croatian, but Debbie did. Her father was attached to the diplomat service and had served in the Australian embassy in Belgrade. She had spent a couple of years in the country, learning to speak the language fluently. But she could not let on that she knew Serbo-Croatian, because that would have reinforced the impression that we were spies.

The conversation became extremely heated. I showed one man our passports. It wasn't enough. A circular conversation continued, marinating in misunderstanding and rising in temperature with each round. He started shouting and becoming very agitated.

What he wanted were the documents for the car. Eventually he used the words 'car documents' in German, another language Debbie understands. She immediately translated it for me. I then went round and opened the boot in a very confident manner and showed him the rental documents for the car, which we had picked up in Italy. He visibly relaxed and a great big smile broke out on his face. He became our new best friend. One could only imagine what the next steps would have been if he and his colleagues had decided against us. It is possible that we could have been taken away, possibly tortured, then, when they realised their mistake, rather than letting us go they could have disposed of us. War can be filled with all sorts of injustices. The arbitrary nature of decisions, particularly when fuelled with hate, can often be extremely callous.

Once we arrived in Sarajevo, we stayed at the Holiday Inn, which is where the journalists had stayed during the conflict. There was an underground car park, and whenever we went down to get the car we would have a horrible feeling that made our skins crawl. It was almost as if the walls were seeping fear. Two years later, we were watching the movie *Return to Sarajevo*. It's a brilliant film, combining news footage and movie-set acting, such that it becomes difficult to tell what is real and what is acted. It turned out the car park had been used as a shelter from the bombing. Hundreds of people would take cover there, crowded and fearful. Somehow, it still held traces of its terrifying history; I think the fear and suffering had leached into the place. It was an awful reminder of what happens when there is no peace. Places and cultures are shaped by war, and the shadow can hang over them for decades, even centuries.

This trip made me realise that in many ways people are shaped by their experiences. My own experiences led me towards finding peace, but in a different set of circumstances I could have been the man on the hill searching for my enemy.

It is tempting to lose hope when faced with inhumanity on the scale of the Bosnian War, but on my travels I am constantly reminded of the resilience of ordinary people and the ability of their better natures to triumph. Sometimes it takes the worst to bring out the best in people.

Another story I would like to share is set in the Tanzanian province of Kasulu. Although not a war story, it did help me understand how small positive incremental actions can have important flow-on effects. For me it was the beginning of thinking systemically. At the time, Kasulu was one of the poorest provinces in Tanzania, then one of the poorest countries in the world. It lies on the border of Burundi, Congo and Tanzania and is remote even by African standards.

It took a three-hour light-plane flight to get there, landing on a dusty, dirty airstrip with no buildings. There was just a car with a driver waiting to pick us up and another hour-long car ride. We went there to review a project we were running that aimed to encourage locals to refer cases of malaria to a clinic so they could be treated. Kasulu had a particularly high rate of malaria infection, which was killing many children. To get the project moving we had to work with the local traditional healers who often used incantations against evil spirits to heal the sick. Because they were the first port of call when anyone got sick we needed to work with them. If we were going to persuade locals to use Western medicines, we first had to gain the assent of those who dispensed African forms of medicine.

Meetings were set up with about 40 traditional healers. What surprised me was the similarity to many situations in the West. Their main concern was job security: they were worried about the impact of the Western health system on their jobs. It was simply a standard industrial demarcation issue. Eventually we were able to persuade the traditional healers to refer children to the clinic when they saw the symptoms of malaria.

One positive experience came from this. I walked out of one of these meetings and about 300 people had turned up to see what we looked like. It was rare to have Westerners visiting. I scanned the group. They were extremely poor, undernourished and dirty because it was the dry season.

They wore the oldest clothes imaginable. But one young woman stood out. She was better dressed, had a bright face and was smiling. She was like a beacon of light. I asked the project officer who she was, and they said, 'Utopia - do you want to hear her story?'

Utopia was HIV positive and because the local population feared AIDS, she had been driven out of the village some years earlier to live on her own. As the knowledge of AIDS increased, many women would worry that they might be HIV positive and would visit her in the middle of the night to discuss their fears. She was intelligent and acted as a counsellor. Eventually word got out and, as AIDS became better understood, she was able to move back into the village.

Because of the respect for her that had developed over time, the project officer decided to give her the title of 'counsellor'. But he didn't have the money to pay her. When we met I was particularly impressed with her intelligence and friendliness. It was clear she had a special quality so I asked her what she wanted. She replied she wished to set up a shop. I decided to give her $400 to do so. It was another 18 months before I returned and one of the first things I did was look her up, and sure enough, there was the shop, fully stocked. But what blew me away was that she had managed to build a small house for herself from the profit. She was also paying for her sister's education at a Catholic boarding school and was in the process of building a house for her father. The natural resilience of people such as Utopia, supported by small amounts of money, can go a long way to rebuild lives, and like people anywhere in the world they know what they can do best.

Cultural differences that make a difference

One of the more profound aspects of peace is being able to account for different cultural perspectives. Diversity is a much-celebrated phrase today, but often means accepting a narrow set of Western progressive values. This was something I encountered again and again in development, eventually leading to the realisation that for peace to take root it's important to work with the existing values of a society, slowly shaping them and moving towards a mutually agreed vision. I would later realise that this was the concept of path dependency in systems thinking.

From my experience, too many Westerners, but by no means all, in Asia and Africa have little understanding of the peoples and the cultures they are setting out to help. We in the West too often go into these places thinking we are brighter, we know more, and all the recipients have to do is listen and their lives will improve. Yet if the necessary cultural adjustments are not made, failure will always be possible, if not probable. I am as guilty of this as many others. The core of the issue lies in our adherence to one-model-fits-all interventions and relying on narrow actions based on our understanding of the causes and their effects, rather than understanding the system. We tend to think 'Here is a problem, here is the solution' rather than trying to understand the way local systems operate, people's beliefs and their encoded norms, and then tailoring the intervention to fit the circumstances.

Often, broad-based cross-cutting themes developed by Westerners are applied to all their projects with insufficient knowledge of the local beliefs or culture. At times the Western values espoused in these projects are at loggerheads with local morals. Without adjustments to the local circumstances, counterproductive outcomes are highly likely. The road to hell is all too often paved with good intentions.

I once visited a remote village in Myanmar where we were putting in pumps to give access to clean water. The chief and his daughter greeted us some 3 kilometres from the village; my daughter Jennayah had come with me. It was impossible for our four-wheel drive to get in over the last stretch of road, so we came in on a bullock wagon. When we reached the village I was met by the local people, and as had happened many times before, I asked them what they needed most. 'Electricity,' said the chief. From a development perspective this was a great answer, and my eyes lit up. I imagined electricity would allow students to continue studying after they come in from the fields at dusk; it would help women to supplement their income with sewing machines; farmers could pump water up from their wells during drought. But I had been tripped up by my Western views again.

'If we had electricity then we could put lights around the pagoda and that would be very good for our merit,' he said.

I was back to trying to understand the system they lived in. They were Buddhists seeking a better life next time around, therefore respect for the Buddha and his teachings was the best form of merit, and much more important than short-term material gain. Without a true understanding of different cultural perspectives, it is impossible to design appropriate interventions.

One way to make the adjustment in the aid context is to design flexible programs that can be easily tailored to local circumstances, and then focus on local-level initiatives as much as possible. Peder Nygaard Pedersen, the chief executive of our family foundation, The Charitable Foundation, argues that the key to success is the quality of the people on the ground. Peder says:

> We can sit in our offices in Sydney, giving money to other people sitting in an office in Sydney because of a well-written project plan. They give money to people sitting in an office in Nairobi, who then give money to people on the ground in western Kenya. But unless the guy on the ground who goes out to the village gains an understanding of the full cultural dynamics, is fully knowledgeable in their field, and is good at doing it, then the results will be suboptimal. It doesn't matter how good the organisation or project is, or how well it's written, it's the people on the ground doing the implementation which makes the difference between success and failure.
>
> We often have projects where we firstly identify the partner on the ground and then look at what they have previously achieved, what their ideas are, and listen to them to understand how they are going to go about doing it. How well do they understand the culture and the way it operates? Only then do we try to find an Australian charity to work through because it is much less important who the person in the middle is. We travel a lot to get down to the lowest levels of implementation to see for ourselves the difference we are making. If we are not making a difference then we try to understand the cultural dynamics inhibiting the project, then change things or get out.

There is a similar need to make cultural adjustments depending on how peace is perceived. Local conditions matter.

Even in the most advanced Western democracies there are large variations in what is acceptable to say and what is not. In many countries it is important to sound politically correct – it could be to avoid criticising minorities, even when that might not be the honest response – or to avoid expressing angry emotions. This leads to what is sometimes called the Bradley effect, named after African American Los Angeles mayoral candidate Tom Bradley, who lost the election despite a clear lead in polls. Many people were not going to vote for him but felt they couldn't say that. It was also seen in the Trump presidential election and the Brexit campaign, where the polls predicted neither outcome. Trump trailed in the polls and the majority of British people surveyed said they wanted to stay in the EU.

Adapting to the complexities of cultural differences is always a challenge when attempting to design global interventions or make global comparisons. However, that does not mean that global surveys are useless, that global values do not exist or that certain initiatives are not globally beneficial and applicable.

I would argue that Positive Peace helps avoid a lot of these cultural issues. Positive Peace is an empirically derived framework describing what sustains highly peaceful societies. It is also statistically associated with many other things that are associated with flourishing societies. The framework reflects universal human desires that can then be adapted to local customs and values. We have conducted Positive Peace workshops in all the major regions of the world and have held them for leaders, youth and the poorest of the poor. Some of the countries where we have conducted workshops are Uganda, Libya, Thailand, Australia, US, Mexico, Kenya and Zimbabwe. Providing that we do not colour in the detail but talk about the broad framework, the participants arrive at locally appropriate interpretations of their own accord. This allows for the necessary cultural and political sensitivities to be incorporated and therefore respected.

The first large-scale workshop we ran was with Rotary International in Uganda. There were roughly 250 people in attendance, and as it was the first one we were struggling with the format and how to get the messaging across.

I gave the introductory overview of Positive Peace and then opened it up for questions. One of the first questions was cynical: 'Isn't war just a natural state, and besides, if you are on the winning side isn't there a lot to be gained from it?'

The audience broke out laughing. Uganda has a violent history and these people had not arrived at the workshop as peaceniks. I realised this was a make-or-break situation, so I walked up to the guy with the microphone, and asked him how many of his family would he willingly see killed for a slice of power. There was silence. I then addressed the crowd and said that our most basic human desire is to be free of suffering and that war is the ultimate suffering, and asked who wanted to live in those conditions. No one raised their hand. After that the workshop progressed well. In fact, it was so successful that they wanted another one, which was held about a year later. We tracked about a dozen peace projects that sprang from this workshop. The groundwork had been laid, Rotary saw the success and embarked on a global rollout of the program.

Since then many other organisations have launched Positive Peace projects. Many are in conjunction with the Institute, but others are from organisations that have heard of our work, studied it and adapted it to their own needs. One example came from a woman called Irene Santiago, who organises a large women's network which is working on peace in Mindanao, in the southern part of the Philippines. It is the second largest island in the country, and it and the smaller surrounding islands are inhabited by roughly 25 million people. It is also considered the breadbasket of the Philippines, with eight of the ten major agri-exports coming from the region.

Roughly 20 per cent of the population of Mindanao is Moro. The Moro people are a Muslim group that kept up a resistance movement against Spanish, American, and Japanese rule for over 400 years. Their long struggle eventually turned into a war for independence against the Philippine state. In March 2014, the Philippines government and the Moro Islamic Liberation Front signed a peace agreement.

Irene is the Peace Adviser to the mayor of Davao City, providing strategic direction to the local peace-building process called Peace 911, which Mayor Sara Duterte-Carpio describes as 'an initiative to change the pattern of development by using a human-centered approach taking in account cultural diversity social justice and participatory decision making'.[4]

After signing a peace agreement with the communist guerilla army, the New People's Army, the city government put a comprehensive development plan in place. It was implemented in a troubled northern quarter of the capital of Mindanao, Davao, with outstanding results. Positive Peace was used as the basis from which to develop and understand what interventions were needed.

In May 2019, Mayor Duterte-Carpio rang a bell to celebrate 12 months without any violence, the longest period of peace in the city in 40 years. The project has been so successful that it is now being considered as a strategy to be rolled out throughout the rest of the Philippines.

4 A.V. Nudalo, 'Peace 911 launched in Paquibato', *Davao Today.com*, 13 May 2018.

CHAPTER 3

What is peace?

Peace is a word much used and its meaning is generally thought to be self-evident. On closer examination, though, it's an elusive word to define, but without a common understanding of what the word means, finding peace itself becomes even harder.

If we examine its etymology, we find that in the 12th century it had a number of meanings including 'freedom from civil disorder'. It was also related to silence: the quiet that comes with the absence or cessation of war or hostility, or from a personal perspective the absence of negative emotions. The word was derived from the Latin *pax* meaning 'compact, agreement, treaty, the absence of war'. Some etymologies suggest that it replaced the Old English word *frith*, which not only denoted an absence of war, but crucially also the nature of social relationships conducive to peace.

Two things emerge from the word's history. One is that it is associated with something that is not there: silence, the absence of violence or the absence of war. The other is that it is considered to be something good in itself, a primary desire of all humans, and is often compared with the desire for happiness and wellbeing. In this sense peace is an enabler. It's the primary condition that enables people to have a better opportunity to fully flourish. Peace directs energy away from anger, fear and suffering towards more productive pursuits.

Assessing peace is different from measuring other social phenomena. If, for example, one were to examine marriage, one could ask people about their attitudes to marriage, measure divorce rates, and consider the composition of family homes, to give some idea of the condition of the institution.

Peace is more problematic. It is usually taken for granted: it's a background condition and often not perceived, but when it is lost, restoring it overrides all other concerns; only those who are deeply damaged psychologically actually revel in violence and chaos.

There are few attempts to collect statistics about how peaceful people feel. It is only when people are confronted by something that clashes with what they consider peaceful, such as crime, that they become interested. Peace is usually only understood through evidence of social breakdown or negative actions, such as the incidence of violence, homicide rates, corruption, justice denied, and institutional deterioration or decay.

Peace is often associated with happiness, but the two are not identical. It is difficult to be happy without peace, but peace doesn't necessarily mean happiness. One method for analysing happiness is to use measures of wellbeing and institutional capacity, such as educational attainment, childhood mortality or housing quality. The second way is through surveys, asking people if they are happy and why. But this can easily become overly subjective. The answer from a Russian and the answer from a Kenyan may be very different, and a person's answer may vary even within one day.

Happiness can also be bound up with desire, and when put into this context it is hard to characterise happiness as a basic human right. It could be framed as the right to 'the pursuit of happiness', which is the wording in the United States Declaration of Independence. But this is associated with Aristotelian notions of happiness: the pursuit of virtue rather than pleasure. The pursuit of pleasure, such as the taking of drugs, is treated as crime, which then leads to the violence associated with criminal activity and incarceration.

There is a Buddhist saying that in pursuit of happiness, blinded by desire, we destroy the very things that make us happy. This saying could equally apply to peace. Our desire for peace causes actions that on many occasions only lead to further violence. The current crisis in the Middle East is a testament to this. In an effort to overthrow ruthless dictators in countries such as Syria or Libya, many more people have died and suffered than probably would have had these dictators been left in place.

What makes people happy and what they need as a basic condition of living are very different. Nobody, for instance, would seriously talk of the right to eat caviar, or the right to listen to Mozart. Yet this may be what makes someone happy.

Peace, on the other hand, can readily be characterised as a fundamental right. This opens the way for considering peace as something that, when present, creates the essential conditions for the possibility of a flourishing life. Peace is an enabler because without it many of the other things we consider important become more difficult, if not impossible, to achieve. Peace allows businesses to grow, communities and countries to cooperate and individuals to flourish.

The importance of peace has been recognised by the United Nations, which defines it in the Sustainable Development Goals (SDGs) as to: 'Promote peaceful and inclusive societies for sustainable development, provide access to justice for all and build effective, accountable and inclusive institutions at all levels.'[1]

The United Nations definition reflects the mutually reinforcing nature of peace, accepting the rights of others, rule of law, development and the absence of physical violence. People need more than basics, such as food, water, shelter, education and health care. They also need peace, dignity, justice and the opportunity to express their concerns and shape their future. Peace is crucial to ensuring the smooth functioning of government and a robust business environment.

Positive Peace

The Institute for Economics and Peace (IEP) has adopted two definitions to cover two different aspects of peace. The first, the 'Absence of violence or the fear of violence', is what we call Negative Peace – measuring the actual violence and the fear of it. The second is Positive Peace, the 'Attitudes, institutions and structures that create and sustain peaceful societies'. This describes the conditions associated with peaceful countries. As Positive Peace increases, so do a society's prospects of peacefulness. It acts as a lead indicator for future levels of peace. When Positive Peace improves it sets the conditions for improvements in many social factors. Positive Peace is also closely correlated with many other things that societies see as important, such as higher per capita income, stronger business environments, longer life expectancy, better measures on inclusion and better environmental

1 Accessed at unstats.un.org/sdgs/report/2017/goal-16/

outcomes. Therefore, Positive Peace can be seen as creating an optimal environment for human potential to flourish.

Positive Peace is bound up with what should be the true purpose of a society: to create an environment beyond conflict where humanity can thrive. The Positive Peace Index provides a comprehensive snapshot of how a society is caring for the interests of its citizenry.

Peace is also inevitably bound up with politics, and here some very real ambiguities emerge. What is understood as peace in an authoritarian regime would be considered unacceptable in a fully democratic system: what is considered peace in military ruled Egypt would be very different from how it is understood in the Netherlands. Moreover, the perception of peace is often related to specific local circumstances, reflecting the different cultural beliefs, power structures and economies of countries. Additionally, impulses buried deep in our subconscious can affect our sense of peace. The collective consciousness of groups can be affected by events such as genocides, sometimes many centuries old.

Personal peace

Although this book mainly considers large social structures at the level of the nation-state, personal peace is also very important. All power structures in the end are composed of people, and serene leaders are more likely to make peaceful decisions. Similarly, peace is an upward and downward phenomenon: the system influences people and people influence the system. There is also a spiritual dimension to peace, which is expressed in all of the major religions.

One of the greatest writers on peace was Leo Tolstoy, the author of *War and Peace*. He was a truly extraordinary character. Born a serf-owning aristocrat who joined the army as a young man to escape his gambling debts, he transformed and became a committed pacifist. Thousands of peasants lined his funeral procession after he died of pneumonia at a train station trying to escape the last vestiges of his aristocratic inheritance. He came to fame through writing the first novel that viewed the world through the eyes of a child. Until then books had been written about children, but never from a child's perspective. It was a clear demonstration of his ability to perceive phenomena in an original way.

Tolstoy realised that peace had a spiritual dimension that could only be expressed through the individual. History, he said, had been about finding evil and attempting to destroy it, but in the process of destroying evil we become the very thing we are seeking to destroy. He said we have been doing this for thousands of years and without success; therefore, we need to find a new approach: we need to find peace within. His perspective was that only when one has become personally peaceful can one truly create peace in the world. In his own words, 'The kingdom of God is within', and that, in its fullest form, is peace.

This is a profound insight and one that reverberates down through history to the present day. It is paraphrased in simple ways such as 'Peace starts within one's self.' One of the most compelling images from my study of Buddhism is of bodhisattva: individuals so moved by compassion and spiritual realisation that their lives are fully transformed and dedicated to alleviating others' suffering, with little to no thought about themselves. Mahatma Gandhi was one such person.

Tolstoy's *A Letter to a Hindu*, written in 1908, highlighted love – expressed as passive nonviolent resistance – as the only way the Indian people could throw off colonial rule. In 1909, Gandhi and Tolstoy began a correspondence regarding practical and theological applications of non-violence. Gandhi saw himself as a disciple of Tolstoy, with both men sharing a strong opposition to state authority and colonialism. They preached non-aggressive resistance and abhorred violence. They did, however, differ on politics: Gandhi called for political involvement, while Tolstoy did not believe in politics.[2]

Very few of us are Tolstoys or Gandhis, let alone bodhisattvas. We are just ordinary human beings caught in the groove of working or bringing up families, or for too many, merely surviving. Our lives offer only limited choices. However, peace does start with the individual, and even in the most mundane of lives it can be expressed in vivid and compelling ways. We all

2 Martin Burgess Green, *The Origins of Nonviolence: Tolstoy and Gandhi in Their Historical Settings*, Pennsylvania State University Press, 1986.

know people who have an uplifting effect on those around them. We have all felt happier because of some little kindness or sweet words given to us. Simply smiling at people who seem despondent, for example, can be of some benefit. When buying goods, make a friendly comment at the sales counter. Such simple acts of kindness can go a long way towards making other people's lives happier, as well as enriching our own. We can all do little acts of peace.

Personal peace is generally associated with being passive, but it does not need to be so. It becomes much harder in competitive settings when the person you are dealing with is not honest, or is excessively aggressive, or is trying to undermine you with misrepresentations. In the face of dishonesty or aggression, passivity can be counterproductive. One needs to be fully engaged, and at times insistent, in order to create a favourable outcome. For me, personal peace is what I aim to feel within. My approach to these people is, wherever possible, not to have strong negative emotions, nor to mimic their behaviour, and not to budge from the path I think is best. Not being overcome by negative emotions really makes for a clearer head and, therefore, better judgement calls. A peaceful world does not come about by empowering the unscrupulous, but personal outcomes can be enhanced through a level of detached involvement, self-understanding and a positive attitude.

We can all have an impact on peace and our happiness is closely intertwined with how we approach our personal interactions. Personal peace and societal peace are both important and inter-reactive: as individuals become more peaceful so too will the system. But the system through its interactions with individuals will also shape their behaviour, beliefs and their experience of happiness and peace. This can be described as a large mutual feedback loop.

The University of Bradford

About four years after the launch of the first Global Peace Index I was invited to the University of Bradford in the United Kingdom to give a talk on the Institute's work to staff and students in the Peace Studies and International

Development program. About 140 people attended and I was chuffed as this was among the first Peace and Conflict centres in the world and one of the most famous. I was invited by one of the leading figures in academia in the field of peace and conflict, Professor Tom Woodhouse. Over the years Tom and I have become good friends and whenever possible we catch up in Barcelona to watch Messi create his magic on the football field. Tom is friends with the Barcelona Soccer Club Foundation, which has an active interest in peace.

One of the more fascinating examples of how difficult it is to establish new social systems and mechanisms of functioning came from Bradford University. In one of our many conversations Tom related the early years of setting up the program and told me that it had nearly folded. Given that it was new, the program's staff and management decided to take an experimental approach to the way it would be run. They engaged with the students so that the students would decide what courses should be taught. It was a true communal approach aimed at fostering greater inclusiveness. To a degree this was creative and stimulated a lot of new perspectives, but a number of competing ideological perspectives emerged among staff and students, resulting in destructive division and factionalism. The competing ideologies and perspectives included pacifists, Third World Maoists and gay liberation activists, along with others who, for example, saw the need to concentrate on different regions and areas as priorities (the Middle East, Africa, or Northern Ireland).

Each group competed for control of the research and teaching program in order to make it fit with their views of what creates peace. Since the students could decide what courses were going to be offered, the professors ended up being run ragged developing some courses for as few as three students, resulting in classes being too small to be viable and an unsustainable workload for the teachers.

During the early stages of the Bradford program, it did indeed seem that Peace Studies was in danger of proving its conservative critics right, that it was not viable or coherent as an academic area of study. The program was restructured to run as any progressive academic department would be. High academic standards in teaching and well-managed research programs were implemented, and from there it flourished, becoming a leading centre for peace research and education internationally.

This highlights the interplay between the members of the system and the system itself – both affecting each other – and the difficulty of finding an acceptable homeostasis as a new system. Eventually, a well-tried model was adopted. There is an analogy here with Positive Peace. It has been derived from studying what has worked; therefore, adopting what has worked is more likely to be successful.

Tom found the work of the IEP compelling and describes his own career and the work as follows:

> I came into peace research in 1974 when, as a then young academic, I was appointed as a member of the team working under Adam Curle to build up the new Centre for Peace Studies at the University of Bradford. Within the Peace Studies Department, I was the founding Director of the Centre for Conflict Resolution, which became a leading player in connecting peace theory with peace-making practice. Working in this field I saw many exciting initiatives in peace research evolve over the period from the early 1990s, especially in the development of conflict prevention systems and structures.
>
> What I began to realise was that while we developed a lot of understanding about how and why violent conflicts happened, we knew very little about what enabled societies to become sustainably peaceful. It was not until I met Steve and came across the work of the IEP and its pioneering Global Peace Index, followed by the Positive Peace Index, that I saw how exciting and innovative this idea of measuring peace was, especially in giving us new ways of thinking and acting, of connecting theory with practice, and of building on Johan Galtung's original definition of positive peace. Still in its early stages of development, the concepts, methodologies and tools provided by the IEP and its eight Pillar model of Positive Peace provides the most advanced system available to us to understand how to do peace-building.

Peace and the crisis in political leadership

A focus on peace is nothing new. The Code of Hammurabi was written 3,700 years ago in Babylon and is the earliest known legal system. It calls on the king 'to bring about the rule of righteousness in the land, to destroy the wicked and the evil-doers... to further the wellbeing of mankind'. In recent centuries we can see the roots of a more proactive and positive conception of peace starting to develop. The Quakers, founded in the middle of the 17th century, developed their pacifist view from Christ's teachings. They repudiate violence in all its forms and have declined to take up arms in any of Britain's subsequent wars.

The origins of the early peace movements came from two strands of thought. One was the secular Enlightenment, while the other was evangelical religious revivals, which also played a role in the abolition of slavery. In 1795, Immanuel Kant made one of the first attempts to codify the requirements for peace, which he thought included democracy and international cooperation, in his ground-breaking *Perpetual Peace: A Philosophical Sketch.*

During the Napoleonic wars, 16 peace petitions were sent to the British Parliament. The first peace movement in the United States was established in New York around 1815. In the 1840s British women formed the Olive Leaf Circles, which were groups of 15 to 20 women who promoted pacifism. The International Peace Congress was established in London in 1843, and by 1900 it is estimated that there were over 400 peace societies in existence. Many political movements have also used nonviolent action as a transformative agent of change, the most prominent being Gandhism in the first half of the 20th century.

The vast majority of peace movements throughout history have been set up in explicit opposition to governments. They might have been against the established order, but it wasn't until the 1960s, boosted by anger at the Vietnam War, that 'Peace' seemed to become an umbrella term for all forms of anti-establishmentarianism: anti-corporatism, anti-authoritarianism, anti-conventionalism and anti-imperialism, to name a few. It was largely a movement defined by what it was against, rather than what it was for. By the 1980s, peace activism had become associated with far-left politics, anti-globalisation and an anti-capitalist agenda, none of which has an intrinsic role in creating or sustaining peace. Peace Studies moved to the fringes of academia, out of fashion and far from the corridors of power. Attention turned instead to national economic advancement and 'national security' as the route to peace.

In Washington, in the first years of the Global Peace Index, I was continually counselled not to use the word 'peace'. For a long time it was considered a dirty word by many establishment politicians in the West. One of my key aims in setting up the IEP and in writing this book is to move peace back into the centre ground.

When considering the word 'peace', it's important to recognise that peace and national security are not the same thing. Security does create a negative peace up to a point, but too much emphasis on security can have the opposite effect. Both Turkey and Egypt had large increases in terrorism after their respective crackdowns. Deaths from terrorism in Turkey increased by 1,600 per cent after Erdoğan's crackdown in 2015, and in Egypt deaths from terrorism increased by 800 per cent the year after al-Sisi came to power. This can also be seen in America's approach in Afghanistan and Iraq, where it was thought that the overwhelming might of American firepower could defeat anyone. If you believe that sheer military strength is the alpha and omega of your own peace, it makes sense to conclude that you can impose peace on others.

As we have seen, this has turned out not to be true. The phrase 'national security', when used in developed Western economies, often means building or applying force, or supporting friendly or compliant leaders who wield force. But it is far from clear how such policies have made American or European society safer or more peaceful. Indeed, Western interventions in the Middle East have resulted in a deterioration of their domestic peace and destabilised their politics. For one thing, it has galvanised home-grown terrorists. The Paris terrorists referred to what was happening in Syria and Iraq as partial motivation for their atrocities.

These policies have also created millions of refugees, a trend that has had a particularly powerful impact in Europe. Most of those refugees are coming from countries such as Syria, Iraq and Afghanistan: countries that have been destroyed by Western military interventions.

The key question is how could escalating violence in countries such as Syria, Libya and Iraq increase the peacefulness of those countries involved in the fight, such as the US, the UK, Russia and others? What is the link? Or is it simply the case, as General Wesley Clark comments, 'that when the only tool you have is a hammer, then every problem looks like a nail?'[3] It seems more reasonable to conclude that in order to enhance peace, the focus should be on what creates peace, Positive Peace, rather than relying solely on the application of ever-increasing force.

The Iraq War fundamentally altered the global political landscape. The failure to find weapons of mass destruction made many uneasy about the single-minded focus on security. Estimates put the cost of the war at more than $5 trillion, while the intervention created the conditions for further conflict.[4] Additionally, large groups of voters in the US and Europe became suspicious of the underlying motives of their political leaders. People were starting to look for new answers. This created room for groups such as the IEP to explore the nature of peace without being impeded by previous ideological noise.

Meanwhile, politics in democratic societies has been undergoing powerful changes. There is a growing lack of belief in our politicians and political systems.[5] It is perhaps unsurprising that the number of people turning out to vote is falling,[6] or that more and more people in advanced democracies perceive their politicians to be corrupt.[7] The Global Financial Crisis added to the perception of a lack of transparency and increasing political dishonesty. The system has been further damaged by eroding employment conditions among those who have benefited the least from globalisation, and the increasing evidence of money in politics, adding to the growing disenchantment with political processes.[8]

---

3 See Youtube video, General Wesley Clark, 'Wars Were Planned – Seven Countries in Five Years', 11 September 2011: www.youtube.com/watch?v=9RC1Mepk_Sw.

4 J. Stiglitz and L. Bilmes, *The Three Trillion Dollar War*, W.W. Norton & Co., 2008.

5 Edelman, 'Edelman Trust Barometer 2014 Annual Global Study', 2014, accessed at www.edelman.com/insights/intellectual-property/2014-edelman-trust-barometer/about-trust/executive-summary/. It is notable that the politicians of the day remain unrepentant. After the release of the Chilcot Report, Tony Blair and John Howard, in the face of the obvious facts, still justified their actions as if nothing had changed since 2004.

6 International Institute for Democracy and Electoral Assistance, 'Voter Turnout in Western Europe since 1945', 2004, accessed at www.idea.int/publications/voter_turnout_weurope/upload/Full_Report.pdf

7 Susan Rose-Ackerman, *Corruption: A Study in Political Economy*, Academic Press, 2013.

8 Russell Hardin, 'Government without trust', *Journal of Trust Research*, vol. 3, no. 1, 2013, pp. 32–52.

Implied in this alienation is the need for a new type of politics that can find new ways of conceptualising the social contract, making it more transparent and inclusive, especially for the middle and lower classes.

This raises a number of important questions. Although the current batch of politicians can see the issues, they seem incapable of addressing them. Why do only a small minority of political leaders act from a long-term perspective, demonstrating a clear sense of ethics? What can be done to restructure and refresh our institutions and restore their vigour and resilience? How can we create truly peaceful societies?

Most of our leaders' world views are trapped in an earlier age. Misconceived Darwinian ideas of the survival of the strongest continue to dominate their thinking. This underpins many of our conceptualisations of international relations, markets, economic performance and trade. However, in an age where we are all interconnected to an unprecedented degree, these ideas are not only inaccurate, they are becoming counterproductive.

Although most people in Western societies are becoming more distrustful of established political leaders, little emphasis is placed on selecting leaders based on their moral capabilities. Too often political campaigns are about attacking the policies or morals of their opposition, with little regard to truth or even offering an alternative. Those who are most on the offensive are often the least moral. Political parties seldom look to the moral qualities of the leaders they select, while the media seldom reviews the moral backgrounds of candidates. In this sense morals are not so much about how a candidate stands on abortion, sexual preference or feminism, but rather a deeper sense of honesty and working for a common good. Political leaders do need to be skilled in their trade: all the moral principles in the world will be useless without the necessary knowledge and skills. On the other hand, a highly skilled person can be dangerous without the right moral compass.

Will humanity adapt so that we can solve our global habitation challenges, or will we compete, nation against nation, into oblivion? What is required is more of a politics of shared, mutual global interest. Yet few leaders seem able to move beyond political ideologies based on outdated notions of national self-interest and competition between states.

Countering violence with violence

Too little thought is given to the underlying social conditions that cause violence to arise in the first place.

The shortcomings of the tendency to counter violence with more violence are nowhere more apparent than in the United States. The number of guns owned by its citizens is rising steadily, and in recent years police forces have increasingly been equipped with battlefield weapons such as armoured personnel carriers and sniper rifles, yet violent crime has started to rise again after more than a quarter of a century of decline. In some areas, notably the murder of African American men, police are perceived to be part of the problem rather than part of the solution. Some police officers, it seems, are acting with a sense of impunity, and it is revealing that the only cases in which they seem to be found guilty of misconduct are the rare occasions when video footage exists. Police need to be trusted or they risk being seen as a vector of oppression.

In justification for the police in the US, assailants can be heavily armed. When police officers pull citizens over in their cars, they may have concealed weapons. It is true that many police do get shot, which creates a heightened sense of fear, and their first instinct is to protect themselves from death. In 2016 in the United States, 64 police officers were fatally shot while on duty.[9] This risk creates a heightened sense of fear, leading police officers to believe they are protecting themselves from death. Tellingly, the North America region, which consists of the United States and Canada, was the only region to suffer a net deterioration in Positive Peace between 2009 and 2018.

One of the indicators in the United States that has been deteriorating is the level of *Group Grievances*. This measures the level of grievances that arise between social classes, religions or racial or ethnic groups. It is clear that these issues cannot be solved with force.

As citizens become dissatisfied, they are more likely to look for more radical alternatives – as evidenced by the 2016 Presidential election. The

---

9 Melissa Chan, 'Number of U.S. Police Officers Killed on Duty Rises to 5-year High in 2016', *Time*, 29 December 2016, accessed at time.com/4619689/police-officers-killed-2016/.

outcome is that the system becomes less predictable and less stable. Making the police more accountable, although a good measure, will not on its own fix the system. There needs to be a move towards articulating and achieving positive changes that undercut the causes of the grievances so that they do not arise in the first place.

This unpredictability is now being played out on the world stage, with the United States pitting itself against its long-term allies, such as the EU, through the creation of trade disputes. Worse is the unravelling of relations with China. They were deteriorating before COVID-19, but the aftermath of it has seemingly put the countries on a collision course. This is creating further disruption, with ramifications that are currently impossible to foresee.

Another regional dispute with the potential for negative consequences is China's approach to the South China Sea. Little compromise is being sought. Instead, China is taking a competitive win–lose attitude to its neighbours. Where this will lead, we do not know, but it is a retrograde step for the development of international treaties and codes of conduct in the region, as well as helping to fuel an arms race.

The outbreak of the COVID-19 virus triggered a global pandemic the like of which humanity has not seen in a century, further highlighting the need for multi-lateral responses. The toll in lives lost is tragic, but it also comes with a crippling economic cost. This will require unprecedented international coordination, common policies and cooperation. This will prove difficult in a world of rising nationalism and protectionism.

One conclusion from the current political ineffectiveness in dealing with international relations and domestic harmony is that there needs to be new criteria for selecting our leaders. We do not seem to choose our leaders based on their ethics or empathy. The documentary maker Adam Curtis comments that politicians have boosted their power and authority by promising to protect the citizenry from hazily defined enemies.[10] Although this may seem like a promise to establish peace, it is very much oriented towards negative peace: using the threat of state violence to counter the threat of violence

10 A. Curtis, *The Power of Nightmares*, BBC documentary film series, 2004, accessed at www.dailymotion.com/video/x20su5f_the-power-of-nightmares-1-the-rise-of-the-politics-of-fear-bbc-2004_news

rather than attempting to establish systemic changes that instil Positive Peace so that less violence arises in the first place.

Values, globalisation and peace

Values, of course, differ from culture to culture, as well as within cultures. So how can we devise a set of leadership values that are universal and transversal? What is unacceptable in one culture can often be permitted, even admired, in another. Dealing with the world's variety of cultural, religious, secular and spiritual differences looks near impossible at first glance.

The concept of peace, however, is a good starting point for defining such common values. It is a core concern across all regions of the world, and for all major religions and cultures.

What, then, are the fundamental values connected to the sort of political leadership that promotes peace? At first glance, these values are associated with compassion and caring for the wellbeing of all members of society, including the unprivileged, but this is not sufficient on its own. Although compassion is of extraordinary value, and a necessary virtue for leadership, it is not sufficient to ensure effective action. If the action is ineffective, regardless of how caring it may be, it could easily lead to less peace. Competence, which is the knowledge gained, both formally and informally, that can successfully be applied to solve problems or issues, is also needed. Without competence, we are left with only good intentions.

To put it metaphorically, the heart and the mind must be combined to create dynamic and effective action.

This is not how politics is currently conducted in most democracies, let alone in non-democratic societies. Compassion is rarely seen as an attractive political virtue. Leaders tend to be promoted for their toughness, with little thought given to their motivation. The moral issues that generally receive the most attention in the media are areas such as gender, same-sex rights, religious orientation, free-market philosophies or socialist ideals. These moral debates are worthwhile, but they can become lightning rods for underlying division. Such friction has come to characterise how we think about politics. One of the most notable features of politics in many Western democracies is a growing divisiveness, as if the business of governing a state were a battle that can only be won by destroying the values of the opponent, not through constructive and collaborative policy.

Leadership values need to be thought of in a more fundamental and peaceful way. For instance, we could easily ask questions such as: What personal virtues do we desire from our leaders? Individuals who care about others or those who are greedy, power seeking and interested in pursuing their own needs?

Peace in its broadest sense can be used as a transcultural reference point, a benchmark against which to test social initiatives. Will leader *x* or policy *y* strengthen overall peace or weaken it? If we can get that right, the benefits of more resilient, harmonious and prosperous societies will flow naturally from our choices. If we are to use peace as a benchmark, we need to be able to quantify progress or regression. That is where Positive Peace can help.

Peace in an interconnected world

The level of integration and interconnectivity in the globalised world has profoundly changed the peace equation. Policymakers can no longer afford to focus on narrow issues of what is best for their country and its people.

Humankind has been shaped by its environment, but recently – at least in the geological and ecological sense – we have acquired the technology and power to shape our environment for better or worse on an unprecedented scale. This time around it is not nature that is causing mass extinctions or climate change, or altering the composition of the air we breathe, but humans. For the first time in the history of the planet, we are finding non-naturally occurring substances in the geological record, from the rising levels of atmospheric carbon dioxide beginning with the Industrial Revolution, to a layer of radioactive isotopes from the nuclear tests of the 1950s, to plastics that do not break down. The occurrence of these substances has given rise to the Anthropocene era, which many are calling a new geological age dating from the time of humans' impact on the Earth's climate and ecosystems.

Our new power, when combined with the forces of the globalised traffic in goods, technology and information, poses novel challenges. What will be the moral compass guiding these developments and the international system to govern and manage them?

The biggest existential threats facing us, including issues such as climate change and nuclear weapons, can only be addressed by the world working in unison for the common benefit. In today's deeply divided world, we seem to be failing even this basic test. However, just as an appeal to peace can provide the common ground to reframe the issues that cause division within nations, it can be used to reshape the global debate and to provide constructive ways forward.

The combination of interconnectivity and the power of modern weapons means that almost any conflict has the potential to spread and kill hundreds of thousands of people and destroy social and practical infrastructure that has taken decades if not centuries to build. Another global war of the magnitude of World War I or II could set the development of humanity back many generations.

The global challenges we face require cooperation on a scale unprecedented in human history, and peace is an essential prerequisite if we are to solve them. Without an ability to create a world that is basically peaceful we will never be able to create the necessary levels of trust, cooperation, inclusiveness and social equity necessary to address the existential threats we face. Peace is a prerequisite for the survival of society as we know it in the 21st century. In the past peace may have been the domain of the altruistic, but in the 21st century it is in everyone's interest.

Conflict, migration and money

The importance of peace in our globalised, interconnected world is especially evident in three areas: the movement of people, the financial system, and the media, including social media.

Growing refugee flows, largely triggered by violent conflict, have profoundly changed the political landscape in many developed nations. In Australia, concern about asylum seekers has become a bipartisan political obsession. One of the underlying reasons for Brexit was the influence of foreign cultures in Britain. Many British people didn't like the changes.

Across Europe, nationalist movements had gained strength because of the heightened fear of refugees performing terrorist acts, not conforming to social norms, or taking jobs. There are reasons for concern regarding violence, but the vast proportion of refugees are ordinary people fleeing conflict, fearful for their personal safety. When the conflicts cease many will return home.

The European Union is especially troubled, wrestling with ways to deal with the flood of refugees fleeing countries such as Afghanistan, Iraq, Libya, and Syria, even though the 1.2 million refugees who claimed asylum in 2016 are equivalent to just 0.2 per cent of the EU population. But despite the angst gripping the EU, none of the five countries hosting the largest number of refugees is in Europe. Turkey has the most refugees at 2.8 million people, mainly those who fled from Syria, Iraq and Libya. It is followed by Pakistan, which hosts about 1.6 million people, mainly from Afghanistan, while Lebanon and Iran each host about 1 million people.[11]

Syria is by far the biggest source of refugees. By 2016, over 13 million people – 60 per cent of the prewar population – were displaced, with 5.4 million of those having fled the country since 2011.[12] This figure truly underlines the extent of the human suffering generated by the conflict. After Syria, the two biggest sources of refugees were Afghanistan (2.5 million people) and South Sudan (1.4 million people).[13]

The political destabilisation that accompanies large refugee movements has become one of the principal political debates in developed economies, but there is too little debate about how to avoid these flows in the first place. How can we spot countries on the brink of failure? What investments could be made in fragile countries to prevent their failure? What can be learnt so that we do not repeat the same mistakes?

Instead, the current focus is on how to keep refugees out, or the merits or otherwise of military intervention. Both solutions shift the immediate problem for host nations but do little to address the underlying causes.

---

11 'Mid-Year Trends 2016', UNHCR, p. 6, accessed at UNHCR website www.unhcr.org/statistics/unhcrstats/58aa8f247/mid-year-trends-june-2016.html

12 Accessed at UNHCR website www.unhcr.org/en-au/syria-emergency.html

13 Accessed at UNHCR website www.unhcr.org/figures-at-a-glance.html

The globalisation of trade and finance means that the costs of conflict are now spread far beyond the locus of any dispute. The US financial sanctions on Russia, for example, have caused problems for German companies associated with the supply of gas to the EU. The impact of growing interconnectivity should provide a powerful incentive for nations to work together to prevent conflict from erupting in the first place.

CHAPTER 4

Measuring peace

The region around Lake Kivu is one of the most unstable places on earth – both geologically and socially. Bordered by Rwanda to the east and the Democratic Republic of the Congo to the west, the lake straddles an active volcanic zone known as the East African Rift. Under the waters of the lake, 60 billion cubic metres of dissolved methane and 300 billion cubic metres of carbon dioxide lie ready to explode, a natural event known as an overturn that could smother the region in a layer of toxic gas 100 metres thick. No one seems to be able to predict when the next overturn event will happen.

Two million people live on the shores of Lake Kivu.

On the Congolese side of the border at the northern end of the lake is the town of Goma, where the instability of the physical environment is matched by the danger and uncertainty of the social environment. North East Kivu is one of the most lawless places in the world. The guesthouse where we would regularly stay was surrounded by armed guards, but they left me feeling less secure, rather than more. It is the sort of place where it is unwise to make eye contact. I remember once walking down the street and glancing at a woman accompanied by a thug, provoking a verbal tirade from the woman that almost turned violent.

These types of environments bring about a heightened sense of awareness, a kind of mental clarity that runs deep. It was while staying in Goma that I started musing on the reasons for such instability. Is there a connection between the geological and the sociological? What were the causes of such a violent social context? There was no lack of emotional strength among the people; indeed, they showed extraordinary levels of resilience at times. So why was there such an absence of peace?

It occurred to me that what creates peaceful societies can be very different to what is needed to stop violence. The sort of strong and forceful security apparatus that would be essential to curb the lawlessness in Goma would likely have exactly the opposite effect were it to be deployed in, say, Scandinavia. The longer I looked at peace, the clearer it became that it was more than merely an absence of violence, but I did not understand what peace actually was.

That was when I realised I wanted to gain a better understanding of peace. But like a doctor recognising that studying sick people will lead at best to an incomplete understanding of what constitutes health, I realised that I would have to start by understanding which countries were the most peaceful and why, rather than undertaking the more common route of studying conflicts.

I did some searching on the internet when I returned to Australia and could find no comprehensive comparisons of nations by their peacefulness. This led to a conversation with Stuart Rees, the founder of the Sydney Peace and Conflict Centre and the Sydney Peace Foundation, about whether there had been any empirical attempts to measure which countries were the most peaceful, as opposed to personal opinions. When he could not find any, I decided to investigate further.

I visited a number of leading peace institutes, asking them whether they thought a peace index would be useful. The response from all of them was that they did not know of such an index, but they all thought it would be beneficial. That is how the Global Peace Index was born. What I like about its origins is that it sprang out of experience. It could easily have been titled the Global Violence Index.

Peace entrepreneurialism

Having a background in computing and mathematics I naturally think in numbers and I have trouble understanding phenomena unless they are quantified. If something hasn't been measured, can it be truly understood? And if it isn't measured, how do we know whether our actions are helping or hindering us in achieving our goals? We simply don't. This applies to peace – if it isn't measured, how can we understand it?

Most formal investigations of violence and peace tended to be conducted by academics or military theorists. As I came from a business background, it was inevitable that I would adopt a different approach.

My professional background was one of researching, writing and then commercialising computer software products. Unconsciously, I started out on my quest to understand peace as I would with any commercial venture, using many of the same techniques that had proved successful for me in the past, especially my experience of successful product development life cycles, management processes and marketing. An example of this would be competitor analysis. The idea is to avoid head-on competition by using analysis to understand which research ideas are original: there is no point in developing what someone else has already done, or undertaking research in areas that are well covered by other researchers. Examples of this would be gender and youth, both worthwhile subjects, but with thousands of dedicated researchers already, IEP's research could only add incrementally to the current body of knowledge.

When I started, little quantitative research was being undertaken on peace, so it was comparatively easy to find areas where it was possible to make a difference. Happily, over a decade on, there is more interest in quantitatively studying peace.

The aim was also to be as factual and neutral as possible and to avoid injecting moral, political or personal value judgements. If the data is to be useful to people with differing values and from different ends of the political spectrum then we cannot afford any hint of partisanship. To illustrate, the following quote is from the 2017 Global Peace Index report:

> Yemen's deterioration has it ranked as the fifth least peaceful country for the first time in 2017, owing to an increase in the *level of violent crime*, *intensity of internal organised conflicts*, and the *impact of terrorism*. Yemen has fallen considerably in the Global Peace Index since 2008.

The observations are grounded in the data and are highly contextualised. We explain the internal logic of Yemen's fall, and leave any value judgements on the moral culpability of the participants to others.

The Global Peace Index

The Global Peace Index defines peace as 'The absence of violence or fear of violence'. The reason I picked this definition is because most people understand and can agree with it as a suitable definition, as well as something that can actually be measured independently. Definitions are really important in the development of indexes, as the indicators will always follow the definition. I would regularly get questioned on why the military was included in the Index, especially in the United States. The answer flows from the definition. There are two reasons why countries have a military: first, aggressively, to use in its national interest; second, defensively, because of the fear of other aggressive countries. The absence of both of these is the sign of a peaceful environment. It's not a moral judgement on the military.

The Index covers 163 countries and independent territories and more than 99.7 per cent of the world's population. Countries included in the Index must have a population of more than one million or a land area greater than 20,000 square kilometres. Microstates are excluded, mainly because it is difficult to get a full range of data.

The Global Peace Index measures peace based on 23 qualitative and quantitative indicators, ranging from a nation's level of military expenditure, to its relations with neighbouring countries, to the percentage of the population in prison. Each indicator is a valid measure, and when combined they can be used to capture complexity and to balance errors in cases where the information is of variable quality. The 23 variables seemed to strike the right balance between using too few indicators, which would risk creating unreliable results because of possible bias, and using too many indicators, which would run the risk of getting 'fuzzy' results. Additionally, the Index uses a combination of quantitative and qualitative data, as this helps to provide balance in analysing countries with unreliable data.

The intention in devising the Index was to create a dataset that could be used to work out what factors are most closely associated with peaceful societies: in other words, the components of Positive Peace. The data for the Index is sourced from a wide range of respected sources, including the International Institute of Strategic Studies, Stockholm International Peace

Research Institute, various United Nations agencies, peace institutes and the Economist Intelligence Unit.

The Index allows us to spot relationships that might otherwise lie hidden. One of the things that quickly became clear is that the data backed up my intuition in Lake Kivu. That is, that the relationships between the different aspects of peace are not fixed but change as other factors shift. It's highly complex and difficult to understand. It can't be put into one simple causal relationship, which many people want to do.

The Index also debunked some persistent myths that have been muddling the policy debate for years. Contrary to popular perception, for example, militarisation has been steadily decreasing since the end of the Cold War. In the last decade more countries have decreased their military expenditure as a percentage of GDP than increased. Similarly, 114 countries decreased the personnel in their armies, compared to only 38 countries that increased it.

Although we may be on the cusp of a new era of militarisation driven by China's rise and a re-emergence of militarism under President Trump in the United States, the longer-term trends are clear. These kinds of insights provide policymakers with a set of tools to make a much more nuanced assessment, helping to guide their actions.

The rollout

When the time came to make the Global Peace Index widely available, I again applied the practices I had learnt in business. In the field of computing, there is a concept known as a minimum viable product. The idea is to release a functional product into the market as quickly as possible rather than aiming for perfection. I didn't worry too much about such things as the depth of additional research; that could come later. A fast release, even if the product is not perfect, beats competitors to market and quickly determines how acceptable the product is to the public. This also provided very fast feedback and ensured that I would not be burning money and time on something that would not gain traction.

The initial product, released in 2007, was based on solid quantification, therefore it was robust. It met the needs of the market as being a viable product, but it was not over-engineered. Other than ranking 121 countries, we did little additional research for the first edition. Since then we have been steadily improving both the measures and the depth of analysis. Each year there have been incremental refinements in how the factors are measured and weighted, as well as an expansion in the number of countries and independent territories covered, rising to 163 in 2015.

However, developing a successful index was not enough: it needed to become well-known. The more people who knew about it, the more likely it would be used to shape policy and the way people think. For me this is a clear measure of success. Again, my business experience helped with valuable insights into defining and solving this challenge.

We started this process by attempting to better define our audience. After much thought, we identified a broad demographic: people who are intelligent, globally aware and positively motivated. The next step was to work out how to communicate with them effectively, en masse and cheaply.

One of the early successes was our first web portal. It gave visitors to the site the ability to navigate the peacefulness of the world through interactive maps. It was amazing how much this feature was used. This focus on making the information accessible was one of the key factors that differentiated our research from more academic approaches.

The use of strict timelines, combined with tight project management, helped keep us focused, but more importantly allowed for regularly timed deliverables that maintained a steady flow of product. Often in academia and think tanks, deliverables have longer time frames. Our approach was to design a series of quick-impact reports and indexes and to time their release to external events, such as a PR campaign, in order to maximise impact. In that way we made sure that over the years there would be a continuous improvement in process, while maintaining the high quality of the product. For the people involved in the process this was all new. For me personally it has been a source of pleasure watching the people around me growing with the organisation's success.

A different approach

Many of the organisations working on peace are somewhat anti-establishment, and when they do focus on business, it is on the damage business is doing and the iniquities of globalisation.

At heart, I am a fairly conservative businessman. I do not have an anti-capitalist bias and I think globalisation is fundamentally a good thing: it has been a mechanism for distributing wealth around the world and drawing many hundreds of millions of people out of poverty. Moreover, the economic interdependence that globalisation brings has raised the cost of international armed conflict, making it less likely.

As for the military, another key target of many peace organisations, to me it is neither moral nor immoral in and of itself. Prevention and deterrence are essential; if there were no military, many parts of the world would be overrun by criminal gangs or militias. Some wars are a tragic waste of human life; others are necessary. Some countries do have better relations with their neighbours, fight fewer wars and spend substantially less on their military. This simply highlights the self-evident truth that leaders can make good and bad choices and that militaries can be a force for either good or ill depending on how they are used.

Our work is not an argument to dispense with armies, which is unlikely to happen anyway. Diverting money from military spending to other areas generally reaps economic benefits, but that is not an argument against maintaining a military capability. Broad moralistic statements such as being 'anti-war', 'anti-globalisation' or 'anti-capitalism' are neither insightful nor helpful. Nations are not about to dispense with armies. Globalisation has already happened, and capitalism will continue to be the dominant form of economic organisation for the foreseeable future, even though the heavy reliance on consumption and materialism has many problems.

Our approach is to avoid moral judgements: to be as dispassionate as possible, assembling and distilling the facts as best we can. One advantage of taking a fact-based approach is that it is possible to derive a disinterested sense of context around politically charged issues. For example, the United States and Russian militaries receive a great deal of attention in the media because of their size, especially in relation to recent events in the Middle

East and Central Asia. Yet it is Israel that recorded the highest level of militarisation in 2016 according to the Global Peace Index. This conclusion is supported by other research such as the Global Militarization Index.[1] Second is North Korea, followed by Russia, the United States, Pakistan, France, India, Syria and Yemen.

Such context can shed light elsewhere. The most heavily militarised countries also tend to score low in other domains of the Global Peace Index, namely societal safety and security, and levels of ongoing domestic and international conflict. Thus, in the 2019 Global Peace Index, Israel ranks 146 on the list of 163 countries and territories. By comparison, the United States is at number 128, India is 141, Russia 154, North Korea 149, Pakistan 153, Yemen 160, Syria 162 and Afghanistan 163.

Reporting on facts in the public domain

The public's perception is largely shaped by the media's coverage of news and current affairs. If the media does not cover a subject, then it is unlikely that it will be understood, let alone debated by the public. The relationship between the media and violence is complex.

Representatives of the media would argue that they are only holding up a mirror reflecting the public's interests. The argument is that if they do not do this then they will not be fulfilling their role. That may be true, but it can also be portrayed as appealing to the public's negative appetites. Humans respond more strongly to emotions such as fear and have a fascination with violence. Nuances are hard to put into a four-word headline that can be rehashed again and again. The only time there is a powerful public appetite for peace is when a country is at war. Otherwise, it is a desirable background condition. In a media sense, peace is not a story. Acts of violence, especially when they are out of the ordinary, are.

If the media concentrates on one area, especially if exaggerations are used, this will lead the public to be overly concerned. The Global Peace and Positive Peace indexes provide a mechanism to engender media coverage

---

1 Max M. Mutschler, 'Global Militarization Index 2016', accessed at www.bicc.de/uploads/tx_bicctools/GMI_2016_e_2016_01_12.pdf

that is based on facts, both positive and negative, depending on what is being covered. It's a factual examination of the world, which is crucial if we are to get a more accurate sense of what is really occurring. It is more than just a corrective against media distortions or the political use of fear to garner votes. It runs to the heart of creating a sustainable world – peace is a precondition for sustainability.

Analysis based on the Global Peace Index and Positive Peace offers the basis for developing a politics that is not based on fear, but rather the deliberate creation of a thriving society and a more peaceful environment.

We must direct resources in ways that will improve all the factors associated with peace. This will not only create peace; it will create the appropriate environment for the development of many other things that societies think are important. It will create an optimal environment for human potential to flourish. Over the longer term, creating societies that are not under the yoke of entrenched violence will lead to higher levels of economic prosperity, countries with stronger soft power and a more stable political environment that is more adaptable to change and resilient to shocks, such as COVID-19. These are all outcomes that reasonable politicians should desire.

The early helpers

Many people have helped to bring this project to fruition. A very early catalyst was Kevin Clements, one of the intellectual leaders of the global peace movement. He has moved seamlessly back and forth from being a practitioner, when he served as Secretary General of International Alert in London, to academia, where he has held chairs in peace studies and conflict resolution in the United States, Australia and New Zealand.

I met Kevin when his career was already well established. He is a tall, friendly New Zealander with an infectious laugh. I was struck by how open and warm he was. Equally impressive was his list of contacts. Once I had described what I wanted to do he opened up his black book and introduced me to a series of people around the world who were at the top of their field. He did this before we had really got to know each other properly; we had only spoken a couple of times on the phone. I will always remember this act of trust. It gave me access to the best people to judge whether the Global Peace Index was a good idea or not.

Having taken a snapshot of what was happening in the field, I set about establishing a structure to oversee the development of the Global Peace Index. Kevin came on board to head up an expert panel to determine how to develop a truly rigorous product. This was important: if it was not rigorous from the beginning, there would be persistent problems later. We began adding people with complementary skills to the expert panel, including statisticians, data analysts and peace experts who widened the range of talents and cultural backgrounds.

I opted for a tripartite arrangement. One part would be the Institute for Economics and Peace, which was initially just me. It would set the basic definitions of peace, including how internal and external peace would be defined, and the outline of the Index, including its coverage. The second part would be an expert panel to determine what indicators we should and should not use and how those indicators would be weighted. The third would be an organisation that collated the data to be reviewed by the expert panel. From this we established a rigorous process.

Chic Dambach was another important early influence and inspiration. Chic had lived several lifetimes before I met him. A champion kayaker who was on the Unites States national team at the Olympics, he went on to revitalise the National Peace Corps Association, fought against bullying in schools, served as chief of staff to a Democratic congressman and founded the Alliance for Peacebuilding. He has dedicated his life to trying to create a better world, at a level that is truly impressive.

Chic was one of the first people I met who I felt really got what we were trying to do. He saw the need to tackle peace from a new angle. We met when the Iraq War was at its height. People like him, who had dedicated their lives to working for peace, were incredibly frustrated. The reason for waging the war had turned out to be entirely false. Chic saw what I was planning as a badly needed new approach. He introduced me to a range of important contacts in the United States, which was crucial to building a base and influence there.

Yet like many things in life that become important, our relationship did not start well. Within five minutes of our first meeting I had come to the conclusion that it was going to be a waste of time. He had tried to get hold of me 20 minutes before the lunch to cancel, because he did not know who I was and he was busy. When we sat down and I told him what we were doing, we did warm to each other a little, but we were still a long way short of establishing a meaningful connection.

As it happened, we were having lunch in a cafeteria in a bookshop at Dupont Circle in Washington. When we were leaving, I stopped him and pointed to a number of books I had read and we started talking about them. Chic later said that as he was listening to me he realised how closely our world views were aligned. That was when he came on board with the project. Before that, in the back of his mind he was wondering whether I was just another businessman with a new angle to make a buck from peace.

One of the more interesting organisations I have dealt with over the years is the Club of Madrid, which has more than 120 former presidents and prime ministers as members. The organisation acts as an advisory group to current world leaders, bringing their collective wisdom to help think through complex and difficult decisions. The organisation itself is low-key, preferring to use its members' profiles where necessary, but often working in the background with no public exposure. It is an organisation I like a lot.

The Club of Madrid was founded by Diego Hidalgo, a man of tremendous vision and success. He created the PRISA media empire, which at one stage was one of the biggest in the world. Once he confided to me over coffee that whenever he set out to make money, he lost it. Twice he had launched a venture because he wanted to make a positive difference and both times he had made a fortune. That was how he had got involved in media. After serving at the World Bank he decided that he would launch a newspaper in Spain with the aim of helping the country navigate from a dictatorship to a democracy. At the time this seemed fraught with risk, but King Juan Carlos, who still held the dictatorial powers he had inherited from General Francisco Franco, had also come to the conclusion that greater democracy was the way forward. The King approached Diego to help guide the country to a more enlightened future. This was how his business empire started. Steering through these difficult waters gave him a strong appreciation of the influence leaders can have, which eventually led to the founding of the Club of Madrid.

Another inspirational helper has been Dr Bill Vendley. Bill at that time was the Secretary General of Religions for Peace, an organisation he joined in 1994 when it was a fledgling operation. Over the years it has grown into the world's largest multi-faith organisation, with chapters in more than 70 countries, counting over 1,200 religious organisations as members. He is one of the pioneers of using interfaith dialogue to build peace and has personally engaged in peace processes in Ethiopia, Eritrea, Sierra Leone, Liberia, Indonesia, Sri Lanka and Iraq, and many other countries.

Our first meeting was in his offices in New York opposite the UN headquarters. Within 15 minutes of talking to him he said, 'I get it, what can I do to help?' It blew me away. Bill's theological knowledge always stunned me, and it was from this deep intellectual base that he was able to build the organisation that he did. Bill can literally pick up the phone and call nearly any of the major religious leaders around the world, from the Pope to the Grand Mufti of Egypt to the Chief Rabbi of Israel.

Developing the Index

An index nearly always has an implicit tension. The aim is to create a simple measure of a complex phenomenon: that is anything but simple. The aim of the Global Peace Index is to take something as complex as peace and to simplify it into a definable and measurable phenomenon.

The first step towards doing it well is to have a robust definition of what is to be measured. For example, if you say, 'I want to measure good government', then you have created a myriad of problems around the word 'good'. With peace, if you get your definition wrong, or worse still, start measuring things without a clear idea of why you are measuring, the outcome will inevitably be amorphous. In a sense, you have to define precisely what you are examining and delineate it. Otherwise, measurement becomes problematic. All too often, indexes do not have clear definitions of what they are measuring, which leaves them open to criticism of subjectivity or leads to ambiguous outcomes. One way of understanding the robustness of an index is to see whether the organisation fully publishes its methodology. If the methodology is not published, then more than likely it is flawed.

Another limiting factor is the quality of the statistics. This can be particularly challenging when compiling and normalising global data. To overcome this, the Index uses a combination of quantitative and qualitative indicators, the latter compiled and weighted by experts. This provides multiple perspectives and contributes to a more robust index.

An excellent example of this is the terrorism indicator. This was originally scored by the Economist Intelligence Unit as an expert score called the *Likelihood of a Terrorist Attack*. Over time we found that it lacked reliability because of the difficulty in predicting black swan terrorist events. However, the University of Maryland started a large project, partly funded by the US government, to compile a database of terrorist attacks by scouring global news sources for reports. Using this database as our source, the IEP developed a quantitative indicator that measured the levels of terrorism. So, rather than being a projection of the likelihood of terrorism, it became a measure of terrorist activity in the preceding year, which is more accurate and more appropriate for an annual index.

In time this new measure led to another index, the Global Terrorism Index, which has now become a major product. It has taken on a life of its own and is used by major intelligence organisations around the world as a key source in their fight against terrorism.

Each indictor in the Global Peace Index is weighted according to the effect it has on society. While homicides have more impact than fear of violence, determining the correct value of the weight is crucial. There are statistical techniques to come up with weightings, but they have their flaws. We decided to use an expert panel to reach a consensus on the relative importance of each indicator.

Our definition of peace as the 'Absence of violence or fear of violence', and the fact that the 23 indicators in the Index are designed to be clearly differentiated from each other, makes us confident that the Global Peace Index is not a proxy measure of something else, such as per capita income.

Prosperity and peace

One of the more interesting and important findings from our research is the strong link between peace and economic prosperity. Since the Global Peace Index is not a proxy of GDP, we could confidently explore the connection. Contrary to my own feelings when I started, the relationship was strong. What's more, there was a tipping point – if peace passes a certain point then economic prosperity takes off. On reflection this was understandable. As economies grow the tax revenues increase, which in turn means better funding of government services, such as the police and judicial systems,

FIGURE 1

Peace and wealth

There is a tipping point. Once peace passes a certain level, GDP growth improves dramatically.

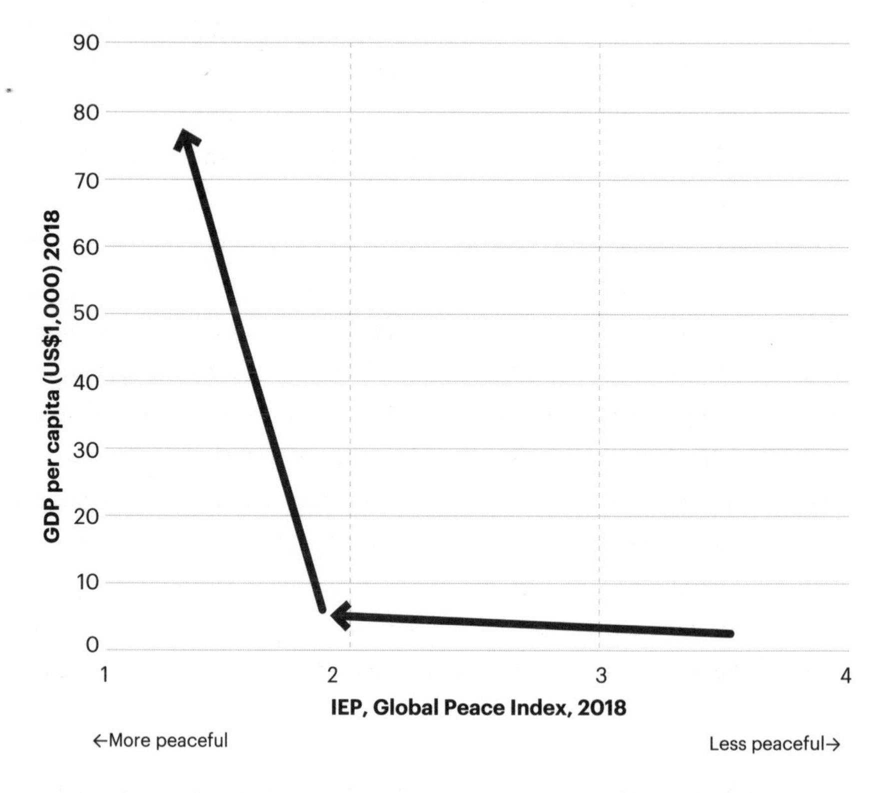

SOURCE: IEP; WORLD BANK

education and health. As the average person's life improves, they are less likely to contemplate violence. A virtuous cycle.

This relationship between peace and economic growth is far from simple. First, ascribing causality is flawed: one does not feed the other; they work as a mutual feedback loop. Also, the other factors associated with Positive Peace need to come into play. A better enforcement of legal contracts and better free flows of information are two examples of items that need to improve so these virtuous cycles can come into play.

The problem with GDP

The most ubiquitous measure of social progress is GDP. For most countries it's the major measure used to determine social health or wellbeing. If it's going up, then the general assumption is everything else is improving too.

However, it has long been known that GDP is simply a measure of transactions and has severe limitations. In the 1960s Robert F. Kennedy commented that it measures 'everything except that which makes life worthwhile'.[2] It only counts human activities that involve the exchange of money, without any consideration of the social value of those exchanges, or even the concept of a national capital account.

GDP first came into its own in the 1940s, when the economist John Maynard Keynes published a pamphlet, *How to Pay for the War*, arguing that there needed to be a proper calculation of what the British economy could produce with its available resources. This led to the first set of national accounts being published in Britain in 1941. Keynes, sensing the limitations of GDP as a measure, did not expect it to be continued after the war was over, but in 1953 the United Nations established the System of National Accounts, which gave a prominent position to GDP.

What started out as a wartime measure became a universally applied yardstick of national output and standard of living. Even Simon Kuznets, who led the postwar transformation of economics into an empirical science,

2 Robert F. Kennedy, speech at the University of Kansas, 18 March 1968, accessed at www.theguardian.com/news/datablog/2012/may/24/robert-kennedy-gdp

warned against equating GDP growth with wellbeing. As the British social commentator George Monbiot puts it:

> The problem with gross domestic product is the gross bit. There are no deductions involved: all economic activity is accounted as if it were of positive value. Social harm is added to, not subtracted from it. A train crash which generates £1bn worth of track repairs, medical bills and funeral costs is deemed by this measure as beneficial as an uninterrupted service which generates £1bn in sales.[3]

As many have pointed out, if businesses used GDP-style accounting, they would aim to maximise gross revenue at the expense of profitability, efficiency, sustainability and flexibility.

GDP makes no additions to take into account the health of the population, the quality of education, the strength of social relationships, the intelligence of public debate or the integrity of public institutions, nor subtractions to account for social strife, inequality or environmental degradation. If a house burnt down, then a new house would need to be built. This would increase purchases of building materials and require labour to rebuild it, thereby increasing GDP. Viewed through this distorted lens, it would be considered a better outcome than if the house had not burnt down. However, there is a net loss in the quality of life.

In the same way, many of the elements of violence, such as expenditure on the military, jails, policing, the judiciary and security will show up in GDP as a positive indicator, a way in which the economy has 'grown'.

Because GDP is a measure of the money being exchanged, and not what it is being exchanged for, it creates a deeply distorted, materialistic picture of what a society is.

When there is a heavy focus on GDP there is also a tendency to reinforce the status quo, the existing transactional system. This is especially obvious

---

3 George Monbiot, 'After this 60-year feeding frenzy, Earth itself has become disposable', *The Guardian*, 5 January 2010, accessed at www.theguardian.com/commentisfree/2010/jan/04/standard-of-living-spending-consumerism

with the environment, where heavily polluting activities are seen as a benefit to GDP because there is already an established set of transactions related to them, such as income from electricity generated by coal-fired power stations. More environmentally friendly substitutes, especially if they are new, are seen as either a drag on GDP or irrelevant because of their negative effect on well-established, high-GDP-generating industries.

Soaring economic activity has depleted natural resources and done inestimable damage to the environment; in many countries much of the newly generated wealth is being shared between fewer people than at any time in the past 80 years; and divisions within and between societies are becoming apparent. Yet GDP has nothing to say about any of this.

It became important as a universal measure partly because its emergence coincided with an era in which far more of human activity became subject to recorded monetary exchanges.

At the end of the 20th century, 90 per cent of the world's population lived within a formal recorded economy, compared with only 40 per cent in the 1970s and ten to 15 per cent at the end of the 19th century.[4] Human activity continues to be absorbed into the formal economy, which has the effect of increasing GDP because the number of recorded transactions are increasing, even if there is little real additional economic activity. The informal economy in developing nations, which until recently primarily consisted of barter or cash, is now being captured and recorded. For example, new technologies such as mobile payments capture transactions that would have formerly been invisible, thereby boosting GDP. This expansion of coverage helps to partially explain high GDP growth rates in the developing world.

It is important to be able to measure economic growth and transactions, but these indicators have become misleading proxies for human progress and fulfilment. The problem is that GDP and its associated measures leave out important and meaningful aspects of human experience.

The Indexes produced by the IEP are not intended to be a replacement for GDP. They are designed to be complementary: to give a broader and deeper view of the state of society when used alongside GDP. The transactional

---

4 G. Mulgan, *Connexity*, Vintage, 1995, p. 54.

economy measured by GDP is just one element of a complex system. The singular pursuit of any goal to the exclusion of all others leads to imbalances. Peace, and Positive Peace in particular, recognises that economic growth is just one measure among many in a system that has to be seen holistically if we are to arrive at an accurate view of what a thriving society looks like.

The Global Peace Index and Positive Peace provide a sound base to attempt to arrive at an alternative view of what a thriving society looks like, but also one with better economic outcomes.

CHAPTER 5

Peace and systems thinking

One of my best memories, and an experience that made me think about systems, occurred in Laos in the early 1990s. At the time, Laos was a closed country for all but a few Westerners and when we visited villages there, sometimes a six-hour drive over dusty dirt tracks, hundreds of people would turn out simply to see us. They always held a welcoming ceremony for us followed by a community lunch. We would sit cross-legged on the floor of the community hall, inevitably a traditional wooden building built on pillars 2 metres high. It consisted of one room, with undulating floors that, like the walls, had cracks that you could see through.

During the feast our hosts would give us copious amounts of highly potent, clear rice wine, chicken and rice. The hospitality was impeccable, but I've learnt to be cautious about food. I have come down with stomach problems four times in Laos and Cambodia and each time it took from four to ten months to recover. We would take the food, pretend to put it into our mouths, hide it in our hands and then put it into our pockets. It meant we couldn't wear the same pants the next day. However, we did drink the rice wine. At the end of the feast, groups of villagers would come up to tie a piece of string around our wrists – up to five people on each wrist at a time – while chanting a benevolent incantation. It was truly moving. These were some of the more exhilarating experiences of my life.

Our Laotian projects were about clean water and mother and child health. One of the components was to encourage the use of contraception to increase the spacing between children. The women quickly understood what contraception meant and its power, but they reasoned that because contraceptives were so powerful, they were better used as a sacrifice to the rice deity. So they would accept the pills and put them on the altar in their fields in the hope that the deity would increase their rice yield in appreciation of such a significant offering.

We looked at it as cause and effect – birth control would improve the spacing of children, therefore fewer babies would die. But that was not what happened in the system. The villagers lived in a world inhabited by deities that controlled their destinies: their encoded norms suggested that powerful objects were best used to keep the gods happy, regardless of the other benefits that might be forgone.

Without a clear understanding of the host system and the ability to work with it, or around it, interventions will always be less effective. The solution may have been to give contraceptive pills while also providing something to sacrifice to the deities, or changing the type of contraception, which is what eventually happened.

This and similar experiences come back to me time and again. To make advances in peace, we must start by understanding the existing social system. It has a path, and understanding that path is vital if we are to promote effective and positive change.

In the same way, without a clear understanding of the systemic nature of peace and the factors that support it, it is impossible to determine what policies actually work best and what programs need to be implemented to support a more peaceful environment. Humanity needs new paradigms to shift the deadlock in our thinking; as already discussed, the combination of Positive Peace and systems thinking provides a factual framework that not only will allow humanity's potential to flourish but will also fit in with the broader systems upon which we depend.

At the heart of a sustainable future is the realisation that we are part of a system, not independent of it.

At one level systems thinking is easy to grasp. Everyone gets the concept of a web of intersecting relationships. However, once one digs below the surface it becomes more complex. This chapter attempts to convey a basic understanding of systems thinking. When it is applied to societies its conclusions often stand in sharp contrast to many of our traditional ways of conceptualising and dealing with problems.

Systems theory

Systems theory originated while scientists were attempting to better understand the workings of organisms, such as cells or the human body. Through such studies, it became clear that breaking subjects down into their constituent parts and using cause-and-effect thinking was inadequate to explain the operation of the whole.

We imagine we live in a simple linear world where we feel we have to pick particular actions to alter the specific cause of a problem. This is played out in many ways: doctors frequently look for localised causes of a disease; politicians get tough on crime; economists assume that shifts in one economic factor, such as an interest rate, can 'explain' everything that subsequently occurs.

The concept of linear causality is deeply embedded in our understanding of the world and the way we interact within it; it is built into our subconscious. We undertake an action and expect an outcome. In the physical world the same actions always result in the same outcome. Throw a ball into the air and gravity will always cause it to fall at the same rate. Ideas of cause and effect also appeal to us because they lead to the creation of apparently persuasive narratives or stories. Like stories, explanations of cause and effect are linear: a cause is like the beginning of a story, and an effect is like the end of a story. The difficulty is that such an approach is partial and incomplete at best.

Understanding the physical world through examining causality has enabled great strides in human progress. Modern empirical science arose because of it. However, there are problems. Causality implies that all effects can be tracked back linearly to initial causes. The logical extension is that we live in a clockwork universe where the conditions are predetermined and there is no room for genuine novelty.

Causality is excellent for explaining discrete and well-isolated phenomena. But as we add more variables, the complexity expands exponentially, making attempts to isolate linear causal effects not just ineffective but potentially misleading. The act of simplification destroys the integrity of the model by denying the importance of its inherent complexity.

Linear causality is not in itself an illusion: the illusion is that we believe we are able to explain the complexity around us by using linear causality alone.

Systems thinking forms the basis of how we think about Positive Peace. An example would be the relationship between the free flow of information and a well-functioning government. Governments can regulate what information is available, but information can also change governments. The two are highly correlated and mutually affect each other. This is very different from causal thinking where the effect does not influence the cause.

More than the sum of our parts

Systems thinking is based on the realisation that not only is the whole greater than the sum of its parts, but that the whole produces effects that are different from what each part would produce in isolation.

Human beings can't be fully understood by dissecting us into smaller and smaller parts, let's say to understand consciousness. We are far more than the sum of our parts and by extension so are our societies. Trying to apply scientific laws to human systems is dangerous because the participants are self-aware and can choose between multiple solutions in reacting to any given situation. Even the reading of this book can act as a simple example. The actions taken by three people reading this book will be different, depending on many factors, including their background knowledge, what they may think of the writer and even their emotions or concentration on the day they read it. If individual human reactions can be so variable, imagine how much more complicated a social system is. Then extend this to the international stage.

Systems theory developed because of the inability of physics to explain biological functions. Linear causality provides an inadequate explanation of the evolution of living organisms. They increase in differentiation and also in complexity. Evolution cannot be explained by looking at its pre-existing conditions and drawing quasi-scientific conclusions about causation.

Our heavy emphasis on linear causality has also led to great specialisation. Subjects are broken down into smaller and smaller parts in order to find out how their constituent parts work. This can be seen in the physical sciences or even the natural sciences. It is no accident that the root of the word 'analysis' means 'to break into constituent parts'.

When we look at the major challenges facing humanity in the 21st century, it is clear that there is an urgent need to understand interdependence, something that is limited by academia's aversion to cross-disciplinary research. This is particularly true in the search for peace. Specialisation blocks our perception and our ability to study and understand interlocking relationships, many of which are vital to managing humanity's shared future. What are the interactions between the way a society operates and the use of fresh water, or between consumption patterns and the acidification of oceans? Recognising and understanding the fundamental interconnectedness around us is vital for our survival.

Systems thinking bridges this gap. It takes into account the large number of interactions and aims to understand patterns and flows rather than individual events. It can be applied not only to the ways societies and ecosystems operate but also to the ways that societies and ecosystems interoperate.

The analysis of systems thinking in this book is not aimed at being comprehensive. Rather, it takes the reader on a journey with an emphasis on understanding the main concepts and how systems thinking could be applied to human societies, especially the nation-state.

Systems thinking can be approached from many directions. One direction is to think of the system as an organisation, rather than a series of events. What is important in a system are the flows and patterns, rather than the events.

Systems are not static. The nature or character of a system changes if anything is added, subtracted or modified. Changes to any one element within the system will cause knock-on effects, changing the interactions and flows of other elements. The system will in some way function differently. Think of the COVID-19 pandemic and the way the virus impacted social relations and mental health, and then the knock-on effects into the economy. One thing we can be certain about is that at the back end of this crisis the system will have altered.

Once a system has changed, it can never go back to its original form. In the march of history, think of the fall of communism in Russia and the rise of capitalism in China: these countries could never go back to what they were. Politicians may make statements like 'Let's make America great again', but if the system that is America is made great again it will be a different system, and a different America.

A system can be seen as moving down a path and cannot be separated from its history. This is a characteristic called path dependency. Paths are deeply embedded within the system and take time to change, meaning that the best method of development is small continuous changes and from multiple directions. This can be described as nudging the system in the right direction, rather than attempting to dramatically redesign it. Many historical approaches to nation-building are aimed at being transformational: some recent examples are the nation-building approaches in Iraq and Afghanistan, or historically our interventions with Indigenous Australians, Native Americans and other Indigenous civilisations. The cultures were smashed in an attempt to bring them into the modern age, leading to much social dysfunction, which is still evident over a century later.

From a systems perspective, it is not necessary to understand each and every causal factor. The system is self-managing. This leads to very different approaches to solving problems. In a world defined by linear causality, getting tough on crime is often seen as the best way of stopping crime. Tough punishment stops people committing crime and takes the bad guys off the street. However, a systems perspective is more likely to look at the underlying conditions from which crime arises, such as poverty or social conditions.

When taking a system-wide approach it is necessary not to get stuck in one point in time. If the intention is to change the system, it is better to look at the system holistically and over a long period. This enables one to understand the momentum and direction of the system as a whole. Is the system on a path of improvement or is it degrading over time? Such a perspective is especially important when trying to understand societal systems, which are less predictable than their physical counterparts.

There is also a concept known as mutual feedback loops. Processes can be mutually causal. Factors such as corruption and business mutually affect each other. For example, as corruption increases or decreases, business reacts and changes its practices in response. These reactions then further modify the way corruption is undertaken. Or consider improvements in health services: better health care leads to a more productive workforce, which in turn provides the government with higher income, which can then be invested back into health. Mutual feedback loops can also be seen in politics: two parties forever changing their tactics in response to each other.

Although it is true that people shape the system, the reverse also applies. People are shaped by the system they have created. There is no simple causality; the two are interacting and creating continual changes in each other. This is another example of the mutual feedback loops that lie at the centre of systems thinking.

The effect is especially evident in the incidence of what we term vicious and virtuous cycles. Often, events transpire in a cyclical process, whereby negative events can make more negative events more likely, creating vicious cycles of violence, while positive events can lead to virtuous cycles. This is where improvements in the system lead to other improvements, and when there is enough positive change it becomes self-reinforcing, causing more positive change. Positive and Negative Peace are similarly linked. Changes in Positive Peace create the conditions for changes in Negative Peace and vice versa.

The US has had one of the biggest falls in Positive Peace in the decade to 2019, recording the 10th largest deterioration. The 2020 race riots highlight the problem in which demonstrators took to the streets in 140 cities, causing many states to call in the national guard. So what are the vicious cycles happening here? Firstly, a lack of accountability of the police forces across the US. There were 1,099 people killed by the police in 2019, yet rarely does a police officer get prosecuted and it seems only when there is independent footage taken and it goes public. The small percentage of sadistic police are then free to ratchet up their offences. Impunity is also more likely to attract more dysfunctional people who can satisfy their violent tendencies on the job. A vicious cycle is created.

Similarly, the public witnesses police brutality, causing anger, and then they want justice, but it doesn't come. Demonstrations ratchet up in intensity and become more violent over the years. The government then feels it has to respond to the violence to quell it. However, the system doesn't change as it's stuck in the status quo. The next time police violence happens it causes more agitation and higher degrees of anger, causing the vicious cycle to repeat with stronger intensity. The outcome from all of this is that people become more alienated from the system. There is also an increase in the distrust of authority which in turn leads to many unintended consequences, none of which make for a healthier system.

Most systems are open; that is, they interact with other systems, interpreting inputs and transforming them. Think of two countries exchanging technology, people and trade.

Unlike causality, where the outcome is fixed, systems interpret an input according to its encoded norms and then may or may not initiate an action. If inflation stays within a certain range, then the central bank does not change interest rates. If the inflation figure moves outside of the set boundaries, then it will take action. It's not the input that determines the output but what happens to the input within the system.

Similar inputs can produce very different actions, but also different inputs can produce very similar actions. Think of two peaceful demonstrations for better health care, one in an authoritarian country and one in a democracy. One is seen as a challenge to the system and is suppressed, the other is seen as an attempt to nudge the system towards improvement.

Systems thinking is a recognition that in the real world nothing happens in isolation; everything exists in a relationship of mutual dependence, both within a system and with other systems. Cells within the body depend on the health of the host, while the host depends on the health of the cells, and the health of the society around him or her. Similarly, countries depend on the health of companies, the education system and policing, as well as the health of the family and individuals.

Systems contain other subsystems within them and are also subsystems of larger systems. Nations are no different. Subsystems could be the family, local communities, businesses, police forces or universities. Some of these subsystems have weaker levels of cohesion, while other are stronger. Examples would be a social network like a yoga group that meets once a week compared to a school, which operates daily and is highly regulated (see Figure 2).

Mutual dependency is part of the nature of a system, whether it's an ecosystem, an atmospheric system or a society.

The nation-state works well as a relatively self-contained system and is the area where we have focused our analysis. It has a concept of self-identity;

FIGURE 2

Systems and nations

Although nations are systems, they exist within other systems. Similarly, nations have systems within them as well.

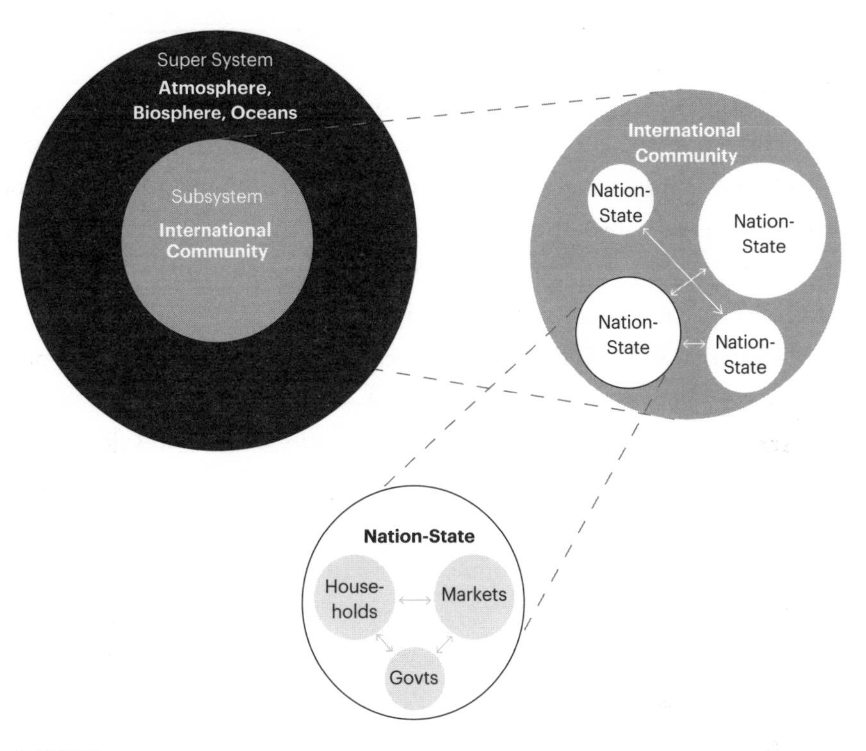

SOURCE: IEP

most of its citizens see themselves as belonging to it; it has control over its territory; and it can regulate. The majority of citizens in the world would first describe themselves by their nationality. Therefore, the nation-state is an excellent starting point in trying to understand systems.

Systems thinking also provides a better model for explaining tipping points, making it easier to understand how small catalytic events can cause significant, seemingly disproportionately large changes. The fall of the Berlin Wall started with the loosening of the authoritarian state in the USSR, leading to demonstrations in East Germany that culminated in the joining of East and West Germany. The Arab Spring started with the self-immolation of Mohamed Bouazizi, a Tunisian vegetable seller. No one could have predicted these outcomes. With peace there are also tipping points. Two of particular note involve the relationship between peace and corruption, and peace and GDP, both of which are covered in other chapters in the book.

Effects of this type are not only nonlinear, but they can also be lagged. Think of education, the full impact of which can only be seen many years after graduation as those who have been educated in new ways of thinking gain power, sometimes decades later, and use their learning to influence the system.

Adapting to change

Another aspect where systems mimic societies is that both constantly exchange matter, energy and information, transforming themselves in the process. Nothing within a system is permanent. For example, societies are always changing. Individuals die and are replaced by the next generation, and even buildings eventually wear out and need to be replaced. Societies also take resources from other systems, most notably the ecosystem. They then transform these materials, thereby improving themselves and their societies.

According to systems thinking, as a nation-state reorganises into greater complexity there will be less structural stability. The additional complexity creates what can be termed jitter because the complexity means more encoded norms, and the responses of the encoded norms will interact with each other. The higher the complexity, the higher the adaptability, because it is more likely that there will be an encoded norm to react to a new or modified input. Adaptability will be a key requirement for the Anthropocene. Think of democracies, which are very noisy, slightly unstable and have political power changing regularly. The high adaptability of democracies explains why they are generally the most peaceful and economically successful form of government.

Political structures are not static: they are dynamic, attempting to adjust to changing circumstances. While our participation alters the system, the system also alters us. One of the ways of understanding the health of a social system is by its adaptability and flexibility. The more adaptable and flexible, the heathier the system, which can be measured through Positive Peace.

Systems thinking provides a philosophical approach for integrating these broader ecological systems with our human systems of government. A balanced relationship between the national systems and other systems, such as the ocean, the biosphere and the atmosphere, is key to the survival of humanity.

That is why it is vitally important to understand the interlocking relationships between these systems and societal systems. What are the most important feedback loops that improve or degrade ecosystems? What are the encoded norms related to them and how do they operate?

Homeostasis and adaptation

Homeostasis is a common term used in systems thinking. Systems like to maintain a steady state. Homeostasis is the process that maintains that steady state. For example, if mammals do not eat, they get hungry and seek out food, thereby restoring the energy needed for the system to function; if inflation rises, interest rates go up, dampening demand and bringing prices back into line. The system makes small adjustments based on the way inputs are interpreted by its encoded norms to maintain the status quo. The same model of understanding can be applied to nations. This can be seen in the legal systems of nations or the moral values of their citizens. They all maintain bounds within society. A simple example is the group reaction when someone pushes into a queue.

Homeostasis on its own is neither good nor bad; it depends on the actions taken through the encoded norm. If corruption becomes entrenched within a system, the system will tend to resist attempts to fight it. Another, more positive, example is a well-functioning education system.

Or alternatively, it could be that if an infectious disease outbreak occurs then medical resources are deployed to fix it, as seen in the response of the medical systems in many countries to the COVID-19 virus. The effectiveness of the responses varied from country to country. Some countries were fast to implement social distancing, mass testing and isolation. Others were slower.

It was the encoded norms within the system that determined the responses. The strength of the shock was enough to cause most countries' systems to modify. The more adaptable the system, the quicker the response. Many of the countries that did little had poorer measures of Positive Peace.

One of the key differences between natural systems, such as the weather or the oceans, and human systems is that human systems have intent. For example, with the abolition of its military in 1948, Costa Rica had a clear intent not to go to war. By contrast, nations that maintain large armies will use them to serve their perceived national interests. This is a different intent. Intention is the focus of political and social commentary: What does Russia intend to do in Ukraine? What will America choose to do next in the Middle East? How will Mexico's government crack down on the drug cartels or respond to calls to pay for a wall?

From a systems perspective, organisms have intent. It is obvious that individuals such as you and I have intent, and by extension societies also have intent in the sense that they have ambitions to be better educated or more powerful. It would be hard to argue that China is not set on extending its influence and dominating the South China Sea, or that the United States wants its allies to buy its military equipment. These desires play a key role in determining how they address policy questions. National intent can be seen as being closely aligned with peace. If a nation believes that a military path is the best option for securing national goals it is unlikely to be peaceful.

If all countries have intent, understanding how to measure and compare national intentions becomes paramount, but amazingly there are few formal studies that set out to systematically map countries' intentions. This highlights how little we actually know about how our societies function.

Humans are not passive; they are primarily active, constantly adjusting their intentions and behaviour. Because we have intent we will consciously disrupt the system to fulfil our aims. When aligned and positively channelled this can be a force for good.

At a personal level, this is self-evident to all of us. We view ourselves as being much more than a group of organs and chemical reactions: we are self-aware. But it is not as easy for us to adopt this view about societies.

Feedback loops and self-modification

When a system is unbalanced, its encoded norms will attempt to rebalance it. When this doesn't work then the system seeks a new balance and attempts to develop new encoded norms. This is closely linked to mutual feedback loops. In the nation-state, this could relate to the status quo between unions and business, or the discourse between the media and the public. Both parties shape their reactions based on the responses of the other group. However, if one becomes too strong they change the system.

Much can be said about the Trump presidency or the rise of nationalist parties in Europe, but both are responding to a persistent mismatch between inputs and encoded norms. For many the encoded norm relating to monetary and social equity is clearly broken and with President Trump and Brexit the system is searching for new ways of re-establishing equilibrium.

Feedback loops are fundamental in promoting constructive modification within the system, allowing the nation to evolve to a higher level of complexity and intelligence. However, when unchecked they can be destructive, leading to runaway growth or collapse. The effect of feedback loops, when they run away, could, for example, be the intensification of poverty, a technological breakthrough, the spread of disease or new ideas, the adoption of new philosophical thoughts or the accumulation of capital in fewer hands. It's neither positive nor negative: that depends on the runaway feedback loop.

There is an encoded norm for what societies consider equitable distribution of a country's resources. Currently more and more capital is being amassed in fewer and fewer hands: prima facie evidence that the ability of this encoded norm to re-establish an acceptable equilibrium is being overwhelmed. The economic fall out from the COVID-19 pandemic may radically alter the encoded norms around what is considered equitable in many countries. A greater understanding of systems dynamics equips us better to analyse the problem and find solutions, providing society with a better chance of surviving and flourishing.

One of the more interesting positive examples of self-modification is happening in parts of the Sahel in Africa. Some years ago a World Vision employee, Tony Rinaudo, was attempting to revitalise the natural landscape in Niger by planting trees. After many years he realised he was not getting anywhere and decided to give up, and as luck would have it he got a flat tyre on a rugged dirt road. As he looked at the tyre he saw a very small green shoot on the road, no more than 5 millimetres high. Fascinated, he started to dig around it and realised that there was a large root system underneath, and that was how Farmer Managed Natural Regeneration (FMNR) was discovered.

Due to over grazing and too many people, most of the trees had been cut down for firewood or eaten by cattle, but the root systems had remained in place. What was more remarkable was that if not interfered with, the trees would grow back to their full size within four or five years. The intervention is simple and the major input is education. Since this discovery Tony has been working with nomadic pastoralists to change the way they operate. When new growth comes through, they should delay cutting it until the shoots are well underway and then cut only one shoot. This created a new encoded norm with the pastoralists. One that improved their environment and their sustainability and livelihoods. Over the last decade FMNR has been successfully adopted in many countries including Kenya, Uganda, Timor-Leste and Mali. In 2017 Niger was the only country to increase its vegetation, mainly due to the FMNR techniques.

Another example of self-modification could be that as the population of a country grows, there is increased stress on its agricultural resources. Its government might respond by developing a manufacturing export industry, which absorbs labour and generates capital to import food. Without the new responses to overpopulation the system would slowly degrade as it fails to meet changed needs.

My experiences in the field have helped me to better understand the importance of systems and to take into account the encoded norms and feedback loops of societies. They have also shown me that relying solely on Western rationalism can be counterproductive. Remember the example from the maternal healthcare program in Laos. We need to consider ideas such as homeostasis, self-modification, path dependency and nonlinearity if we are to make better sense of what is happening in societies.

Africa and the Anthropocene

Africa is usually painted as a continent plagued by violence, poverty and famine. All these things are present, but from another angle it is vibrant, flexible and full of optimists who take their setbacks with an exceptionally good sense of humour. In the 30 years I have been visiting the continent, the positive changes have been remarkable. The Africa I see is developing and there are signs of a better future.

One initiative, which comes from the plains of Samburu County in northern Kenya, especially gives me hope. The people of the area are nomadic tribal herders with a strong history of tribal conflict and intense resource competition, both between different groups and with local wildlife. The local environment has been devastated by over grazing – the native flora was being profoundly damaged – and conflict between tribes was increasing.

Groups of farmers, villagers and the government came together in the late 1990s to find ways to create a sustainable ecosystem that balanced the long-term interests of the environment, including endangered wildlife, with those of the herders and the local farming communities. The positive changes there have been truly profound and serve as a case study, or model, for a way to craft a future in the Anthropocene.

In 2004, the Kenyan government created an umbrella group called the Northern Rangelands Trust (NRT), with responsibility for setting the overarching policies and approaches for managing sustainability, development and conflict. The NRT now includes about half a million people and covers approximately 44,000 square kilometres in 33 conservancies, each of which is managed by local members of the tribe, who form a committee. Among other things, there is a local governance index that measures the performance of each of the trusts. Many of the trusts have their own game park lodges, which provide them with tourist revenue. These hotels are leased and the income is derived from having large amounts of game with the profit going back to the tribe. Therefore, there is a vested interest in maintaining and increasing the wildlife population.

Dispute mechanisms have been set up to discourage tribal conflict and cattle rustling. There is investment in improving the water catchment areas, which means that more cattle can be supported. As well, separate troughs are set up for cattle and wildlife, which means that there is less competition between the two.

Because of the additional water, small agricultural holdings are now springing up. More education is being provided, which improves the skill sets of the next generation. Dense grazing techniques have been introduced that replicate the historical migratory impacts on the plains. The land is slowly regenerating; elephant sightings in Sera Conservancy more than quadrupled between 2006 and 2011, for example.

It hasn't all been peace and harmony. One morning in September 2009, 15 people were killed, and there have been other incidents. But the institutions set up by the NRT, along with the trust and the relationships between individual groups – all important elements of Positive Peace – allowed the conflict to be defused and progress to continue. The new encoded norms of the NRT area have helped people to accommodate droughts more successfully than their southern neighbours.

The key to the success of the NRT is that the various factors were all regarded as constituents of a single highly inter-reactive and interdependent system: the farmers, the villagers, the government and the herders; the environment that sustained them; and the industry that provided them with income. When the encoded norms of the old system were unable to cope with the challenges of encroachment, the system self-modified to establish a more resilient and complex structure. The path dependency of tribal society was respected in the establishment of the committees, which in turn provided efficient feedback loops to adapt when it suffered shocks, helping to create a new homeostatic equilibrium in the aftermath. The result has been a virtuous cycle that has improved the lives of the local people, the health of the environment, and the income of both the tourism industry and the government.

More traditional linear thinking might have led the government to regard the encroachment of the herders as the problem and provoked an attempt to restrict them, or encouraged the herders to see the game reserves as the cause of their hardship, leading to the sort of violent clashes that have happened elsewhere. Where linear thinking may have encouraged division and confrontation, systems thinking provided a long-term sustainable peace.

How replicable this is in other areas of Africa or in other parts of the world remains to be seen, but without appropriate sustainable management humanity is in dire trouble.

To meet our global environmental challenges, we must have major structural changes. Our systems must self-modify if they are ever going to reach the levels of resilience and adaptability needed. It is evident that the way we do business today will not be sustainable. We will need to find more nuanced ways of measuring success beyond merely making money or boosting GDP. Positive Peace is an excellent starting point for these much needed changes.

It may turn out that many of the early changes will start locally and be driven by local communities. What is evident when looking at Africa is that when decision-making is closer to the community, even relatively uneducated communities can make the right decisions in their own self-interest.

The COVID-19 pandemic may be the start of this. Our concepts of social equity may be changing. The Australian government, within weeks after starting its lockdown, reversed long-standing policies. They doubled the unemployment benefit and offered free child care. When proposed previously, these changes had been labeled as socialist waste, but faced with unprecedented hardship the government's view on what is equitable has shifted. Reversal of positions such as these are happening with many governments.

The economic aftermath of COVID-19 could easily become a breaking point for many countries. In 2020, the global debt of governments, corporations and individuals was 320 per cent of global GDP. How this plays through the system is anyone's guess, but it will be a different system.

COVID-19: Look to the system

There is much to be learnt from the COVID-19 pandemic. The first lesson is that it was predictable. World leaders, such as Barack Obama and Bill Gates, had commented on the need to improve the preparedness of their health systems or warned of a future pandemic. Nor is it the first pandemic. AIDS has killed 34 million people since its arrival in the late 1970s, while H1N1/09, better known as swine flu, killed 18,000 people in 2009, and an outbreak of Ebola in Western Africa killed 11,000 people in 2013. To date we do not know the real number of deaths from COVID-19, but what we do know is that it will be measured in the millions, if not tens of millions or more.

How does COVID-19 compare to other causes of death? Hunger kills nine million people annually, while cardiovascular diseases kill 18 million per annum. Suicide results in about one million deaths each year and road accidents kill 1.4 million people annually. Given the seriousness of the pandemic, robust responses are required.

Sadly, it is clear that it has moved from being a pandemic to an endemic virus. In other words, without a cure we will have to live with the virus. People have adapted to endemic diseases before, such as malaria, HIV-AIDS and other infectious diseases. We will need to do it again.

The global responses to the pandemic in many ways are similar. Lockdowns have been implemented in countries ranging from Australia to Zimbabwe to the United States and with very similar protocols. However, the outcomes have been very different. One of the more startling findings from our research is that there is a strong correlation between the number of aeroplane travellers and how quickly the virus spread. This explains why the highest rates have been in developed countries with comparatively good health-care systems, such as Spain, the United Kingdom, Italy and the United States. They have the busiest airports in the world. The disease will spread more slowly in the developing world, but will be more difficult to eradicate.

How well governments have dealt with the crisis has varied considerably. Australia and New Zealand have the best responses in the developed world. On the day that the United States recorded its 120,000th death, Australia's death toll was 100 and only ten new cases were recorded. Bang for the buck the United States has one of the worst health systems in the world, while Australia has one of the best. In Australia, politicians put down their partisan divides and the state and the federal governments developed a coherent strategy quickly, which all signed onto. In the United States it was a different story: some states and cities responded strongly, although probably not swiftly enough; others did little. It soon became a partisan political issue, with the subsequent economic downturn being blamed on the Democratic states' lockdowns. Even the stimulus packages became partisan. It is no surprise that both the United States and Brazil, the countries with the largest number of deaths from COVID-19, are amongst the ten countries with the largest declines in Positive Peace in the last decade.

The underlying systems within these countries have, in many ways, defined how they have responded to the pandemic and the subsequent economic shock. Although data was still sketchy at the time of writing this book, the countries within the Organisation for Economic Co-operation and Development (OECD) with the strongest Positive Peace were the ones that responded best. This was especially true for countries with higher levels of *Well-Functioning Government* and *Strong Business Environments*, where the countries that were high in these Pillars tested more people than countries that were not.

As the shocks of the pandemic vibrate through the world it will become a very different place and as we have learnt, once a system changes it cannot go back to what it was. Some countries will pass tipping points, while others will build new capabilities and will become more resilient.

What is certain is that this crisis is unlike anything that has been experienced before. The United Kingdom is experiencing its sharpest downturn since 1706, while the United States has recorded its largest increase in unemployment ever. With a world mired in heavy debt, sluggish economic growth before the crisis and interest rates so low that there is little room to ease them further, it is likely to be many years before the economy returns to the 2019 levels. This leaves an uncertain future and one that is inherently unstable.

More worrying are the parallels to the 1930s, a severe economic recession combined with increasing levels of protectionism, a loss of support for the international system – a system that, over the last 70 years, has overseen an unprecedented period of wealth creation, and an increasingly belligerent relationship between the world's two major powers. However, most governments do seem committed to whatever stimulus is needed to keep their economies afloat which means we should not sleep walk into another depression.

The short-term outlook is dire, but it is also a chance to reassess global and national systems. Dissatisfaction with the political system in developed countries has been increasing for some time. Hostilities will increase in the short term, but the countries that can adapt and seriously address the causes of their problems will be the ones that thrive in the longer term.

The pandemic has highlighted how interconnected, fragile and complex the global socio-economic system is. In a matter of weeks, global travel and trade systems collapsed, social norms changed radically, rights and liberties that had been taken for granted, such as the freedom of movement and association, were revoked and social values re-oriented. It also became apparent that the world lacks a credible approach to dealing with this crisis. The uncertainty, along with the impact of the virus and subsequent economic losses, is likely to sharpen the focus on other socio-economic factors that have been brewing, such as the growing inequality in wealth, deteriorating labour conditions in developed countries and the alienation with the political system.

A little known fact is that in the decade to 2020, the number of demonstrations, riots and general strikes increased globally by over 240 per cent. The largest number of incidents was recorded in Europe,[1] although Europe also had the least number of violent incidents. Without addressing the underlying causes of these demonstrations they are likely to become turbo-charged.

As these dynamics play out the world will become a very different place. Political instability will only get worse before it improves.

What we can see is that the crisis is systemic, highly complex, and the processes of dealing with the problem and finding solutions are interconnected. This is where Positive Peace comes in. Countries that focus on Positive Peace specifically, or unwittingly, because of the strength of their societal attitudes and internal cohesion, are likely to recover more quickly and will be better equipped to thrive afterwards.

It is easy to see how *Well-Functioning Government* is vital for economic recovery, while *Good Relations with Neighbours* is the antithesis of trade

1 2020 Global Peace Index Report

wars or another super-power cold war. *Equitable Distribution of Resources* determines how equitable access is to the health system. It will be crucial to see whether the future high levels of unemployment lead to a better compact between governments and their citizens or is used to grind down wages and employee entitlements. The *Free Flow of Information* is critical for societies to trust the health measures being implemented and to understand the economic debates. A *Strong Business Environment* is essential to achieving a faster economic recovery and building bonds with other nations, while *Higher Levels of Human Capital* means that better educated people and inventive societies are more likely to find the best avenues to progress their country.

A country's ability to develop Positive Peace in the past has paved the way for its current successes, so too will the current strength of its Pillars determine its responsiveness to the current crisis. Those countries that can improve their Positive Peace through the crisis will be the ones best placed to reap the rewards afterwards and better placed to deal with the other global challenges facing humanity later in the 21st century.

Personal experiences of the system

One of our earliest projects was in Kasulu, and I have already mentioned Utopia, who turned a few hundred dollars to good use. In our malaria project we were seeing many cases of severe malnutrition. It mainly affected boys. In some parts of the world the girls are better fed than the boys, simply because the women have the responsibility for cooking, so they have first access to the food in the kitchen. Women are disadvantaged in many other ways, but not always in this area.

The malnutrition was so severe that in many cases the muscles in the stomach wall would become extremely weak, leading to herniation. The boys had stomach hernias that were about ten centimetres long, which would hang down from their bodies. We asked if there was anything we could do and were told no: the hernias could be sewn up, but they would pop back out again, because of the poor nutrition.

It was a shocking sight. We started a child-survival project that looked at how to improve nutrition by building agricultural capacity and improving crops, spending more than $2 million on the project. The aim was to introduce crops that had higher yields, were hardier, and that provided a more balanced and nutritious diet. This is a textbook example of linear thinking: malnutrition can be cured with more nutritious crops.

When I visited five years later, I could see no discernible difference. Looking back, I realise now that the project did not take into account the local societal system. We should have asked: What were the foods they liked that were nutritious enough? Instead, we introduced crops with higher nutritional content. The local people simply didn't like the taste of the new foods; their taste buds had to adjust to different tastes. It was a salutary lesson: their encoded norms preserved homeostasis by rejecting the new crop. Never underestimate the barriers that come up when people have to change their habits, attitudes and beliefs. It would have been better to understand what crops they liked and had the highest nutritional content, and then built the program around it.

We learnt the lessons of Kasulu and the importance of systems thinking. More recently our family foundation has been working with a group called the One Acre Fund, which works to increase the capacity and profits of local farmers in western Kenya and Rwanda. The Fund provides farmers with seed and fertiliser banks and offers training in low-tech farming techniques to grow the crop and improve the yield. The farmers were used to paying top prices for seed and fertiliser in the planting season, and they were frequently funding this by taking out loans, which meant that a failed crop could lead to bankruptcy.

Through the One Acre Fund, we created a capital fund and encouraged farmers to come together in cooperatives, which then established seed and fertiliser banks. The cooperatives could buy cheap seed and fertiliser out of season, making the farmers less dependent on loans. Alongside addressing the cost side of the equation, we worked to improve water supply, taught farmers to use better spacing between plants, and helped them optimise the use of fertiliser and water.

These initiatives alone increased crop yields by over 30 per cent. It wasn't long before the cooperatives were in a position to repay their initial capital, which could be directed to other interventions. We did not make the same mistake of trying to change the system by bringing in new crops that the locals had no history of eating.

It is easy to see, even with this simple example, how a holistic approach allows for the right initiatives to support each other. The farmers realised they could get increased yield from the better seeds, fertiliser and training, and they could more easily pay for the goods and services from their realised profits because they were operating at higher margins and without being dependent on the mortgagers. Eventually 30,000 farmers were organised into cooperatives.

We had nudged the system forward and helped the farmers improve their resilience. In doing so, we had given them the space to address deeper systemic challenges.

Midway through the project I sat down with about 30 farmers to discuss how their program was progressing. I try to do this as much as possible, partly because I like learning about the local customs and cultures, but also because it provides direct feedback on the benefits and shortcomings of our programs.

As I asked the farmers questions about the difficulties they faced, we suddenly moved from the micro to the macro. The root of many of their problems, they said, was the size of their landholdings. The convention of the local culture was that when children became of age, their parents would give them some of their land. The dramatic improvements in child survival rates over the previous 40 years meant that the average size of a family block had become too small to be economically viable. The cultural tradition was being abandoned because of necessity; people were being forced to migrate to the cities. Once again I was finding out first hand the effects of overpopulation. Although we had taken a holistic approach to their agricultural problems, it was only a system within a broader system. The key systemic problem was that there were too many people. The solution was beyond the scope of a simple agricultural program.

There has been a huge drive for efficiency over the past few years, in everything from business, to aid, to social reorganisation. Efficiency is excellent for getting the most 'bang for the buck', but it also reduces the number of alternatives in the event of a failure: it makes the system less adaptive and more brittle. Diversity is important to systems as it allows more options when coping with change. We will need to learn these lessons globally as the larger environments change and transform. Our ability to adapt to these changes will become paramount, and that will involve ensuring our systems retain a degree of redundancy and diversity, rather than giving in to the current trend for optimisation and specialisation.

Just as diverse natural systems possess greater resilience, so do diverse human systems. This is one of the imperatives of life in the Anthropocene. Artificially created monocultures are more fragile and are less likely to prove sustainable as conditions evolve. One of the better examples from history is the Irish potato famine in the 19th century. Ireland has rich soil and once supported a diversified agricultural industry. However, with the rise of the British Empire specialisation was pushed and pushed hard. Many parts of the Empire had their own area of specialty, based on what they did most efficiently. Ireland was the best place to grow potatoes, and other crops were dropped. By 1840 nearly 40 per cent of the Irish population were dependent on a single variety of potato called the Irish Lumper as their primary food source.

When the potato plants got a form of blight, the crops started to fail. There was nothing else for the Irish people to eat. It is estimated that a million people died and two million emigrated; the population of Ireland did not recover to its pre-famine levels until the beginning of the 21st century, some 170 years later. The problem was exacerbated by British incompetence and mendacity, but if there had been greater crop diversity, millions of lives would have been saved.

COVID-19 is teaching us a similar lesson. When one province in China, Wuhan, went into lockdown the global supply chain for many items stopped. The outcome of this is that many countries and companies are now considering how to build more diversity into their supply chains.

CHAPTER 6

Discovering Positive Peace

The origins of Positive Peace as a concept lie with Dr Martin Luther King, Jr, as explained in Chapter 1. The Norwegian sociologist Johan Galtung took the concept further in 1964, defining it as 'the integration of human society', which led him to develop the concepts of structural, cultural and indirect violence. These terms pertain to situations where there may not be physical violence but high levels of fear, little personal freedom, or environments in which the structural aspects of society, including the culture, lead to higher levels of violence than necessary. Much of this work is normative, and although a lot of it is good, it's based on the shifting sands of moral perception, with little empirical work behind it.

The IEP adopted the term 'Positive Peace' and defined it as 'The attitudes, institutions and structures that create and sustain peaceful societies'. Positive Peace in this sense is about actions that create a sustained peace. The starting point for the IEP was the desire to create a simpler framework, one that would be useful and practical, derived from data and mathematics, and involving systems thinking. We use Positive Peace with capitals to denote the IEP's particular form of Positive Peace. We also acknowledge that like all concepts, including the word 'peace', Positive Peace is evolving.

We can draw a parallel with medical science to show how we arrived at Positive Peace. Pathology – the study of disease – has led to breakthroughs in our understanding of how to treat and cure illness. However, it was only when medical science started to look deeper into healthy human beings – the study of wellness rather than illness – that we gained a better understanding of what we need to do to stay healthy and avoid sickness. This could only be learnt by studying what was working. We would never learn this from studying people who were on their deathbeds. In the same way, the study of violence is different from the study of peace.

The parallels between physical health and social health also illustrate two other key aspects of Positive Peace. Just as exercise and a healthy diet build physical resilience to the onset of disease, Positive Peace builds social resilience to the onset of violence: it is preventative. The second insight is that just as we can score the healthiness of apparently healthy people by looking at cholesterol levels or performance on a treadmill, we can measure Positive Peace by comparing levels of governance or the acceptance of the rights of others. Peace, like health, is a measurable phenomenon.

Positive Peace is also associated with many other social characteristics that are considered desirable, including better economic outcomes, measures of wellbeing, the levels of gender equality and environmental performance. In this way, Positive Peace can be thought of as creating an optimal environment in which human potential can flourish.

Iceland

Iceland is a great case study of resilience and adaptation. The Global Peace Index has ranked it as the most peaceful nation in the world for the last ten years. It also ranks 7th on the Positive Peace Index. The country has a number of natural factors in its favour: it has a small population and a large landmass. South Korea is roughly the same size and has 150 times as many people. The climate is not friendly to prolonged military escapades. Many have joked it is so cold no one ever goes outside, therefore how can they fight? Still, the nation has an enviable record of peacefulness. The bloodiest battle in the island's history killed 110 people, and that was in 1264.[1]

A few years after the Global Peace Index was launched, I was in Reykjavík to speak at the Spirit of Humanity Forum. It was organised by a beautiful person called Scherto Gill, whom I have since come to know well. Scherto is a soft person with a marvellous way of articulating what is most difficult to articulate, namely the spiritual aspects of peace.

The forum left me with a few days' holiday to see different parts of the island. Until recent times, it was quite acceptable in Iceland to seek shelter

1 J. Johannesson, *A History of the Old Icelandic Commonwealth: Islendinga Saga*, University of Manitoba Press, 2014, p. 261.

in someone else's house. As I travelled around Iceland, the reason for such generosity became obvious. It has one of the world's most unforgiving climates: storms can come in quickly and they often turn into blizzards. As Iceland is sparsely populated, anyone caught in these storms would head for the nearest shelter, even if the occupants were not at home. Sadly, the custom of leaving one's house unlocked in case someone needs to take refuge is in decline, but the legacy of social cohesion and trust that it represents is still alive. As the country modernised, life has become easier but the cultural integration has largely remained.

Iceland's history has other interesting features that left a deep imprint on its encoded norms. Viking settlers founded the world's oldest parliament, the Althing, in the 10th century. Although the Vikings had a fearsome reputation as raiders on their British neighbours, Iceland had a long track record of solving its internal differences nonviolently.

The benefits of such a history became evident in the wake of the 2008 Global Financial Crisis. Iceland's economy collapsed under the weight of debt equivalent to seven times the country's GDP. The country defaulted on its loans, which meant it could not raise more commercial debt and had to be bailed out by the International Monetary Fund (IMF). The country was effectively bankrupt. The crash resulted in great hardship, but although there were some demonstrations, they were not particularly violent. Also, the protesters were specific in their demands. In highly peaceful societies, protest movements tend to be less violent and their goals are narrower and better defined than in less peaceful countries. This can be seen from the IEP's studies of civil resistance movements.[2] In peaceful societies, there is a continual negotiation occurring between the different constituencies, which narrows the gap in potential grievances. That is exactly what happened in Iceland.

The next step was the emergence of a new political party, which went on to win the next election and form the government. The processes for peaceful systemic change, in other words, were present. Iceland was able to come up with a coordinated response to its severe banking distress

2 Institute for Economics and Peace, *Positive Peace Report 2015*.

that was more effective than those of other nations that were under considerable stress.

As Spiegel Online commented, what happened in Iceland between 2008 and 2011 is regarded as one of the worst financial crises ever to befall a nation, and one of the greatest recoveries:

> It seems likely that never before had a country managed to amass such great sums of money per capita, only to lose it again in such a short period of time. But Iceland, with a population of just 320,000, has also staged what appears to be the fastest recovery on record. Since 2011, the gross domestic product has been on the rise once again. What's more, salaries are rising, the national debt is sinking and the government has paid off part of the billions in loans it received in 2008 from the International Monetary Fund ahead of schedule. It's a sign of confidence.[3]

The high levels of external peace in Iceland can partly be explained by its geography. One of our more intriguing findings is that island states tend to be more peaceful. They have no land borders, which limits cross-border contagion and provides a degree of protection from criminal activity and hostile nations. However, while these factors are important, they do not explain why internal peace in Iceland is so strong.

The Pillars of Positive Peace

The distinguishing feature of the IEP's work on Positive Peace is that it is empirical and uses quantitative analysis techniques wherever possible.

Historically, Positive Peace has largely been understood qualitatively and has been based on idealistic concepts of what a peaceful society is. Instead, the IEP's approach is based on statistical analysis by identifying the quantitatively definable common characteristics of the world's most

---

3 G. Mingels, 'Out of the abyss: looking for lessons in Iceland's recovery', Spiegel Online International, 10 January 2014, accessed at www.spiegel.de/international/europe/financial-recovery-of-iceland-a-case-worth-studying-a-942387.html

peaceful countries. In order to find out what they are, the IEP utilises the time-series data contained in the Global Peace Index, in combination with existing peace and development literature, to statistically analyse the key characteristics common to peaceful countries and identify the key drivers of peace. The IEP has roughly 50,000 datasets at the country level, of which 25,000 are used to identify Positive Peace.

The aim, as best as possible, is to avoid the value judgements inherent in our team and our understanding of the world.

Human beings encounter disagreement regularly – whether at home, at work, among friends, or on a more systemic level between ethnic, religious or political groups. But the majority of these differences do not result in violence. Positive Peace recognises that nonviolent disagreement can be constructive because it offers an opportunity to negotiate or renegotiate relationships in ways that improve mutual outcomes. Built within societies are certain aspects that enable or encourage this, such as attitudes that discourage violence or legal structures designed to reconcile grievances. These informal and formal values and structures facilitate nonviolent change and adaptation.

The Global Partnership for the Prevention of Armed Conflict's review of the role of civil society in peace-building found that, 'When tensions escalate into armed conflict, it almost always reflects the break down or underdevelopment of routine systems for managing competing interests and values and the failure to satisfy basic human needs.'[4] Positive Peace provides a framework to study and strengthen these qualities.

To identify the key components of Positive Peace we ran multiple correlations against the 25,000 datasets used in the Global Peace Index to ascertain which aspects had the strongest statistical correlation with peace. We then ran further analysis to eliminate spurious results and multiple measures of the same thing. The results were then clumped together and analysed using principal component analysis, a form of statistical analysis, to help in determining how the factors related to each other so that relevant

---

4 Catherine Barnes, *Agents for Change: Civil Society Roles in Preventing War and Building Peace*, Global Partnership for the Prevention of Armed Conflict, 2006, accessed at www.peaceportal.org/documents/127900679/127917167/Rapport2_2.pdf

factors could be grouped together, which then became the Positive Peace framework pictured below.

FIGURE 3

The Pillars of Positive Peace

The factors comprising Postive Peace. All eight factors are interconnected and interact in varied and complex ways.

SOURCE: IEP

The IEP has identified eight key domains, or Pillars, that comprise Positive Peace:

- **WELL-FUNCTIONING GOVERNMENT** – A well-functioning government delivers high-quality public and civil services, engenders trust and participation, demonstrates political stability, and upholds the rule of law.
- **SOUND BUSINESS ENVIRONMENT** – The strength of economic conditions as well as the formal institutions that support the operation of the private sector determine the soundness of the business environment. Business competitiveness and economic productivity are both associated with the most peaceful countries, as is the presence of regulatory systems that are conducive to business operations. This Pillar also measures the freedom of individuals to work, produce, consume and invest.
- **EQUITABLE DISTRIBUTION OF RESOURCES** – Peaceful countries tend to ensure broad access to resources such as education and health, as well as, although to a lesser extent, better income distribution. Social mobility is a key factor.
- **ACCEPTANCE OF THE RIGHTS OF OTHERS** – Formal laws that guarantee basic human rights and freedoms and informal social and cultural norms that relate to behaviours of citizens serve as proxies for the level of tolerance between different ethnic, linguistic, religious and socio-economic groups within the country. Similarly, gender equality and workers' rights are important components of societies that uphold acceptance of the rights of others.
- **GOOD RELATIONS WITH NEIGHBOURS** – Peaceful relations with other countries are as important as good relations between groups within a country. Countries with positive external relations tend to be more peaceful and politically stable, have better-functioning governments, are regionally integrated and have lower levels of organised internal conflict. This factor is also beneficial for business and supports foreign direct investment, tourism and human capital inflows.
- **FREE FLOW OF INFORMATION** – Free and independent media disseminates information in a way that leads to greater openness and helps individuals and society work productively together. This is reflected in the extent

to which citizens can access information, whether the media is free and independent, and how well informed citizens are. This leads to better decision-making and more rational responses in times of crisis.

- **HIGH LEVELS OF HUMAN CAPITAL** – A skilled human capital base reflects the extent to which societies educate citizens and promote the development of knowledge, thereby improving economic productivity and care for the young, enabling political participation and increasing social capital. Education is a fundamental building block through which societies can build resilience and develop mechanisms to learn and adapt.
- **LOW LEVELS OF CORRUPTION** – Low corruption can enhance confidence and trust in institutions. In societies with high corruption, resources are inefficiently allocated, often leading to a lack of funding for essential services. The resulting inequities can lead to civil unrest and in extreme situations can be the catalyst for more serious violence.

In line with systems thinking, the relationships between the Pillars are complex and contain elements of both cause and effect. For example, *Well-Functioning Government* is both a symptom of a healthy nation and a cause of it.

What is appropriate in one country may not be appropriate in another. The ways in which *High Levels of Human Capital* or *Acceptance of the Rights of Others* manifest in each society will have unique factors. The indicators chosen to measure each domain are based on the factors with the strongest statistically significant relationship with peacefulness, and as such form both a holistic and an empirical framework.[5]

Complex systems are much more than the sum of their component parts. When analysing system complexity, and how it pertains to conflict-affected or peaceful environments, it is not possible to simply isolate causes from effects and then act accordingly. Not only are there a multitude of ways in which different variables react with each other, but also the 'components' of the system are not just unthinking biological entities. They are people

5 Measured as the correlation between each Positive Peace indicator and internal peace scores from the GPI. The GPI includes measures of both internal and external peace, with internal peacefulness accounting for 60 per cent of a country's overall scores.

who are self-aware and conscious of what is being done. How they react will change the system, and the system will change how they react as well: a mutual feedback loop.

To have a lasting effect on peace, it is necessary to work as much as possible on all eight Pillars simultaneously, thereby addressing the whole system. One of the shortcomings of development aid is that it generally tends to work on only one problem at a time, rather than the whole. This can mean that the problem returns, even if the particular project seems to have been successful.

An intervention should stimulate as many of the Pillars as possible and should satisfy three key criteria: it should be substantial, acceptable in the current political environment, and lead to relatively quick impact.

The eight Pillars capture the *attitudes*, *institutions* and *structures* that are strongest in the most peaceful societies. High levels of Positive Peace occur where attitudes make violence less tolerated, institutions are more responsive to society's needs and structures underpin the nonviolent resolution of grievances.

- **ATTITUDES** refer to norms, beliefs, preferences and relationships within society. Attitudes influence how people and groups cooperate in society and can impact and be impacted upon by the institutions and structures that society creates.
- **INSTITUTIONS** are the formal bodies created by governments or other groups, such as companies, industry associations or labour unions. They may be responsible for supplying education or administering the rule of law, for example. The way institutions operate is affected by both the attitudes that are prevalent within a society and the structures that define them.
- **STRUCTURES** can be both formal and informal and serve as a shared code of conduct that is broadly applicable to most individuals. Informally, it could be as simple as politeness and the protocol for greeting people, or more formally, as complex as tax law. Interactions are often governed by societal views on morality, which lead to the acceptance or rejection of others' behaviours.

Attitudes, *institutions* and *structures* are all highly interrelated and can be difficult to disentangle, but in the context of systems thinking that is less important than understanding what affects them and how they interact as a whole. Positive Peace is a generalised framework, where many paths can be taken to accomplish the same goal. These paths are dependent on the cultural norms and specific situations within any particular society.

The Positive Peace Index

Once we had developed the concept of Positive Peace and a way of measuring it objectively, the next logical step was to create an index. The Positive Peace Index became a major conceptual breakthrough because it allowed us to compare Positive Peace to a range of other social phenomena.

The Positive Peace Index and the Global Peace Index stand as two complementary bodies of work. The Global Peace Index acts as a measure of the current state of peace at the national level, whereas the Positive Peace Index provides insights into the underlying health of the nation and how it is progressing in terms of building the appropriate structures to sustain peace, resilience and the broader foundations for societal development.

The Positive Peace Index consists of the eight Pillars, with each domain containing three indicators, making a total of 24. The three measures chosen for each domain are the most statistically significant, which eliminates personal biases, while the weightings of each indicator are based on the strength of the statistical relationship, thereby further reducing the potential for bias. This also means that the indicators may change over time as new measures are developed or underlying associations change.

It soon became evident that we had developed something that was more than a framework to describe peace. The Positive Peace Index was also statistically correlated to many other socially desirable outcomes, such as higher per capita income, better performance on environmental management, better health outcomes, and many others. Therefore, we coined the phrase 'Positive Peace describes an optimal environment for human potential to flourish.' Although we had started with peace, what we discovered was something much more profound.

The Positive Peace Index takes into account many of the things that are associated with peace in the popular mind, but which are not in themselves directly linked to stopping violence: equal treatment, justice, good international relations, better economic opportunity, lower corruption, free speech and legal protections. Positive Peace can also be used as a proxy for measuring a country's social resilience – its ability to absorb and recover from shocks. It can also be used to measure fragility, which in turn helps to predict the likelihood of future conflict, violence and instability, making it an excellent basis for analysing risk.

When the levels of Positive Peace are lower than the actual peace, as measured through the Global Peace Index, it indicates a higher risk of substantial falls in peace.

Positive Peace is systemic

Positive Peace and systems thinking, as applied to nations, are still in their infancy. Concepts will evolve, new approaches will be developed, but the thrust of the research is clear. Conceptually this approach gives a clear, informed and useful way to understand the forces governing the operation of our societies.

A systems view of Positive Peace recognises complexity, but that complexity itself can make identifying entry points for change appear to be difficult. The IEP has identified a number of approaches for catalysing systemic change in complex systems – one that emphasises depth, one that emphasises breadth and one aimed at the local level. The first approach focuses on a society's weakest Pillars and is appropriate where one or two Pillars are much weaker than the rest. This approach is illustrated by a short case study of post-conflict improvements in peace in Nepal, where a 30 per cent improvement in the *Free Flow of Information* was a leading indicator for a significant improvement in both *Acceptance of the Rights of Others* and *Equitable Distribution of Resources.*

The second approach involves stimulating the entire system simultaneously. This approach takes each of the eight Pillars of Positive Peace and defines an action for each Pillar that is substantial, can be achieved in the current political environment and will have an impact within a reasonable amount of time. A good example of this is Peru. It has emerged as one of Latin

America's most prosperous countries following decades of military coups, violent insurgencies, social unrest and macroeconomic fluctuations. With a population of 33 million people and covering an area of 1.3 million square kilometres, Peru is the third largest country in South America. Its Positive Peace score has been steadily improving and the country is now ranked 72nd in the Positive Peace Index. This is the fourth highest rank within South America. Much of the improvement in Peru's Positive Peace scores occurred prior to 2008. Examples of actions taken for four of the Pillars are:

- **GOOD RELATIONS WITH NEIGHBOURS:** In 2004, after decades of border disputes, Peru and Chile signed a statement expressing their intent to forge closer ties and develop bilateral relations. Peru is a member of Mercosur, the Pacific Alliance, the Community of Andean Nations, the Asia–Pacific Economic Cooperation, the Community of Latin American and Caribbean States and the Forum for East Asia–Latin America Cooperation, among other international bodies. Over the past decade, Peru has improved 22 places in the *Good Relations with Neighbours* Pillar.
- **WELL-FUNCTIONING GOVERNMENT:** Peru created the Acuerdo Nacional, a consultative body comprising representatives from various sectors that defines long-term government reform objectives and policies. Meetings of the body are attended by high-ranking members of the country's political parties, the workers' union, business and professional associations.
- **SOUND BUSINESS ENVIRONMENT:** Macroeconomic reforms halted hyper-inflation in the 1990s and opened Peru to international trade and investment. From 1990, then President Alberto Fujimori implemented a series of deregulation and privatisation measures that unencumbered the local business sector.
- **EQUITABLE DISTRIBUTION OF RESOURCES:** In 2005, Peru's Ministry of Development and Social Inclusion (Ministerio de Desarrollo e Inclusión Social, MIDIS) implemented Juntos, a conditional cash transfer program that provides monthly support to impoverished families.

Innovation in Africa

The third approach is to apply the eight Pillars to a community project. This was first developed in the field by a young Rotarian, Jude Kakuba, who did a training course in Positive Peace. He was a school teacher and his local Rotary club had been funding a project for education in a very poor school in Uganda but without much success. After the course Jude examined the project, looking at it through each of the eight Pillars of Positive Peace. This provided a much better understanding of the inhibitors to education and changed the approach to the project. He and his team provided interventions for all eight Pillars. This provided new and successful insights into the schooling system, resulting in a much more holistic approach. Many of these interventions would not have been carried out without the framework, but two of the interventions really struck me. The first was for the Pillar *Acceptance of the Rights of Others*. Looking through this Pillar the number one priority appeared to be that the girls felt excluded from school and the reason turned out to be the lack of sanitary pads. When they had their period they would not go to school. So the project provided sanitary pads and the attendance rates increased.

The second was for the Pillar *Good Relations with Neighbours*. They were having trouble with the neighbours. The school was in a rural setting and the kids were stealing fruit from the neighbours' trees for lunch. Given the poverty in the region each apple or orange was meaningful and this had led to conflict between the school and its neighbours. The problem was that the kids were hungry. The area was so poor that most families couldn't provide food for lunch. Many kids didn't go to school because they had to scrounge to find their own food. The school introduced porridge for lunch and planted the same types of fruit trees in the school grounds. The porridge literally costs cents per day per child. The attendance rates increased because the parents encouraged the children to go to school as it was one less meal they had to provide. The upshot of these interventions, and the others, was a stunning improvement in attendance and scholastic scores. In 18 months, attendance rates jumped from 327 students to 805, while the percentage of students scoring Grade 1 and 2, the two highest grades of the five grades, increased from 30 per cent to 62 per cent: one of the best rates in the district. The meal at lunchtime meant that the students had a recharge of nutrients; therefore their concentration didn't wane in the afternoon. All eight interventions were important, but these two stood out. They would not have occurred in the standard models to improve literacy.

Each Pillar of Positive Peace represents a complex set of social dynamics. For example, overhauling all aspects of corruption or resource distribution in a country simultaneously is not only often politically impossible, but is also likely to be destabilising. Some improvement will always be possible, but the project should aim to be evolutionary rather than revolutionary, recognising that path dependency takes time. Through stimulating the whole system, it is possible to start or enhance a virtuous cycle, in which conditions act in a reinforcing manner, thereby continually improving each other.

Zimbabwe: a practical approach

The Pillars of Positive Peace are designed to transcend the infinite variations in encoded norms between nations as best as possible. However, the way they are stimulated will have features unique to different societies.

Our first practical attempt to apply the framework of Positive Peace and systems thinking was in 2016 in Zimbabwe, where we worked with the National Peace Trust. Although the recommendations that were developed have yet to be implemented, the development process demonstrated Positive Peace's potential to bridge long-standing divisions and create a space for progress where none had existed before. The framework also proved to be culturally appropriate and worked in the local setting.

The political discourse in Zimbabwe had been toxic for many years. President Robert Mugabe was reaching the end of his tenure in power; he was 91 at the time. Both the government and society were looking towards the future and change. It was generally agreed within the ruling party, ZANU–PF, that the land reform initiatives had been a disaster in execution if not in principle.

In their view, the principle of taking the land off white farmers and giving it to Indigenous Zimbabweans was just and appropriate. Most Zimbabweans had supported the move because, in their eyes, white colonialists had seized the land from their ancestors in the first place. The acquired land was distributed among 600,000 families, so in one way it was equitable. It certainly brought a lot of loyalty for ZANU–PF, partly helping to keep them in power for many years afterwards. The redistribution covered ten per cent of the voting population.

However, the policy led to Zimbabwe being isolated from the international community and this, along with the ensuing collapse in farm production, provoked economic breakdown. Before the redistribution, Zimbabwe was a thriving economy with a strong primary export sector. But the new land-holders had no experience in farming and the lots were too small to generate any of the economies of scale needed for export. Much of the land went to waste and the export sector has never recovered. The collapse of the economy led to the worst inflation rates ever experienced by any country, peaking in November 2008 at almost 80 billion per cent: prices were doubling every day.

At the time of independence in 1980, one Zimbabwean dollar was worth one US dollar. In 2009, a friend gave me a Zimbabwean note worth 200 billion dollars, so bad had hyperinflation become. The economy was eventually stabilised through the adoption of the US dollar, but when we did the workshop Zimbabwe was still toxic in the eyes of the international investment community.

The Positive Peace conference in Zimbabwe came about because of the work of Trust Mamombe, an exceptional Zimbabwean who had successfully navigated the politics of his country, eventually developing good relations with all sides of politics. Trust did six months of background work, bringing together leading academics and thinkers – from Zimbabwe, Botswana and Zambia – to arrive at an understanding of how Positive Peace could be applied in the local setting.

The first phase was to determine whether the Pillars were applicable to Zimbabwe. Did the Pillars relate to Zimbabwean culture, and was there a need for inclusions or deletions? The experts agreed that the Pillars worked, did not need modifying and were culturally acceptable. They also agreed that an initiative would be developed for each Pillar that would be substantial, could be implemented in the current political environment and would have an effect quickly.

What I found striking was that representatives of the government, the opposition and civil society were all able to agree on these initiatives. What made this possible was the way the process was conducted. It looked for actions that could be carried out which would stimulate each Pillar. It was also practical as the interventions would have to be achievable in the current political setting. It was forward looking. It was a way to overcome the hostile nature of past clashes between government, opposition and elements of civil society.

Previously any attempt to discuss problems broke down into mutual recrimination.

Generally, people look backwards in an attempt to understand the cause of a problem. The people associated with its causes become defensive, setting off a new cycle of recrimination. This underlines one of the issues with causal thinking. In the systemic approach we look forward, to the emergent qualities. What factors would best stimulate the system? By asking this type of question there is no need to apportion blame. This is another example of how systems thinking can radically change the way we approach problems.

The then Vice-President Emmerson Mnangagwa opened the Positive Peace conference. It was attended by a number of government ministers, leading members of the opposition, the Movement for Democratic Change – Tsvangirai, business leaders and civil society. We found a common willingness to entertain the prospect of developing Positive Peace among people who had not sat in the same room or found common ground since independence 35 years earlier. Even if nothing else transpired, re-establishing a forum for civil discourse was a success in itself.

An action was developed for each Pillar based on the three principles outlined – *substantial, could be achieved in the current political environment, and have impact in the near future*. They were presented at the conference, they were discussed, and accepted. The actions ranged from a recommendation to create a process to mediate conflicts related to land use and access under the *Equitable Distribution of Resources* Pillar, to training women's clubs for engagement with traditional leaders, under the *Acceptance of the Rights of*

Others Pillar, to encouraging community involvement in planning local government budgets under the *Well-Functioning Government* Pillar.

Although the conference and the development of the action items were a success, and follow-up meetings are continuing; implementation is proving challenging. The frozen nature of the political system makes change extremely difficult. This highlights the systemic nature of the country's challenges. Years of Mugabe's rule have eroded its adaptive capability and the encoded norms are so strong and rigid that the capacity for self-modification to a more sophisticated system is currently limited.

We have since run workshops on the application of Positive Peace for young Libyans, Mexicans and Ugandans, among others. Some examples of workshops are set out below.

Moroto Workshop, Karamoja region, Uganda

The Karamoja region in northeast Uganda is one of the poorest areas in the country and one of the least developed areas in the world. The illiteracy rate for the Karamoja people is 81 per cent. School attendance in primary and secondary is low, with primary education attendance at 6.7 per cent. The people are predominately pastoralists, and economically, the region depends on livestock herding and trade.

Karamoja has been marked by a recent history of conflict including intercommunity livestock raiding. The issue has become more acute through the spread of small arms and light weapons in the area. Peace is fragile due to many factors, including competition for critical and depleted natural resources, and longstanding intercommunity grievances.

Over three workshops in October 2018, in the Moroto region, the IEP along with The Charitable Foundation and the Danish Refugee Council introduced the eight Pillars of Positive Peace to 120 participants, discussing the factors that sustain peaceful societies, and how the Positive Peace model applies to local environments.

Workshop evaluation surveys showed that there was a 54 per cent increase in participants who correctly identified and defined Positive Peace. As well, more than half of the survey respondents said they had new ideas for projects or activities to build peace in their communities after the workshops.

Libyan Youth workshops, Tunisia

In March and April 2018, in collaboration with UNICEF and the Nicosia Initiative, the IEP conducted a series of four workshops for Libyan youth. After a successful pilot, 180 young people were flown to Tunis in Tunisia from Libya because it was too dangerous to train them there.

Since the overthrow of Muammar Gaddafi in 2011, Libya has been mired in violent conflict. Various militias and brigades control different areas within Libya, and many of the communities from which the youth came were in conflict with each other.

The workshops gave participants from cities across Libya the chance to sit at the same table and discuss their different experiences and perspectives. Through the IEP's Positive Peace framework, participants were able to see common problems facing their cities. After the course, many people said they never thought they would be in the same room with some of the other participants, let alone agree on approaches to common problems.

At the conclusion of each of the four workshops, participants were asked to develop and present their own projects based on the Positive Peace framework. This exercise allowed them to consider the challenges they face systemically and respond with actions aimed at building the Pillars of Positive Peace. Of the 40 projects submitted, 13 were selected to be funded as part of the initiative. Project grants, awarded by a multi-stakeholder committee, were based on the project's potential to build Positive Peace in Libyan towns and cities.

Prior to each workshop, participants responded to a survey that measured perceptions of cohesion across communities. The same survey was also completed at the end of each workshop. The results show a marked increase in intergroup cohesion and positive perceptions of other communities, as a result of participation in the workshop.

Mexico workshop

Mexico ranked 137th out of 163 countries on the Global Peace Index 2020 due to high levels of organised crime.

The IEP, Rotary International and Universidad de las Américas Puebla convened more than 300 young members of Rotary, university students and youth leaders for an intensive Positive Peace workshop, titled 'A Stronger Mexico: Pillars of Positive Peace'.

The workshop aimed to provide youth leaders with the knowledge and tools needed to improve peace. The group learnt about the Mexico Peace Index, as well as topics such as social entrepreneurship, civic engagement and leadership, and took part in breakout sessions on each Pillar of Positive Peace. Participants identified peace and development-focused projects to pursue in their own communities.

Following the workshop, participants reported increased familiarity with Positive Peace, conflict resolution, project management and fundraising, peace-building and leadership. All respondents reported that the knowledge they gained through the workshops was pertinent to their work, studies or projects.

Positive Peace and resilience

The resilience of societies is crucial in an age where we are preparing – or should be preparing – for an onslaught of environmental and societal challenges that have been building for decades. Such problems do not respect human borders. Therefore, building adaptive capabilities and stronger resilience into as many countries as possible is vital to our collective survival.

There are many different types of resilience – ranging from conflict, to natural disasters, to economic downturns, to name a few. We decided to assess whether Positive Peace accurately reflected a society's ability to mitigate the effects of these types of shocks. To do this we measured a variety of types of shocks, including violent civil resistance movements, natural disasters and genocide.

The first set of tests we did was in connection to violent conflict. There is a strong statistical correlation between lower levels of Positive Peace and the onset of societal conflict. Countries high in Positive Peace performed better in preventing, coping with, and recovering from the type of shocks that might tip weaker countries into conflict.

Positive Peace and resilience are inter-related in the following ways:

- High Positive Peace countries are more likely to maintain stability, adapt to and recover from shocks.
- High Positive Peace countries are more likely to maintain high levels of peace after a shock.
- Of the major political shocks analysed in the study, 97 per cent occurred in low Positive Peace countries because they had lower resilience.
- The number of lives lost from natural disasters was 13 times larger in low Positive Peace countries than in high Positive Peace countries, a disproportionately high ratio when compared with the distribution of incidents.
- High Positive Peace countries have fewer civil resistance movements, those campaigns last for a shorter amount of time, are more limited in their goals, are more likely to achieve some of their aims and are far less violent.
- Of all primarily violent resistance campaigns, 91 per cent were waged in countries with weaker Positive Peace.[6]

Violent political shocks such as regime changes, coups d'état and revolutions are more prevalent in countries with lower Positive Peace, with only three per cent occurring in countries with higher Positive Peace. Countries that are very high in Positive Peace do not experience genocides or violent conflicts, and rarely have political shocks.

Genocide is the worst type of systemic breakdown. According to metrics developed by the Center for Systemic Peace, there have been three genocides since 2005: in Sri Lanka in 2008 when the state initiated an offensive against the Tamils; in the Central African Republic following the forcible

---

6 Institute for Economics and Peace, *Positive Peace Report 2016.*

displacement of the Bozizé regime on 24 March 2013; and the targeting of the Yazidi minority in Iraq by Islamic State in 2014.[7]

Genocide and other forms of violence are much more likely in countries with lower Positive Peace. This highlights two important aspects of resilience. First, that building resilience does not have to be direct. By applying systems thinking we can see how improvements in one area can strengthen resilience in another.

Second, by building Positive Peace a country can shift the way it responds to political shocks, such as revolutions and regime changes, to nonviolence, such as political or economic transitions.

A key element of resilience is the ability to adapt to new circumstances. For millennia, history was defined by a battle for survival between humankind and the forces of nature. There was a need to conquer a harsh and dangerous world in which resources appeared boundless and infinite. The battle was to tame the physical world sufficiently to reap its rewards, a world where the strong and most aggressive triumphed, while the weak struggled to survive. The commonly held belief was that humanity had survived because we were the strongest and smartest.

Darwin's groundbreaking research on the evolution and survival of species upended this assumption, recognising that the key to survival was not strength per se but the ability to adapt: the ability to 'fit' in to a permanently changing environment. Changing habitats create risks for the species that populate them and those that cannot adapt will not survive.

In the 21st century things are very different: we now must manage our own fate, including managing nature itself. It is clear that resources are finite and shrinking daily, mainly driven by overpopulation and overconsumption. Species no longer die off because they fail to adapt to nature. Rather, they die off because they are unable to adapt to the accelerated change caused by humankind. With the outbreak of the COVID-19 virus the resilience of many countries will be tested and from multiple directions. The effectiveness of health systems will be tested first, mental stress will increase, jobs will

---

7 EMAT, INSCR, UCDP and Reinhart and Rogoff, accessed at www.foreignaffairs.com/articles/syria/2017-06-08/isis-yazidi-genocide

become insecure and financial systems will be stretched. The resilience of their systems will largely determine which countries will cope best.

It is easy to see how the Pillars affect many of the necessary capabilities needed to deal with the crisis. A health system that has broad coverage and is effective is a measure of *Equitable Distribution of Resources. Free Flow of Information* allows the dissemination of reliable information while *Well-Functioning Government* is needed for a well orchestrated and managed response.

Countries high in Positive Peace will be more likely to have the necessary societal factors and resilience to best deal with the crisis. Its full effects will take many years to move through the system, with some countries passing through a tipping point.

There is now a much greater level of interconnectedness between people and countries than in the past, and this has changed both the threats to humanity and our options for survival. Diseases and pollution do not respect national borders. Conflicts in one country inevitably have effects for neighbours, creating instability either directly, through armed conflict, or indirectly, with the movement of people escaping the conflict or ecological collapse.

Many of our political ideologies were formed in an era when survival was a battle with nature, rather than with ourselves. These ideologies are losing their relevance: consumption economics, for one. That is one of the reasons why there is a growing discontent with political systems in otherwise peaceful countries. The traditional definitions of 'left' and 'right' politics are breaking down. There are few remaining communist countries and the advanced Western democracies all believe in some form of social services.

We are entering a new age of epochal change that can only be compared to the end of feudalism 500 years ago and will be markedly different from the industrial age. In this new age commerce and business will not disappear, nor will the accumulation of wealth. These have been with humanity from the beginning, but the modern capitalist world based on overconsumption will come to an end. This change is inevitable, and the adaptable societies are the ones most likely to thrive.[8]

8 P. Mason, 'The End of Capitalism Has Begun', *The Guardian*, 17 July 2015, accessed at www.theguardian.com/books/2015/jul/17/postcapitalism-end-of-capitalism-begun.

Positive Peace, development and the UN's SDGs

We compared Positive Peace to a large range of development variables and found that many development outcomes that we value are closely correlated and empirically linked to Positive Peace. These included areas such as competitiveness, social progress, food security, happiness and environmental performance.

In addition, Positive Peace is associated with many aspects that are priorities for the United Nations' Sustainable Development Goals (SDGs), such as improved access to water, energy resources, health, gender equality, education and better business outcomes.

Goal 16 – to 'Promote peaceful and inclusive societies for sustainable development, provide access to justice for all and build effective, accountable and inclusive institutions at all levels' – marks a huge stride forward by the UN acknowledging the centrality of peace to social and economic progress. It would not have been possible without a broad and measurable definition of peace. Goal 16 contains a collection of measures, many from the Global Peace Index, which could be defined as measures of Negative Peace, such as homicide rates and the availability of guns. Goal 16 also includes measures from Positive Peace, such as rule of law and lower levels of corruption, and many other positive aspects that create peace.

Positive Peace can also be used as a lens to critique the 17 SDGs. The SDGs were the result of a series of negotiated compromises, rather than coming from a clear conceptual framework; therefore there are gaps in their coverage. Corruption represents the largest gap. Of the 169 targets in the SDGs, only one target directly references corruption: Goal 16, the peace and justice goal. Reducing corruption is clearly a key requirement if we are to obtain better development outcomes, and the lack of a strong focus on the issue is the Achilles' heel of the SDG agenda.

Another area that has little coverage is press freedom. Goal 16 calls for countries to 'ensure public access to information and protect fundamental freedoms'. This is particularly important at a time when world media freedom is declining. In its 2017 World Press Freedom Index, Reporters Without Borders said press freedoms had declined in 62 per cent of countries,[9] while Freedom House's 2016 *Freedom of the Press Report* stated that press freedoms were the lowest in 12 years and the situation hasn't improved since then.[10]

Further complicating the achievement of successful outcomes is the sheer number of SDG measures, 169 in all. How many countries have the statistical capacity to measure this many targets? It would be difficult even for the developed nations, let alone developing countries. Which targets should be prioritised? The temptation would be to pick the easiest rather than more important but more difficult goals.

Additionally, success will be measured by the countries themselves. Even if the statistical capacity can be built, the temptation to 'cook the books' to cover up failures would be irresistible to some struggling governments. It will be important for professional independent bodies to measure the SDGs to provide accountability and independent verification.

Positive Peace provides an alternative measure of progress, one that can be compared to improvements in SDG measures to better gauge the veracity of the improvements.

The importance of timing

Systems have tipping points – the same action taken at different times can have drastically different outcomes. Nelson Mandela was a transformative figure and had the knack of understanding the right timing. He was highly strategic. It was not so much a case of the depth or brilliance of his thoughts – although he was both deep and brilliant – but rather his ability to know the right action to take at a given time.

The first example of his sense of timing is well known. When he became President, the Afrikaans-speaking population was not on his side. They were highly suspicious and anything could have happened, including a descent into serious violence. In 1995, after years of sporting isolation, South Africa hosted the Rugby World Cup. At the time, South African rugby was still a white man's game – 'the quasi-religion of the ruling class', as one journalist

9 Accessed at rsf.org/en/2017-press-freedom-index-ever-darker-world-map
10 Accessed at freedomhouse.org/report/freedom-press/freedom-press-2016

described it. Most black South Africans played soccer. Rugby was so closely associated with the apartheid regime that members of the African National Congress discussed stripping the team of its iconic and emotionally charged symbol, the springbok.

The World Cup final pitted South Africa against Australia in a stadium packed to capacity. Five minutes before the kick-off Mandela appeared on the playing field to meet the teams. He was wearing a Springboks shirt sporting the number 6, the captain's number. The overwhelmingly white crowd surged to its feet chanting, 'Nel-son, Nel-son.' The team went on to defy the odds and win the championship. 'When the whistle blew, South Africa changed forever,' as Francois Pienaar, the Springboks captain, said. Mandela's gesture convinced many Afrikaners that he was President for all South Africans. If he was not going to attack their cherished game, then he was not going to attack them.

The Springboks' World Cup campaign had started with an aspirational slogan that had a clear political subtext: 'One Team, One Country'. With an inspired gesture at an inspired moment Mandela had made it real.

The second story is less well known. Mandela spent 27 years in prison, 18 of them in the grim surroundings of Robben Island, which is situated 15 kilometres off the coast of Cape Town. In 1985, five years before his eventual release, the leaders of the white political establishment came to him and said that they were willing to release him if he would renounce his principles and retire in silence.

Mandela realised the time was not right. Their offer was aimed at helping to prop up the failing establishment and he refused it. When they finally returned in 1990 with an unconditional offer, Mandela knew the time was right. He also realised that if he tried to get agreement from the other prisoners who were his close confidants – Thabo Mbeki and the others – he would not be able to come to a solution. They all had different ideas about how to approach the negotiations and take advantage of the opportunity. So he decided not to tell them. He knew them so well he could anticipate what they would accept. He entered, alone, into three months of negotiations with the establishment, crafting a deal that he knew his fellow prisoners would accept. Only then did he take them into his confidence.

They did want some changes, but they were all minor. That is how he was able to get the peace deal done.

This is a fine example of a tipping point. The intervention was the same – releasing Mandela – but at different times there would have been very different outcomes. His sense of timing and a view of how the whole system operated were crucial.

Transformation

As Mandela's spectacular political career showed, peace can be transformational. Yet the rarity of leaders as wise as Mandela also demonstrates that our leaders are missing something. I would strongly argue that what our politicians lack is an understanding of Positive Peace.

Failed states cost the international community dearly. All too often governments intervene only when they realise implosion is imminent, but by then it is too late to change the course of events. Without understanding what will truly create peace, and then developing it, any improvements in a country's resilience are only accidental or the by-product of another activity.

The deficiency in proactive investment in peace is profound and is probably best highlighted by one single fact. Only 0.17 per cent of the total global cost of violence is spent on peacekeeping and peace-building, which includes government and UN peacekeeping forces. Without money and investment loaded up front, it is unlikely that lasting peace can ever be created.

To aim for Positive Peace is to aspire to many of the economic and social benefits that are universally desired. It should not be lost on politicians that these are the same things that help them get elected.

Most policy seems to be driven by electoral expediency, rather than any deep commitment to a political philosophy. Political parties undertake polling and canvass their financial backers, and then use the results to guide their policies. Positive Peace does not fit well into this type of environment. Peace as an idea may have popular appeal, but the realities of modern politics mean that the project of creating resilience gets lost in the immediacy of day-to-day politics. Consequently, many politicians, when seeking popular support, interpret peace as: 'Let's find the bad guys and whack them.'

For example, Australia has one of the lowest homicide rates in the world: 227 people were murdered in 2017, a rate of less than 0.8 per 100,000 people,[11] and the rate keeps falling. Yet Australian news is dominated by stories of murders, creating the impression that homicide is becoming more common, making tough law-and-order policies easier to sell to the Australian electorate. In fact, the incarceration rate jumped by 57 per cent from 2012 to 2018.[12] There is also a time mismatch. The low homicide rate in Australia has evolved over decades, as do most aspects of Positive Peace, and is thus barely perceptible: it has become background noise.

For individuals or families caught up in tragedy, the story of the homicide will dominate their life. For the community, which fears violence, the story that they are vulnerable is likewise real and compelling. However, these stories do not translate into a general truth. When a broader snapshot is taken, moving beyond the individual stories, it becomes evident that Australia is relatively free from this kind of violence and in many ways the country is improving.

Unfortunately, many of the policies that grab media attention, such as mandatory sentences for crimes, do not really work. The judicial system generally cries foul at this approach, because it does not take into account individual circumstances. Was this a one-off offence? Was there provocation? What was the background? Does the culprit support others who will be impaired by the loss of their support? The media and much of the public like punishment, but it does come with costs. Positive Peace not only takes a broader view; it also promotes the sort of environment where crime is less likely to be committed in the first place.

To fulfil the transformational potential of Positive Peace, leaders and the general public must be aware of its benefits. It is a way for political leaders to achieve a better understanding of their purpose. For leaders to make the decisions that will lead to Positive Peace, however, they will need to be backed by informed citizens.

The Positive Peace Index and the Global Peace Index are used in thousands of university courses around the world. This is a start. As we

---

11 Australian Bureau of Statistics, '4510.0 - Recorded Crime - Victims, Australia 2016', accessed at www.abs.gov.au/ausstats

12 Australian Bureau of Statistics, '4517.0 - Prisoners in Australia, 2019', www.abs.gov.au/ausstats

have already seen, education is lagged and nonlinear, so hopefully 20 years from now the fruits of this effort will become apparent.

The IEP has also decided to train one million people in Positive Peace. This is a huge undertaking, but well underway. We have produced online tutorials, as well as specialised versions that have been developed in conjunction with our partners. One of these specialised versions was created in conjunction with Rotary International. We have developed a four-hour introductory course on Positive Peace to be rolled out through its 35,000 clubs around the world.

Changes in the Positive Peace Pillars

The good news is that globally Positive Peace is rising, with 75 per cent of countries improving their Positive Peace scores between 2009 and 2018. The two indicators that have made the largest gains over the decade are *Sound Business Environment* and *Free Flow of Information.*

Moreover, seven of the eight Positive Peace Pillars improved. The only Pillar to decline was *Low Levels of Corruption.* However, *Well-Functioning Government* had only a very slight improvement. Post-conflict countries such as Rwanda, Côte d'Ivoire and Georgia have made some of the biggest improvements in their Positive Peace scores, although that is in part because they started from a low base. This does not mean that these countries will not experience problems in the future – Myanmar also showed a big improvement but still has ongoing conflict.

There are significant regional extremes in Positive Peace. Nordic countries tend to rate highly; in the 2018 report, five of the top ten countries were from this region. However, for a number of them their Positive Peace scores have started to decline. At the other end of the scale, sub-Saharan countries tend to dominate. There were seven sub-Saharan African countries in the bottom ten, with the three other countries located in the Middle East, North Africa and South Asia. In the decade from 2009 to 2018, the Middle East and North Africa had the highest proportion of countries deteriorating, while Eurasia had the greatest percentage improvement, but off a low base.

The countries that experienced the greatest shifts in scores, either positively or negatively, were spread across many regions, income groups and starting levels of Positive Peace.

When reviewing the decade to 2017, we found that for most countries Positive Peace scores changed slowly. There were, however, cases where the levels of Positive Peace did improve more quickly. Examples were Côte d'Ivoire, Georgia and Rwanda, while on the negative side countries such as the Central African Republic, Yemen and Equatorial Guinea had some of the largest deteriorations.

FIGURE 4

Changes in the Pillars of Positive Peace, 2009–2018

Seven of the eight Pillars have improved since 2009; *Low Levels of Corruption* was the only Pillar to deteriorate.

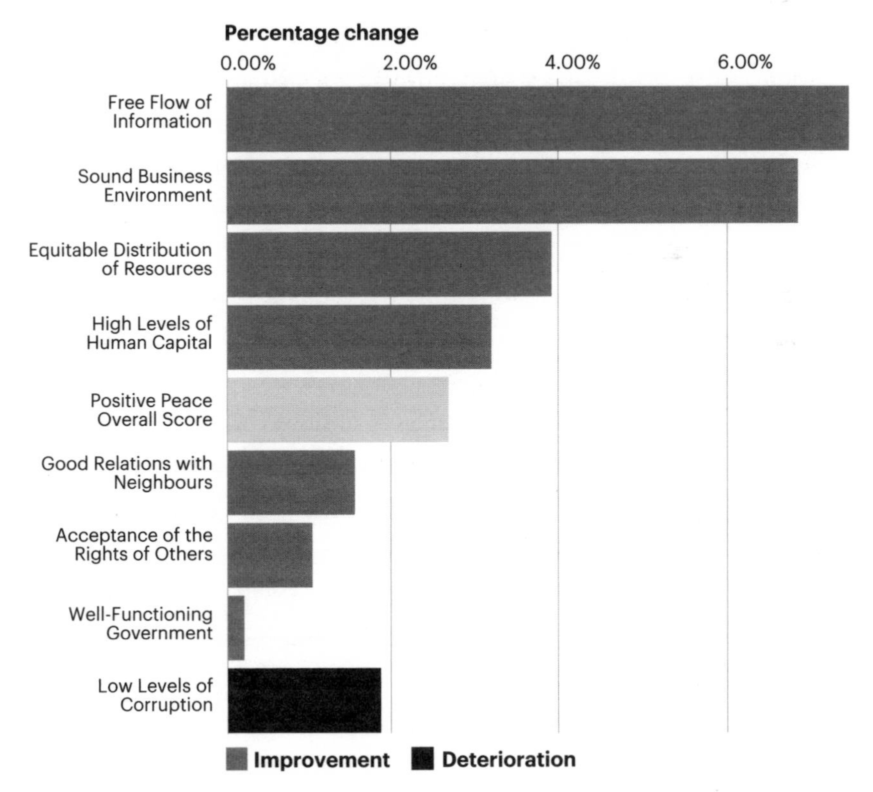

SOURCE: IEP

Additionally, the various indicators that make up Positive Peace also changed at different rates. Mobile phone connections, which is one of the measures in *Free Flow of Information*, has seen the largest improvement, mainly on the back of the roll-out of mobile networks in the developing world. Other measures, such as the levels of corruption within a society or the revenue raised from the tax base, tend to change more slowly.

The concept of Positive Peace is not new, but the ability to ascribe a numerical value extends it into new territory. By moving the discussion of peace beyond the simplistic binary model of being in conflict or not, it better reflects the complexity of the world we see around us. It allows policymakers and the public to better measure the impact of their initiatives in improving the lives of their citizens; helps foreign donors to assess the best interventions; and gives strategic analysts and investors a valuable measure of the ability of societies to absorb shocks without falling into conflict.

CHAPTER 7

The economic value of peace

The economic argument for peace is compelling.

Nobel laureate Joseph Stiglitz said it was 'nonsense' to think that World War II ended the Depression and had this to say about the Iraq War: 'Whichever way one looks at it, the economic effects of war with Iraq will not be good. Markets loathe uncertainty and volatility. War, and anticipation of war, bring both.'[1]

The data bear him out. In the 16 relatively peaceful years between 1980 and 1996, the Dow Jones Industrial Average increased by 670 per cent. Between 10 September 2001 and September 2017, it grew by 145 per cent.[2]

Economist James Galbraith observes that wars create inflation because that is the only way to pay for them.[3] Robert Reich, professor of public policy at the University of California, has commented that 'having a giant undercover military jobs program is an insane way to keep Americans employed'.[4] Economist Dean Baker notes that America's military spending lowers economic growth and increases unemployment.[5] Economists Robert Pollin and Heidi Garrett-Peltier, at the Political Economy Research Institute at the University of Massachusetts, have argued that non-military spending creates more jobs than military spending.[6]

---

1 J. Stiglitz, 'The myth of the war economy', *The Guardian*, 2 January 2003.

2 'Dow Jones – 100 Year Historical Chart', Macrotrends, accessed at www.macrotrends.net/1319/dow-jones-100-year-historical-chart

3 www.washingtonsblog.com/2011/01/war-causes-inflation-and-inflation-allows-the-government-to-start-unnecessary-wars.html

4 R. Reich, 'America's Biggest Jobs Program – the U.S. Military', 11 August 2010, accessed at robertreich.org/post/938938180

5 D. Baker, Centre for Economic and Policy Research, accessed at cepr.net/publications/op-eds-columns/defense-spending-job-loss/

6 R. Pollin, H. Garret Peltier, 'The U.S. employment effects of military and domestic spending priorities: An updated analysis', Political Economy Research Institute, October 2009, accessed at www.peri.umass.edu/fileadmin/pdf/published_study/spending_priorities_PERI.pdf

I am not anti-military and this doesn't mean that countries shouldn't have armies. Sadly, they are necessary in the world we live in, and some wars do need to be fought. Still, if we lived in a world with reduced military spending and less war it would certainly be a more productive and wealthier place.

The message is clear: what creates peace also creates a thriving economy. To gain a more nuanced understanding of this, we should examine the limits of the term 'economy'. Increasingly, the way we understand the world is with reference to economic and financial statistics; they have become ubiquitous scorecards. The expansion of the global market system has meant that much of how we understand what is happening in the world today is dictated by measures of monetary exchange. It has encouraged us to think of the 'economy' first and society second, which is putting the cart before the horse. The economy is only transactions created by a society. This is something we tend to forget in the consumer economies of the developed world.

Geoff Mulgan, a former policy adviser to UK Prime Minister Tony Blair, observes that a rising proportion of our human activity is being absorbed into the system of monetary exchange.[7] One of the problems with this, as Mulgan notes, is that traders often seem to be 'the least concerned with the behaviour of the system as a whole'.[8] This is particularly apparent when it comes to so-called 'common goods', such as air or water quality. The markets have yet to find a way of putting a price on pollution, so it remains free to pollute, yet we all suffer the costs of smog and ocean acidification.

If taking a systems approach is the key to developing sustainable peace, then to some extent the overemphasis on transactions in the market as the central organising principle of society is not conducive to a better understanding of society or peace. We need to regard monetary transactions as a second-order effect, not the primary cause of things.

Contractions in GDP are associated with rises in unemployment, and when countries do go into recession – technically defined as two consecutive

7 G. Mulgan, *Connexity*, Vintage, 1995, p. 54.
8 Mulgan, p. 81.

quarters of negative GDP growth – the government's chances of re-election falls dramatically. Therefore, politicians are keenly focused on GDP. But GDP is a misleading measure of national wealth and wellbeing, as explained in an earlier chapter. Many key goods, including peacefulness, environmental protection or family bonding, are not measured in GDP because they do not involve transactions. In fact, GDP includes pollution, crime, the health costs of cigarettes and environmental disasters as 'growth' because they generate spending. Disasters, indeed, are especially good for GDP. Cleaning up the 2010 oil spill in the Gulf of Mexico was 'worth' more to GDP economically than the carbon absorption provided by the Amazon rainforest.

This highlights some of the faults of GDP, but it has become such a pervasive measure that societal happiness is equated to it. Probably its biggest flaw, after not counting what makes us happy, is that it's only a measure of consumption; there is no capital account. If you had a car accident and went to hospital that would be good for GDP; you would have to buy a new car and spend money on doctors. But it would be a negative for you, physically, emotionally and financially.

Nor does GDP take into account the sustainability of the resources used in the consumption or whether it's even good for society.

These glaring faults of GDP as a measure of societal wellbeing have long been known, but it has still managed to become the pervasive global yardstick for progress. Because of this, in order to mount an economic argument for peace, we are forced to begin with its impact on GDP. Given the centrality of the measure, any arguments for peace will not be taken seriously unless presented through this prism. Therefore, the IEP decided to develop a model that estimates the cost of violence to the global economy, using the Global Peace Index as the basis.

Quantifying the economic impact of violence

The sums lost to violence are huge. We calculate the economic impact of violence on the global economy at nearly 11.2 per cent of world GDP, or US$14.1 trillion in 2018, equivalent to the combined economic output of Canada, France, Japan, Germany and the United Kingdom. About

40 per cent of the expenditure is accounted for by military spending, with homicide and violent crime accounting for 17 per cent, and internal security officers, including police, accounting for 29 per cent.

The IEP was the first organisation to try to calculate a holistic figure for the global expenditure on violence. This may seem puzzling at first, but what we did was collect statistics for 23 different domains and for 163 countries and territories. Having these figures by country gave us the underlying metrics to create a global cost model. The other innovation was to create a measure that included the costs of violence, as well as the costs of protection against violence, and the flow-on effects through the economy.

This meant that we needed a new term that embraced the broader definition. We settled on 'Violence containment' and the 'Violence containment industry'. We define the violence containment industry as: 'All economic activity related to preventing violence, perpetuating violence and dealing with the consequences of violence.' This includes military expenditure, exports of arms, the number of police, the number of people in jail, the costs of homicides, violent crime, sexual crimes, security guards, refugee and internally displaced persons (IDP) costs, and much more.

This approach enabled us to capture the economic impact of violence in a way that had never been done before. It also enabled a better understanding of the economic impact resulting from improvements in peace, thereby allowing for a better understanding of the cost-benefit trade-offs of policy interventions.

Our study does not make any moral judgements about the size of the violence containment industry in any particular country, as many factors determine its size. Ugly neighbours make a strong military necessary and violent criminals do need to be in jail, but if constructive policies can resolve international tensions and government policies can reduce the causes of violent crime, then the savings can be diverted to more productive activities.

Previous studies concentrated on the national level or, when they were done globally, they only covered a particular category, such as the military. Despite their narrower scope, many of these studies were useful and had considerable impact. For example, in 2008 Joseph Stiglitz and Linda Bilmes calculated that the true cost of the Iraq War was $3 trillion – later updated to $5 trillion – not the $50 billion projected by the White House at the start of the war.[9]

Bilmes and Stiglitz shone a spotlight on expense items that had been largely hidden from the American taxpayer, including the cost of replacing military equipment, which was being used up at six times the peacetime rate, and the cost of caring for tens of thousands of wounded veterans for the rest of their lives. They then added up the cost in lives and economic damage within the region. Finally, they measured the opportunity cost of diverting funds from more profitable investments elsewhere in the economy to pay for the war. At the time of the calculations the war had cost a staggering 60 times what the estimates were at the start of the war.

Over half of the $14.1 trillion cost of violence comprises direct and indirect costs while the rest is a partial estimate of the lost opportunity cost. This is the loss of the additional economic activity that would have occurred had the funds been invested in more productive economic activities. Examples of this would be the benefits of redirecting expenditure used to build a jail to building a rapid transit system, or redirecting money from building a frigate to funding skills training or measures to support business.

If violence containment is considered as a separate industry, it is the largest industry in the world. To put this into perspective, the global violence containment industry is more than twice the size of the next largest industry, retail and food, and ten times the size of the oil industry. Another, more sobering, way of looking at it is that the total of global foreign direct investment in 2019 was only ten per cent of the cost of violence, and global Official Development Assistance (ODA) is equivalent to just one per cent of the cost of violence containment. Imagine the extent of the economic stimulation that would follow from a ten per cent reduction in global violence.

It also equates to $1,853 per annum for every person in the world. Compare this to the income of the richest and poorest people in Figure 5 and Figure 6.

As huge as they are, our economic impact estimates are conservative. There are many things that have not been counted in this analysis, as we

---

9 J. Stiglitz and L. Bilmes, *The Three Trillion Dollar War: The True Cost of the Iraq War*, W.W. Norton & Company, 2008.

FIGURE 5

Countries with the highest household and personal income

Median figures based on responses from at least 2,000 adults in each country.

	Median household income	Median personal income
Norway	$51,489	$19,308
Sweden	$50,514	$18,632
Luxembourg	$52,493	$18,418
Denmark	$44,360	$18,262
Finland	$34,615	$15,725
United States	$43,585	$15,480
Canada	$41,280	$15,181
Australia	$46,555	$15,026
Netherlands	$38,584	$14,450
Germany	$33,333	$14,098

SOURCE: DATA AGGREGATED FROM 2006–2012, GALLUP, IEP CALCULATIONS

FIGURE 6

Countries with the lowest household and personal income

Median figures based on responses from at least 2,000 adults in each country.

	Median household income	Median personal income
Liberia	$781	$118
Burundi	$673	$129
Mali	$1983	$165
Burkina Faso	$1530	$168
Madagascar	$1013	$205
Sierra Leone	$2330	$233
Rwanda	$1101	$235
Benin	$1502	$237
Togo	$1571	$279
Zambia	$1501	$287

SOURCE: DATA AGGREGATED FROM 2006–2012, GALLUP, IEP CALCULATIONS

can only count the data we have. Costs related to property crimes, such as motor-vehicle theft, arson, household burglary, larceny or theft, are not included. Some of the costs associated with preventative measures are absent, such as insurance premiums and the cost of surveillance equipment. The direct costs of domestic violence in terms of individual expenditure and costs to health providers are left out, as are some of the indirect costs, such as lost wages from lower productivity and absenteeism. Household security systems, security guards, badge-only access at workplaces, guard dogs, neighbourhood-watch programs and time spent seeking safer travel routes are all responses to violence that are difficult to count. Forgone revenues for the travel and tourism industry as a result of a terrorist attack are likewise not included. It is easy to see from this list that there is much more that could be counted if the data were available. We believe that if all aspects and ramifications of violence were accounted for, our estimates would rise by between 50 to 100 per cent.

It should be stressed that it will never be possible to reduce expenditure on containing violence to zero. Obviously, no society wants to have dangerous criminals roaming the streets and there will always be some violent people. There will also be a need for police to apprehend them, courts to try them, jails to lock them up, and prison guards to ensure they stay there. Similarly, it would be unrealistic to expect nations to forgo their military defensive capacity. However, the less that is spent on violence containment, without increasing violence, the more money will be available to invest in other, more productive areas.

The question revolves around the balance between violence containment expenditure and funding policies that enhance Positive Peace. If there is a large investment in, let's say, a $14-billion aircraft carrier, it can be seen as a trade-off against expenditure on improving infrastructure, or tens of thousands more university places, or skills retraining for the recently unemployed, or substantially improving the health system. All of these lost opportunities would have substantially improved the economy. The most that can be hoped for from the aircraft carrier is that it will not be used. If it is needed to thwart destruction from an aggressive neighbour the investment will have been worthwhile, but all too often politicians fail the basic actuarial test of balancing the real strategic risk against lost opportunity to invest in the welfare of society and the economy.

Many argue that military research and development leads to technological breakthroughs that have uses for broader society and so has value independent of military applications. There is a level of truth in this argument. However, if the same money was invested in well-targeted research it would, in all likelihood, create more innovation, resulting in a larger payback to society because that was a specific aim of the investment, not a by-product.

Almost universally, the data shows an overemphasis on containing violence rather than trying to prevent it from arising in the first place. Direct expenditure on the military is more than 12 times global expenditure on foreign aid.[10]

When examining violence containment spending there is a U-shaped curve in terms of its effectiveness. Finding the optimal level of violence containment spending is difficult. No country that spends less than 0.8 per cent of GDP on internal security is considered a highly peaceful country. However, no country that spends more than two per cent of GDP on internal security is highly peaceful either. There is a trade-off. Very low levels of expenditure mean that criminals run rampant, but if there is too much security then it can be used to suppress people. Countries with the highest levels of Positive Peace spend between one and two per cent of GDP on internal security.

Unsurprisingly, countries experiencing armed conflict, such as civil war or large-scale insurgencies, expend a larger proportion of their GDP on violence containment. In Syria in 2015, violence containment spending accounted for 54 per cent of the nation's GDP, rising to 67 per cent in 2016. In Iraq, the equivalent figure was 58 per cent, in Afghanistan 52 per cent, South Sudan 36 per cent, and Somalia 33 per cent. These are not countries with good economic prospects.

10 As measured by Official Development Assistance (ODA).

FIGURE 7

Breakdown of the global economic impact of violence, 2018

Government spending on military and internal security comprises approximately three-quarters of the global economic impact of violence.

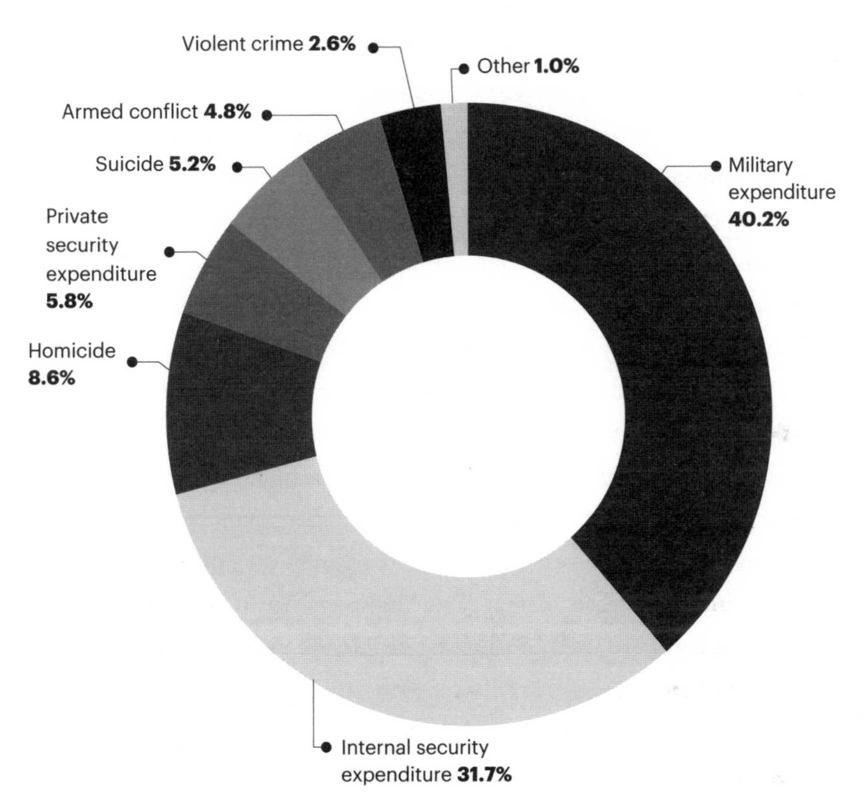

SOURCE: IEP

Income, type of government, and peace

Governments stand and fall on how well they manage GDP. It is one of the major measures of societal success. Despite its flaws, governments still see it as the Holy Grail, building their policies around it, lauding its benefits, believing it to be a source of substantial political capital. This strong dependency on GDP is tied to the population's dependency on employment: higher growth means lower unemployment. Per capita income is seen as a clear measure of individual wealth, although growing inequality in the developed world has blunted its usefulness as a barometer of national wellbeing. The larger the average per capita income, the more influence governments have on the international stage, through both soft and hard power. It also enables a larger tax take, which in turns funds more government services, increasing the government's esteem in the eyes of their citizens.

What is important to acknowledge is that long-term sustainable improvements in living standards do not occur through one or two wise policies. The whole system has to be taken into account.

The per capita income of a country is closely associated with its levels of peace. As peace increases so does the per capita income. This is not surprising, because as information flows improve so does business transparency; as human capital grows so does the sophistication of the workforce; as corruption falls business transactions become more efficient. It's systemic.

Countries with improving Positive Peace had almost two percentage points higher annual growth rates in per capita income than countries with declining Positive Peace when measured over an 11-year period. This demonstrates the close links between improvements in Positive Peace and a robust business environment.

Not only do high-income countries rank highly on Positive Peace, they also perform well on the Global Peace Index, while low-income countries tend to be both less peaceful and lower on Positive Peace. Only one country in the Global Peace Index's top 30 in 2019 – Bhutan – does not have a per capita income above $15,000.

There is also a clear statistical relationship between Positive Peace and the type of government in a country, with full democracies scoring the best. Authoritarian regimes, on average, recorded the worst scores, reflecting the low adaptive capacity of many of these governments, although there are some exceptions such as Singapore.

Democracy seems to provide a more flexible dispute-resolution mechanism. A democratic political culture represents a society's attitudes towards, and mechanisms for, citizen participation in government. This is much more than voting in elections. These findings suggest that democracy is often conducive to creating more robust and accountable government, including an independent judiciary, effective service delivery, participation and accountability.

When a government is responsive to the needs of its citizens, it is better able to support the Pillars of Peace, including a *Sound Business Environment*, facilitate the *Free Flow of Information*, support *High Levels of Human Capital*, reduce corruption and promote a variety of other Positive Peace factors. These factors also support a more robust economy.

Future employment

Positive Peace can contribute to economic resilience. This will be crucial in the coming years when the changing shape of employment will require greater adaptability and flexibility than has occurred in the past. Information technology has upended the shape of the jobs market, especially in the past 25 years, with possibly even greater change to come. Many professions have disappeared, while new specialties have been created.

The coming wave of automation will further reduce the amount of physical effort needed to produce; more will be produced with less and this development will come with a lower number of workers. Unless there is a deliberate effort to distribute wealth through the community or to create new jobs, the productivity gains will be captured by a wealthy few, making them even wealthier, while leaving the majority unemployed, underemployed and moving in and out of jobs, thereby providing little security and dramatically increasing poverty. This is evident with the rise of the gig economy. These jobs are steeped in uncertainly. Workers are hired on a casual basis and the number of hours worked each week is not assured, nor are there any of the normal benefits, such as sickness benefits or holiday pay, because the workers are hired as contractors. That is hardly an environment in which a consumer-based economy will flourish. The economic devastation caused by COVID-19 will only exaggerate this trend.

The term the 'precariat' has been coined to describe the emergence of a class of people who face lives steeped in insecurity, transiting in and out of jobs that give little meaning to their lives. This is the potential breeding ground for future social instability and political extremism.[11]

---

11 G. Standing, *The Precariat*, Bloomsbury Academic, New York, 2014.

Google's favourite futurist Thomas Frey believes that two billion jobs may disappear by 2030 because of robotics, automation and artificial intelligence. Currently there is little thinking about the sort of sociopolitical framework that can deliver equity or meaning to the billions of people whose work will be displaced. Societies that are adaptable and have robust systems are the ones most likely to be able to make the necessary changes.

These and other seismic shifts will change the nature of economic activity and the associated political doctrines. There will be a need for new approaches to governance.

Rather than government policy mainly being directed at questions of economic growth, governments, businesses and citizens will need to debate fundamentally new ways of measuring success and understanding future challenges. We will need new models for understanding what equitable distribution means. In an age of potentially very long lives, who will get them? Just the rich?

We will have to ask fundamental questions: What kind of society do we want, and what type of society will be sustainable? What type of society will be most adaptable? What is society's concept of equitable distribution of its resources and capital? The answer to these questions, and more, will inevitably involve new approaches to societal development. Positive Peace can play a strategic, defining role in how we approach these challenges.

What is also certain is that doing business as usual is no longer feasible. The falling levels of belief and trust in our institutions demonstrate this.

Developing the figures

To estimate the global economic impact of violence, the IEP uses 14 different dimensions:

- The number of deaths from internal conflict
- The number of deaths from external conflict
- The level of violent crime
- The level of expenditure on the military
- The number of refugees, stateless and internally displaced persons

- The number of homicides
- The number of internal security officers and police
- The extent of the jailed population
- Private security forces
- The costs of terrorism
- The economic cost of conflict to the economy
- The costs associated with fear from violence
- The cost of funding UN peacekeeping missions
- The number of suicides.

There are many technical challenges in compiling a global picture of the cost of violence. For example, in many countries there are no reliable data on the cost of many of the items that we measure, such as homicides. How, for example, can we arrive at a figure for the cost of a homicide in Thailand?

In the United States, there is a lot of excellent research on the cost of homicides. In the 2016 Global Peace Index, the direct and indirect costs of a homicide in the United States was estimated at $8,888,692, while each violent assault injury was $120,622. These figures were the median from a range of studies.

The direct costs are fairly low; examples are the cost of police attending the crime scene and follow-up, and medical services related to crime. The indirect costs, by contrast, are substantial.

The indirect costs include the lost lifetime earnings of the murder victims. Most victims die young. If the average age was 25, then that would represent 40 years of lost lifetime earnings to the economy. There are also flow-on effects for family and friends, because there is a loss of productivity for a period of time while they go through their grieving and mourning. If we think about someone who has a relative who was murdered, while they are at work their mind will naturally go to their grief and suffering. For a time, they will be extremely distracted, which will mean they work less and their productivity will fall, although as time passes their productivity might be restored.

These figures are then used pro rata to calculate the cost in other countries according to the differential between the levels of per capita income in that country and the United States. For example, if Thailand's per capita income were 18 per cent of that in the United States, then we would multiply the costs from the US study by 0.18. The result is then multiplied by the number of homicides to arrive at the total cost of homicide to the Thai economy. This approach can be taken for many of the indicators, such as violent crime, battlefield deaths or deaths from terrorism. We were able to do this type of scaling across all of the 163 countries to create a consistent methodology.

A more difficult area to cost is the fear of violence. In the United Kingdom, it has been estimated that the average annual health costs of being fearful of crime is £19.50 per capita per annum.[12] Fear of falling victim to violence changes consumption and work-related decisions. It leads to increased transportation costs, and reduced productivity and consumption. Fear of victimisation can also lead to adverse mental health effects such as anxiety, anger and reduced mental wellbeing, all of which have productivity implications. In addition, the social cost of the fear of violence manifests itself in reduced trust in society and the erosion of social cohesion.

The economic impact of the fear of crime is high in regions with high levels of violence, and most likely higher than the UK study. It is therefore easy to see that fear has a tangible cost. On average, 55 per cent of the people in South America, and approximately 49 per cent in Central America and the Caribbean reported a fear of violence.

Business and violence

Much is made in economic theory about the centrality of rational self-interest. Certainly, it is true that self-interest is what drives markets, although it can hardly be described as always being rational. The father of modern capitalism, Adam Smith, argued that there is also a collective interest that is crucial to the proper functioning of an economy. In his seminal book *The Wealth of Nations*, Smith stated:

---

12 P. Dolan and T. Peasgood, 'Estimating the Economic and Social Costs of the Fear of Crime,' *British Journal of Criminology*, vol. 47, no. 1, 2006, pp. 121–132.

> The expense of defending the society, and that of supporting the dignity of the chief magistrate, are both laid out for the general benefit of the whole society. It is reasonable, therefore, that they should be defrayed by the general contribution of the whole society, all the different members contributing, as nearly as possible, in proportion to their respective abilities. The expense of the administration of justice, too, may, no doubt, be considered as laid out for the benefit of the whole society. There is no impropriety, therefore, in its being defrayed by the general contribution of the whole society.[13]

In this excerpt, Smith made the argument in support of raising money from the general public to pay for goods such as defence spending and the justice system.

There are some services and activities that are of benefit to all society, yet they are too expensive for any individual or group of individuals to afford. This is what Smith referred to and what became known as a public good. Peace can easily be viewed as a public good, perhaps the primary one. Smith's logic could easily be extended to Positive Peace.

Developing a better understanding of our collective self-interest is one reason for measuring the economic impact of violence and the costs of containing it. If nothing else, it can inform business about its lost opportunity costs and how much bigger its markets could potentially be in an environment of high peace. Surprisingly, even though the headline figures presented in this book are striking, there has actually been little work done on estimating the specific impacts for different companies or industries on improvements in peace. This is an area that is ripe for future research.

Much is made about the role and obligations of business in creating peace. Peace is good for business, and vice versa. A robust business environment is not a desirable spin-off of Positive Peace, but a core element of it.

---

13 A. Smith, *The Wealth of Nations*, Book V, Harvard Classics, New York, 1909, pp. 767–768.

In the modern world, business is seen as the key engine of change and growth. However, business has traditionally been wary of getting too involved in social policy, preferring to focus almost exclusively on the Pillar of Peace we have called *Sound Business Environment*. But in a world of systems thinking this is too limited. Other Pillars are also important: *High Levels of Human Capital* create a better educated workforce that is more efficient and more flexible; *Low Levels of Corruption* cut costs; *Good Relations with Neighbours* decrease the likelihood of supply chain disruptions; and *Well-Functioning Government* provides a predictable and equitable regulatory and trading environment. These are some of the ways Positive Peace is good for business and good for shareholder value.

If one looks at the bigger picture, businesses need societies that are resilient to the inevitable shocks of the future: if a society is tipped into conflict, businesses are often the first to suffer. On a less dramatic level, boosting Positive Peace in all its manifestations strengthens resilience and fosters adaptability. Industries, like nations, need to adjust to changing technologies, climatic conditions, new discoveries and demographic shifts, to name some examples. Positive Peace provides an optimal environment for social adaptation.

These are long-term goals that require business to extend its time horizons. Fortunately, many businesses do have five, ten, and 20-year business plans. One of the core functions of a good CEO is balancing the long-term against the short-term focus on quarterly earnings.

Industry associations provide a powerful platform from which to lobby governments for change. It is not only legitimate for business to lobby for a better educated workforce, or for less corruption, but also for other aspects of Positive Peace. This argument need not be limited to domestic investments. In a world of rising nationalism, diplomatic pressure is less effective than it once was in effecting social change. The influence of potential investors, on the other hand, is growing.

Governments need to listen to corporations, and not only because they are the key generators of GDP growth. Business is a vital part of the encoded norms of a society, and if a government wants to effect positive and sustainable change it has to work with industry rather than against it. When seen through the prism of Positive Peace and systems thinking, business becomes a partner in peace rather than a passive bystander or an obstacle.

However, there are limits to what should be expected from the private sector. There is a widespread assumption that business has a moral obligation to create peace. It is certainly true that business has an obligation to do no harm, but it is unrealistic to expect companies to be creators of peace. Business is good at business. Its role in a modern society is to innovate, create wealth and distribute it through employment, taxes and profits. It is impractical to think business has a special obligation to create peace over and above the rest of society. The whole of society has an interest in creating peace, and business shares this responsibility, but only as a part of society.

It is self-evident that countries with high levels of violence will have lower investment rankings and more difficulty in attracting capital. The assessment of risk and reward is central to the asset allocation strategies of institutional funds. However, usually their focus is on sovereign risk, which looks at the likelihood of countries defaulting on debt payments. For a business considering investing in a country, that is only one risk. There are many others that should be considered. Some of these risks can be better understood from the datasets in the Global Peace Index and the Positive Peace Index. The data can be harmonised and analysed in different ways to best reflect a specific investment focus. This provides better insights into the countries that are likely to rapidly deteriorate or inversely the countries that are likely to improve.

Multiplication sums

The multiplier effect is a commonly used economic concept. It describes the extent to which additional expenditure has a flow-on effect to the wider economy. For example, a dollar spent on infrastructure has flow-on effects for the economy by decreasing travel times, thereby enabling businesses to be more efficient. Every dollar spent on infrastructure might be worth an additional $2 to the overall economy.

It can be assumed that expenditure on containing violence will have a much lower multiplier effect than most other types of economic activity because it is generally less beneficial for the wider economy than most other forms of business activity. Most estimates place the multiplier effect for defence spending at less than one, implying that a dollar spent generates less than a dollar in direct economic benefit. Research by Robert Barro and Veronique de Rugy into the effects of a proposed reduction in US defence spending in 2013 estimated that every dollar cut from the defence budget would generate an extra $1.30 in spending elsewhere in the economy.[14]

If a military action acts as a deterrent, then there is limited measurable economic benefit because nothing will have happened.

Compare this with the injection of income for infrastructure development, education or business stimulus. It creates employment, better productivity and further income, and results in additional spending. This is why a dollar of civil expenditure will in most cases create more than a dollar of economic activity.

When it comes to peace, the exact magnitude of this effect is difficult to measure, but peace adds to the multiplier effect across the board, something we call the peace multiplier. In more peaceful environments, individuals spend less time and resources protecting themselves and contribute more to the wider economy as a consequence of lower levels of injury and death. There is greater confidence that investments will pay dividends. As well, there are likely to be other substantial flow-on effects for the wider economy, as money is directed towards more productive areas.

The missed opportunities of violence containment spending are only one half of the equation. If a homicide is avoided, the direct costs, such as the money spent on medical treatment, criminal investigation and the funeral, could be spent elsewhere. However, the biggest benefit to the economy comes from the inclusion of the lifetime income of the victim if they had not been murdered. Violence also stunts economic activity, such as when Mexicans are afraid to go out at night because of potential violence.

---

14 R. Barro and V. de Rugy, 'Defense Spending and the Economy', Mercatus Research, 2013, accessed at www.mercatus.org/system/files/deRugy-Barro-Defense-Multiplier.pdf

There is strong evidence to suggest that violence and the fear of violence can fundamentally alter the incentives faced by business. An analysis of 730 business ventures in Colombia from 1997 to 2001 found that new ventures were less likely to survive higher levels of violence.[15] Increased violence also led to lower levels of employment and economic productivity over the long term.

When one assesses the costs and benefits of a specific initiative, there is inevitably an asymmetry of information. The cost of violence containment can be estimated, but the benefits are usually unknown. If, for example, heavy investment in surveillance results in no terrorist attacks, how do we know that the absence of a terrorist attack was due to the surveillance? Might it have simply been that no terrorists had plans to attack? It cannot be known if there is a linear relationship between money expended on violence containment and the level of actual violence. Even if we assume that there would have been a terrorist attack but it was successfully prevented, how do we know what the financial impact would have been? It might have resulted in heavy loss of life and the destruction of infrastructure, or it might not have. This highlights the difficulty in trying to calculate the benefit. Governments by nature are cautious; given the lack of counterfactual estimates their bias will generally tend towards tighter security.

This does not mean that the benefits of violence containment are not real. It just means that they are not reflected in the transactions. This highlights the need for far better analysis to understand where the optimum point is for violence containment expenditure.

What is the appropriate level of violence containment spending? This is challenging. There is a trade-off. Very low levels of expenditure frequently mean underpaid police and judges, or none at all. Too much often indicates that security is being used as an instrument of suppression.

If we shift gears and start to see violence as systemic and by using the Pillars of Positive Peace as our lens, we gain a truer, and wider, picture

---

15 S.R. Hiatt and W.D. Sine, 'Clear and present danger: Planning and new venture survival amid political and civil violence', *Strategic Management Journal*, 21 February 2013, accessed at onlinelibrary.wiley.com/doi/10.1002/smj.2113/abstract

of how to improve social benefit, as well as alleviating the underlying environment from which violence springs.

All in

Violence affects all parts of society, so understanding its economic impact is of universal interest. For governments, an economic assessment furnishes greater insights into the costs and likely benefits associated with domestic and international policies. For the international community it enables a better understanding of the economic benefits that can accrue from development assistance. For business, it provides a more detailed profile of an individual country's risk factors and the likely impact on its business outcomes. For civil society, it clarifies the economic benefits of peace-building initiatives, such as mediation and prevention programs.

Many of the items used to calculate the cost of violence are also used as measures in the Global Peace Index. Therefore, it would be expected that a close relationship exists between peacefulness and the percentage of GDP spent dealing with or containing violence. That proves to be the case. As a country becomes less peaceful the costs of violence containment as a proportion of GDP tend to increase. Many of the countries with the highest violence containment costs are also some of the most violent. These are mostly concentrated in the Middle East and North Africa.

A stark illustration of the human and economic value of peace is the case of Sierra Leone. The Sierra Leone civil war lasted for 11 years, from 1991 to 2002. Even though the end of the war brought back economic growth, by 2010 GDP per capita was still 31 per cent lower than what would have been expected had the conflict not happened.[16] The negative economic impacts from the conflict were mirrored by the trends in human development as measured by the UN's Human Development Index, with Sierra Leone's levels of human development lagging behind regional averages and only improving after the cessation of conflict.

16 Institute for Economics and Peace, *Global Peace Index 2015*, p. 68.

FIGURE 8

Change in Sierra Leone's GDP

The cumulative economic cost of conflict in Sierra Leone in terms of GDP losses from 1991 to 2014 amounted to US$113 billion, which is equivalent to over seven times its 2014 GDP.

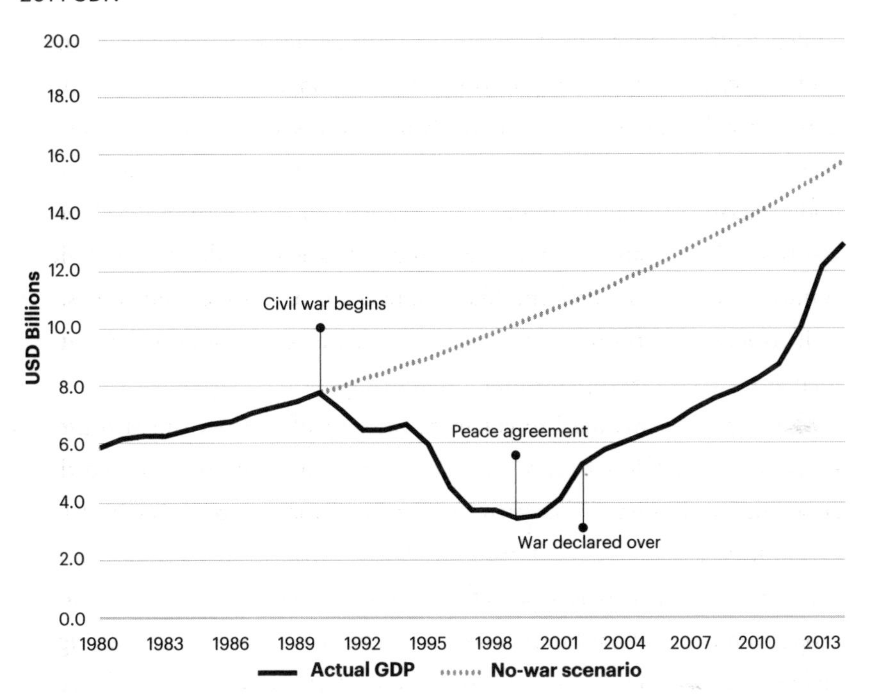

SOURCE: PENN WORLD TABLE 9, SCPR, IEP CALCULATIONS

The impact of violence and war on developing countries is well documented. Perhaps less well known is that the largest absolute economic gains from a reduction in violence containment expenditure would go to the world's largest economies. This is a by-product of their high per capita income. The United States has the eighth highest cost of violence containment per capita, mostly attributable to its heavy military expenditure, the world's largest jailed population, and the heavy costs of gun violence. Middle Eastern nations also feature as high per capita spenders on violence containment, which is attributable to these nations' high incomes, high levels of military spending and high expenditure on internal security.

A comparison between Germany and the United States is instructive. The United States spends nearly three times more per person than Germany on violence containment. This can partly be explained by America's higher spending on national defence, but America also spends significantly more than Germany on 'Other Public Sector Security Spending'. This includes local police, justice and correction services. America's private expenditure on violence containment is, as a proportion of GDP, almost twice that of Germany's. This is, in effect, the price of the absence of peace.

The global challenge

Violence comes with an unacceptably high cost. At $14.1 trillion in 2018, as previously stated, it is equivalent to four and half times the size of the global agriculture sector[17] and 100 times what is spent on Official Development Assistance (ODA). Mark Adelson, the former chief credit officer of Standard & Poor's, estimates that total global losses from the Global Financial Crisis could be as much as $15 trillion for the 2007–2011 period.[18] That is only about quarter of what violence cost the world over the same period.

Given the magnitude of the cost it would be prudent to analyse where the expenditures are occurring and what can be done to reduce them. Sadly, that is not common practice.

The violence containment industry is a major economic force in most developed democracies, with a compelling narrative regarding its relevance and importance. For example, Norway, a small nation, is the seventh largest exporter of military equipment in the world. The Norwegians put a lot of emphasis on being peaceful, and they place many restrictions on where their weapons can go. Yet its arms manufacturing industry is part of the nation's industrial fabric. The country is intent on increasing its market share.

Similarly, the prison industry is big business. In the United States it has an estimated turnover of $74 billion a year.[19] Privatised prisons have revenues

17 The World Bank estimates that the agricultural sector added US$3.2tn dollars in value in 2016, accessed at data.worldbank.org/indicator/NV.AGR.TOTL.CD

18 A. Yoon, 'Total Global Losses from Financial Crisis: $15 Trillion', *Wall Street Journal*, 1 October 2012.

19 B. Kincade, 'The economics of the American prison system.' *Smartasset*, 21 May 2018, accessed at smartasset.com/mortgage/the-economics-of-the-american-prison-system

of $7.4 billion annually. The cost per inmate varies widely, from $14,000 to $60,000.[20] The same goes for the security industry. Spending on security officers and police globally is $1.3 trillion, or more than two per cent of global GDP. Australia, with a fast-rising prison population, has the highest prison privatisation rates in the world. The largest market share in Australia is held by the American public company GEO, which has 20 per cent of the market.[21] .

Given the difficulty of calculating the benefits, the 'right' level of violence containment expenditure will always carry a significant element of value judgement. Often these trade-offs are more than mathematics. When looking at the billions invested in anti-terrorism operations, the number of victims would not seem to justify it. But that kind of metric, although reasonable enough, is far from adequate. The simple truth is that the value of human life cannot be adequately represented by monetary indicators alone, nor can the feeling of not being fearful. The public wants to feel safe. These and many other reasons mean that arriving at the true cost-benefit is complicated and, in the end, must partly be a value judgement.

If there is one clear lesson to be learnt from our research, it is that if even a small proportion of the nearly $14 trillion that goes into violence containment globally was invested in Positive Peace, the economic and social outlook for the entire world would be vastly improved.

---

20 Kincaid, 'The economics of the American prison system'.

21 J. Andrew, M. Baker, P. Roberts, 'Prison Privatisation in Australia: The State of the Nation', The University of Sydney, 2016, accessed at business.sydney.edu.au/__data/assets/pdf_file/0008/269972/Prison_Privatisation_in_Australia-_The_State_of_the_Nation_June_2016.pdf

CHAPTER 8

An entrepreneurial approach to peace

The success of the inaugural 2007 Global Peace Index had energised the whole team. But a question remained: How could we move from a single product launch to creating an ongoing field of study?

Initially I felt that the right home for the Global Peace Index would be a university. The idea of creating a Chair of Peace Economics appealed to me because at that time I had never come across one and it seemed like a big and important field of study. The thinking was that I would endow a chair and a couple of researchers; it would have a home and grow from there.

It was always considered strategic to have our work taught in university courses as a way of propagating a better understanding of peace. Today, we estimate that thousands of university courses around the world include some of the IEP's work in their curricula, especially the data and analysis from the indexes and economic costings. I still get a kick when I meet someone who has studied or used our work at university and found it interesting. It amazes me how regularly this occurs.

Over the next few years I met with the vice-chancellors and deans of universities in Australia, the US and the UK but I could not find the right fit. As the years passed, each marked with a new edition of the Global Peace Index, the project started to take on a life of its own, its resonance increasing and suggesting new possibilities for original research. I could see the potential opportunity expanding. At times, I was dumbstruck by how little quantitative knowledge existed on peace.

After some years, I realised that the gap between my vision and the way universities functioned meant the fit was never quite right. After a couple of successful launches, I knew that publicity had to be integral to the project if it were to be an effective tool to enhance peace. Universities were more introspective and conservative. The concept of launching a global publicity campaign, structuring headline-grabbing sentences and then spending 30 per cent of the time travelling around the world to speak about the results was not the way they worked.

The other defining factor was that my imagination was running wild with the potentialities, especially in relation to the concept of Positive Peace and how it could change the way societies frame and deal with the challenges they face. These thoughts had sprung from my own background and circumstances and were mainly still in my head. It was hard enough for me to fully articulate them, let alone have someone else develop my line of thinking.

Some three years after the first Global Peace Index launch, I decided to create the Institute for Economics and Peace, and to base it in Sydney.

Business success for me just happened. In many ways one needs a big element of luck to be successful. A bad decision early on or a delayed sale is all it takes for a start-up company to fold. I often compare a small start-up to a baby – it's fragile, easily broken and requires nurturing. The same analogy can be applied to a new idea – it needs to be nurtured and built up before being attacked. Too often creative ideas die early because too many people only want to focus on why it won't work rather than what can be done to make it succeed.

It was not until many years later that I realised how much my business background had influenced the way I had conceptualised and managed the Institute. I found my experience in developing products and creating brands around them highly applicable to indexes. The indexes are products; the IEP is an institution. Both can be viewed as brands and there is a lot of knowledge and tried and true ways for building successful brands and brand images.

The branding of the Institute is a more holistic process based around a clear vision, mission and messaging. From this we framed a simple but compelling vision statement:

> *We aim to create a paradigm shift in the way the world thinks about peace. We use data-driven research to show that peace is a positive, tangible and achievable measure of human wellbeing and development.*

To achieve this, we had to build a presence in people's minds and a reputation that was reliable, ethical and had a unique focus on peace. The IEP is a research institute and a think tank. It is non-aligned, therefore wherever possible we do not make value judgements.

This organisational mandate flows into the language in our products. It can even apply to the use of the word 'only', as it may imply a value judgement, such as 'Only 14 per cent of the global impact of violence results from homicides.' This statement would imply it is of less consequence than other costs. In practice, we have found that the presentation of the facts leads most people to the same conclusion. When the facts have multiple interpretations, we do not try to impose or suggest any particular conclusion. This means that the work has the widest appeal and we rarely get caught in cross-value fights and arguments.

In establishing the IEP, as with any organisation, it was essential to assemble a small, highly motivated team with complementary skill sets, and maintain the strategic focus during a period of rapid expansion. Through my experience in business, I've found that people with the right skills will always come along but the key to success is the necessary dedication and work ethic. Too often start-ups fail because the people fit is not right and managers will not make the tough decisions. Two of the core qualities of success are hard work and adaptability, because start-ups require so much more work than an established organisation. It was no different for the IEP.

Clyde McConaghy, a business associate, joined me to help in the early years. Clyde's work was very useful in the setting up of the IEP, especially the legal requirements. He went on to work for me for the next six years, mainly managing many of my business interests and family office and also some aspects of the IEP.

During the first year's launch I met Camilla Schippa, who became a director at the Institute for Economics and Peace and worked there for ten years. She managed our global partnership and outreach activities. When we first met, she was the deputy head of the UN Partnership Office. Her main client was Ted Turner, who in 1998 famously donated US$1 billion to the United Nations.

Here is Camilla's recollection of our first meeting:

> He was such an atypical person. I had at that point been working for about ten years within the office of the Secretary-General, so I was used to people talking in a certain way and behaving in a certain way. And what really struck me was how – and I noticed it right away the first time we got into an elevator – that Steve was talking in exactly the same way to everybody. To the guy who was operating the lift, to the way he talked to the Under-Secretary-General. It was clear he was interested in talking to everyone in an environment which is incredibly bureaucratic and hierarchical. I felt this was something different and somewhat unsettling.

I was looking for the UN to come on as a partner in our initial launch, but Camilla recalls that there was a lot of nervousness about the Index because the countries at the bottom of the Index were unlikely to be happy about it. The conclusion was that the UN could not align itself with it because of the political implications, but there was a recognition of its worth. Kofi Annan only gave his personal endorsement for the Global Peace Index when he stepped down as Secretary-General of the UN. As time went on this attitude changed and the Index became more accepted. Today we do a lot of work with many of the departments in the UN.

We adopted a fairly simple but effective strategy at the IEP, which is still core to the functioning of the organisation today:

- Our skill set was quantitative analysis, with a backdrop in economics.
- We would focus on a core set of products: peace indexes, the economic cost of violence, and what creates peace.
- The products would have a continual evolution with defined release dates.
- Global PR would be used for all major products.
- We would also always have someone from the core team travelling around the world.
- On these trips we would have meetings with multilaterals, policymakers, other think tanks, academia and the media, with the aim of getting as many speaking opportunities as possible.

Rarely a month went by without a round-the-world trip to present our information. This was a lesson I had learnt from building Integrated Research and its software products: that travel was essential to scale from a small business into a global company. When developing Integrated Research, I would spend four or five weeks living in hotels and airports, meeting four or five people every day, repeated every three months, never staying in the same city for more than two days.

The IEP's voice emerges

The IEP has come a long way and is now one of the world's leading peace research institutions.

Our research is used extensively by governments, academic institutions, think tanks, non-governmental organisations and multilateral institutions such as the OECD, the Commonwealth Secretariat, the World Bank and the United Nations. The Institute has been ranked in the top 20 most impactful think tanks under $5 million in revenue in the world on the Global Go To Think Tank Index for the last four years.

Probably one of the most pleasing milestones during our journey was the inclusion of peace and governance as one of the 17 goals in the UN's Sustainable Development Goals. Goal 16 aims to 'Promote peaceful and inclusive societies for sustainable development, provide access to justice for all and build effective, accountable and inclusive institutions at all levels.'

The IEP's work had helped to remove one of the largest barriers to peace being included as a viable target. One of the arguments consistently put forward against the inclusion of peace as a goal in the development agenda was that it was not technically possible to measure it.

Prior to the establishment of the IEP and the Global Peace Index, no reliable measures of global peace existed. Without reliable measures, it is impossible for those engaging in peace and development activities to know whether they are achieving their desired outcomes, and without a certain level of peace, development is impossible to achieve.

What our work has done is create a much richer understanding of what peace is and how to measure it. The 12 measures outlined in Goal 16 are a mixture of the measures in the Global Peace Index and Positive Peace. Although Goal 16 lacks the same conceptual clarity as these two IEP products, it is still a major breakthrough as all nations are now committed to measuring their performance towards peace.

This has been a long time coming. The United Nations was established after the end of World War II with the aim of stopping a repeat of the tragedy. Highlighting this, the first article of the Charter of the United Nations is explicitly based on the need to create external peace. The UN's founding aim was:

> To maintain international peace and security, and to that end: to take effective collective measures for the prevention and removal of threats to the peace, and for the suppression of acts of aggression or other breaches of the peace, and to bring about by peaceful means, and in conformity with the principles of justice and international law, adjustment or settlement of international disputes or situations which might lead to a breach of the peace.[1]

Yet peace was notably absent from the Millennium Development Goals (MDG), which were the goals and targets 190 governments agreed to in the year 2000. Although the MDGs provided a successful road map for development over the subsequent 15 years, a broad agreement on a mutually agreed definition of peace was just too difficult to include at the time of their inception in 2000.

The UN's summary report of the achievements for the MDGs stated that conflict remained the biggest threat to human development.

> By the end of 2014, conflicts had forced almost 60 million people to abandon their homes – the highest level recorded since the Second World War. If these people were a nation, they would make up the 24th largest country in the world. Every day, 42,000 people

1 *Charter of the United Nations*, Chapter 1, Article 1, accessed at www.un.org/en/sections/un-charter/chapter-i/index.html

> on average are forcibly displaced and compelled to seek protection due to conflicts, almost four times the 2010 number of 11,000. Children accounted for half of the global refugee population under the responsibility of the United Nations High Commissioner for Refugees in 2014. In countries affected by conflict, the proportion of out-of-school children increased from 30 per cent in 1999 to 36 per cent in 2012. Fragile and conflict-affected countries typically have the highest poverty rates.[2]

Additionally, for multilaterals and governmental Official Development Aid programs it is vital to know which countries to target. It is too controversial for organisations such as the UN, the World Bank or the OECD to rank their member countries by their levels of peace.

Other reports

Today the IEP aims to produce four major reports a year and a number of minor ones. A major report would be the Global Peace Index, the Mexico Peace Index or the *Positive Peace Report*, while minor reports would include papers on peace and corruption, key questions regarding the role of religion in conflict, and how to better assess the risk of a country falling into conflict.

Some reports are reactive. Once the UN had made peace one of its Sustainable Development Goals, we thought this would be worthy of a new report, so for the last four years we have produced a report on 163 countries' progress towards the goal. Our yearly *SDG16 Progress Report* looks at a country's performance against the official SDG 16 targets, examines the challenges of data collection, and reports on the country's progress towards the targets in the prior year.

2 United Nations, *Millennium Development Goal Report 2015*.

Peace and corruption

Another example is our 2015 *Peace and Corruption* paper. This research first isolated the tipping point for peace. This was exciting and was our first glimpse into the systemic nature of peace. What we found was that there is a consistent and statistically significant relationship between peace and corruption. It became clear that as corruption increases it has only a marginal effect on peace until a particular point, after which small increases in corruption generally result in large deteriorations in peace. The main factor causing this steep fall off in peace, after the tipping point, is corruption within the police force and the judiciary. Once corruption within these organisations passes a certain threshold, they create an environment of impunity, or worse still, the police are the ones committing the crimes.

This leads to an important question: what affects corruption? Our view is it's a systemic problem and needs to be addressed through the lens of Positive Peace. From a systems perspective all factors interact, and the best way of tackling corruption is systemically.

Using just three Pillars it is possible to demonstrate the difficulty in attributing causality: *Free Flow of Information*, *Well-Functioning Government* and *Low Levels of Corruption.*

A free press affects government policy, which in turn affects corruption, but education also affects what people think is good government and corruption. However, government does set the education priorities and can control press freedoms. It's impossible to untangle the causality. These interactions are classic mutual feedback loops.

The interaction of these factors of Positive Peace sets out the shortcomings of using simple causal analysis. Although systems thinking is more complex, and it is more difficult to identify relationships and patterns, it leads to a better understanding of how to implement successful change.

Corruption in the police and the judiciary has been established as especially harmful to peace, but the ways of addressing such problems are not always simple, particularly in cultures that do not have a long history of an independent judiciary or where the government's tax receipts are not enough to pay adequate wages to the police. Although analytics can provide valuable context, it is important to remember that different cultures have different understandings of corruption and justice. The core of the problem is that corruption undermines faith in the processes of the justice system and creates inefficiencies. But the justice system, and its crucial role in moderating the relationship between citizens and the state, is also affected by culture. This underlines the importance of soliciting local input when designing interventions.

Two incidents in Samburu, a semi-nomadic area in northern Kenya, show these difficulties. We were working with a tribe trying to cure trachoma, a bacterial infection of the eye that can lead to blindness if untreated. Samburu had the highest rates of trachoma in the world at that time. Just before I arrived there had been an issue with someone breaking in to a dispensary and stealing a substantial quantity of drugs. They intended to sell them on the black market.

When the police arrived, they arrested five people, taking them 200 kilometres from where they lived. They were sentenced to three to six months in jail. Yet according to the locals, three of the five were innocent. The tribes were left wondering what was going on. Historically, such situations would have been handled internally by the tribe. If found guilty the offenders would have had to hand over some of their cattle. Because people were being sent to jail, all their cattle were rustled. These people, some of whom were entirely innocent, had to support their families but had lost the means to do so. Instead, the community now had to look after the families.

So it became a struggle against the justice system itself. Instead of the elders of the tribe administering justice in the traditional way, which would have punished the offenders and maintained community cohesion, a method of punishment was used that set the people against the system.

Another incident, which happened at about the same time, highlights the limits of the tribal justice system in relation to sexual practices. When the men reach puberty, they go through a ceremony in which they become warriors. The women do too, in a separate ceremony. Having come of age, the warriors are meant to have sex with as many people as possible in order to show their manhood. But one boy objected, because it could involve rape. In response, a group of the other young men beat him up so badly that he died. The tribal elders came down to discuss what had happened. It was a lengthy and serious debate. In the end, the three men who beat him to death were required to give over a large amount of cattle to the grieving family.

What was sad was that while traditional justice was capable of punishing murder, it was blind to the evils of institutionalised rape. These examples highlight the difficulties of the two systems coming together. Both need to adapt and change.

It is hard to understand a culture from the outside. Understanding and dealing with circumstances like this requires situational intelligence. Analysis of context can define general frameworks, but it is always necessary to look closely at the situation, rather than try to shoehorn everything into one understanding of the way the world is.

The drivers of corruption are multifaceted, complex and systemic. To address corruption effectively, it is necessary to improve the underlying structures of the overall societal system. But this needs to be done with an understanding of the particular society's unique culture and history. As has been mentioned, the idea from a systems perspective is to constantly nudge the system forward, not radically change it, as that will only smash the system, leaving an uncertain replacement.

More reports

As the IEP developed, we expanded our areas of expertise. One of my favourites was the annual Global Terrorism Index, which we started in 2013 in response to the alarming upward trend in terrorist attacks. The aim of the report is to provide a factual context to what has become an extremely emotive and politically charged issue. The Index summarises trends in terrorism since 2000 and analyses changing patterns by geographic activity, methods of attack, the organisations involved, and the national economic impact and political context, as well as providing insights into major terrorist groups. Another chapter in this book is dedicated to terrorism, where the findings and results are explained in detail. For many countries, terrorism is their number one domestic security concern.

Some IEP reports seek to provide context about 'hot button' issues, especially in the media. Our 2014 report, *Five Key Questions Answered on the Link Between Peace and Religion* set out to re-examine some of the myths surrounding the religious roots of violence, including:

1. Is religion the main cause of conflict today?
2. Does the proportion of religious belief or atheism in a country determine the peace of the country?
3. In Muslim countries, does the demographic spread of Sunni and Shia determine peace?
4. Is religion key to understanding what drives peace?
5. Can religion play a positive role in peace-building?

The report covered conflicts in the years 2012 and 2013 and provided new insights. Contrary to the public's general perception of religion, the study found that the relationship between violence and religiosity is weak. There was little evidence that religion caused conflicts and we found no statistical relationship between the presence or absence of religious belief and conflict. Although there has been sectarian violence between Shia and Sunni groups in the Middle East, there is no evidence that it is inevitable. The conclusion is that religion is rarely the key factor in conflict, although it did play a part in about 60 per cent of conflicts. Other factors, such as corruption, state-sponsored terror against its citizens, group grievances, economic inequality and political instability, are much more closely correlated with conflict. On the positive side, religion can play a constructive role in improving social cohesion: countries with higher membership of religious organisations tend to be slightly more peaceful.

The evidence presented in the IEP's *Religion and Peace Report* runs somewhat against public perception. Yet the fact that the picture is complex is scarcely surprising. A glance at history suggests that religion has been the motive for many wars and conflicts, yet it has also been pivotal in the development of the concepts of peace and nonviolence. Many major religions advocate nonviolence, yet some of their adherents are extremely violent. In assessing religion and peace, we need to take a more sober approach as the realities are highly complex.

Other IEP reports address broader historical issues, taking more of a longitudinal approach. *The Economic Consequences of War on the U.S. Economy* (2011) examines the widely held belief that war and military spending have been key drivers of America's economic growth. It's now over 17 years since the invasion of Iraq and the countries involved, especially the United States, have expended vast sums of money while their economies have remained in the doldrums. Perceptions are now starting to change.

America spends more on its military than any other country, representing about 37 per cent of global military expenditure,[3] so an examination of the economic consequences of its heavy investment is important.

The report begins by considering the macroeconomic effects of government policies and spending during the major periods of conflict over the last 70 years. These fall into five periods: World War II, the Korean War, the Vietnam War, the Cold War, and the Iraq and Afghanistan wars. The report focuses solely on the economic impact of these wars had on the US economy and makes no moral, philosophical or political comments on the justification of these wars, nor the human costs.

To determine the overall economic impact the following indicators were analysed:

- GDP
- Public debt and levels of taxation
- Consumption as a percentage of GDP
- Investment as a percentage of GDP
- Inflation
- Average stock market valuations
- Income distribution.

One of the most commonly cited claims is that war is good for the economy because it leads to higher GDP growth. This is often claimed to be true throughout all of the conflict periods, other than in the Afghanistan

3 National Priorities Project, 'U.S. military spending vs. the world', *National Priorities Project*, accessed at www.nationalpriorities.org/campaigns/us-military-spending-vs-world/

and Iraq war period. It is also often said that World War II catalysed the economic growth that ended the Great Depression.

World War II is also associated with a sharp decline in income inequality, a trend that lasted to the end of the Cold War. The levelling of income inequality, it is claimed, created the ideal conditions to build a vibrant, consumer-driven society.

How valid are these claims? The higher level of government spending associated with war does seem to generate some positive economic benefits in the short term, at least if economic benefits are measured in terms of GDP growth. There is often an increase in economic growth when conflict spending booms. But there are many negative, unintended consequences that either occur concurrently with the war, or develop later as residual effects, thereby harming the economy over the longer term. This also highlights the limitations of using GDP as the single measure of a country's success.

The macroeconomic effects varied for each conflict because there were different approaches to financing the additional government expenditure. But during each war, gross investment either declined or grew at a very slow rate, and in all cases, apart from during the Iraq and Afghanistan wars, consumption stalled.

The truth is that war created a burden on the American government and the economy. In most cases there was an increase in public debt and taxation, a fall in consumption as a percentage of GDP, a decrease of investment as a percentage of GDP, and an increase in inflation.

War has not necessarily been good for American financial markets either. There does not appear to be a consistent relationship between average stock market valuations and conflict periods, other than for companies involved in the armaments industry. During World War II, stock markets did initially fall but recovered before its end. During the Korean War there were no major corrections. During the Vietnam War and afterwards, stock markets remained flat from the end of 1964 until 1982.

War and the economy

When we consider what happened in each war, it is clear that war is not the great economic good it is thought to be. World War II was financed through debt and higher taxes. By the end of the war, American gross debt was over 120 per cent of GDP and tax revenue increased more than three times to over 20 per cent of GDP. GDP growth soared to over 17 per cent in 1942,[4] perhaps another instance of the flawed nature of GDP as a measure of social benefit, but consumption and investment contracted. Unemployment was all but eliminated, but recovery was well underway prior to the war, and the key counterfactual is whether similar spending on public works would have generated even more growth.

The Korean War was largely financed by higher tax rates, with GDP growth averaging 5.8 per cent between 1950 and 1953 and peaking at 11.4 per cent in 1951. Investment and consumption both stalled. The government was forced to implement price and wage controls in response to the inflation that occurred as a consequence of government spending.

The Vietnam War ramped up slowly, so its impact was different. It was largely funded by increases in tax rates and an expansive monetary policy that led to inflation. Unlike prior wars, consumption remained unaltered, but investment fell. GDP growth increased and peaked at 7.3 per cent of GDP in 1966.

The Afghanistan War, which started in 2001, and the Iraq War, which began two years later, have been accompanied by weak economic conditions following the bursting of the high-tech asset bubble that led to the 2001–2002 recession. It was probably the first time in American history when taxes were cut during a war, so both conflicts had to be completely financed by deficit spending.

What would have happened in economic terms if these wars had not happened? It can reasonably be concluded that taxes, budget deficits and inflation would all have been lower, while consumption and investment would have been higher.

---

4 Institute for Economics and Peace, *Economic Consequences of War on the US Economy*, accessed at economicsandpeace.org/wp-content/uploads/2015/06/The-Economic-Consequences-of-War-on-US-Economy_0.pdf

Some wars must be fought and the negative effects of not fighting these wars can far outweigh the costs of fighting. World War II, the Korean War and the Gulf War are examples. But in purely economic terms, if there are other realistic options than war, then it is prudent to explore them first.

The IEP has also produced a number of country-specific reports, most notably for the United States, the United Kingdom and Mexico. These reports are intended to provide a measure of national levels of peacefulness, providing insights at the sub-national level and contributing to a more meaningful policy debate. Each of these reports includes an analysis of the statistical factors most closely associated with peace, as well as the economic cost of violence by country. The reports always provide new insights and a conceptual framework for understanding peace at the sub-national level. The IEP's main country reports are discussed in more detail in a later chapter.

Analysing risk

One of the newer areas of research within the IEP is focused on assessing the potential risk of countries having substantial falls in peace. This has come about because of the realisation that Positive Peace is a measure of resilience. Therefore, if a country is much more peaceful than its Positive Peace factors say it should be, it runs the risk of its peace deteriorating. Conversely, if the underlying Positive Peace factors are improving, then the likelihood of substantial falls in peace will be diminishing.

Using data collected since 1996, the Institute developed two methodologies to identify countries most at risk of experiencing large increases in violence. To test the models, they were compared to the actual falls in peace since 2009. The most accurate model predicted falls in peace for nine of the ten countries with the largest peace deficits. The beauty of this model, known as the 'Positive Peace Deficit model' is its predictive capacity. It forecasts many years into the future, which means that there is time to take preventative measures.[5]

5 Institute for Economics and Peace, *Positive Peace Report 2019*, accessed at visionofhumanity.org/app/uploads/2019/10/PPR-2019-web.pdf

It's important to understand that the risk methodology doesn't make judgements about particular governments or particular ideologies. The positions that countries are in are not necessarily the fault of the governments of the day. Often, they can have a long legacy.

Launching the Global Peace Index

'If it bleeds, it leads,' as the newsroom mantra goes. Selecting stories because of their violence or tragedy seems to be a guiding principle for many news outlets. This creates a dilemma. How can we publicise peace, particularly its positive aspects?

Research by the Pew Research Center has shown that crime stories are consistently the largest single area of news broadcasts, usually averaging about 8 to 15 per cent of broadcasts.[6]

In 2011 the IEP, in conjunction with Media Tenor, produced a study that looked at the coverage of conflict and violence by the major global news services. The study, *Measuring Peace in the Media*, came to a number of conclusions and many are not especially surprising, but the report does shine a light on how peace is positioned in the media relative to conflict. The major findings were:

- War, conflict and violence are the most widely covered news stories.
- International news coverage in relatively peaceful countries tends to be dominated by stories of exceptional violence or disasters.
- The number of violence reports for international coverage compared to total reports approximately aligned to the proportion of the actual level of violence in the country covered, as measured by the Global Peace Index.
- Based on the Pillars of Positive Peace, critical topics such as the *Equitable Distribution of Resources* received very little coverage.
- On average, the number of negative reports far exceeded those which were positive in tone.

---

6 Mark Jurkowitz, et al., 'The Changing TV News Landscape', Pew Research Center, 17 March 2013, accessed at www.stateofthemedia.org/2013/special-reports-landing-page/the-changing-tv-news-landscape/

- Countries with the largest declines in peacefulness received approximately 14 times more coverage than the countries that had the largest improvements.

To better understand the media's reporting on violence, the ratio of the number of international news stories on violence was compared to the total number of international news stories for that country. We didn't include domestic stories as we felt this would lead to bias. The aim was to see whether the level of news coverage of a country could be used as an indication of the level of peacefulness for that country. We expected that the more violent a country is, the greater the proportion of violence-related international news stories there would be, and this was generally true. For example, Afghanistan, which had high levels of violence at the time, also had a high percentage of violence-related news stories. This contrasts with Sweden, which attracted little coverage of violence in the international press in the years covered by the study.

Stories related to violence receive the most coverage for several reasons. They tend to be more dramatic and shocking, often invoking primeval emotions concerning life and death. Across all topics, there were three times as many negative stories as positive stories.

The implication is that the instinctual appeal of violence leads to an inherent bias in the media. As is well known, the media are mainly interested in the number of viewers or readers, because that drives advertising revenues, underpinning their business model. This slants coverage towards what will maximise the number of consumers viewing their publication or program. Positive human-interest stories, by contrast, make up only a fraction of the output. One of the more interesting findings was that there is a greater tendency for English-speaking countries to report violence. Out of the ten news programs with the highest violence-reporting percentages, seven were programs from the United States or the United Kingdom.

According to journalist and author Ulrik Haagerup, the media's inclination towards negativity has a number of root causes.[7] The first was the emergence of tabloid media that concentrated on crime, scandals, sex, celebrity and sport.

---

7 U. Haagerup, *Constructive News*, InnoVatio, 2015.

> It focused on the little man against the system, simplifying issues and turning political coverage into matters of persons rather than visions and ideology. This approach quickly spilled over into local TV news and from there, into mainstream media.[8]

These trends have, if anything, intensified as mainstream media have come under increasing commercial pressure from the growth of the internet and social media. The problem with the media's focus on violence – other than creating the impression that the world is a much more violent place than it actually is – is that it represents a great challenge for the promotion of peace as a political and social imperative. This was the main hurdle we were facing as we attempted to promote the first Global Peace Index.

How can the right policy decisions be made if people are not aware of advances in peacefulness, or have the false impression that violence is significantly worse than it actually is? If, for example, the general public hold the false impression that violent crime is getting worse, governments are tempted to resort to more punitive measures or politicians might hammer a strong law-and-order agenda, thereby creating unnecessary costs and undesirable side effects.

This has been seen in the US on its 'war on drugs', which incorporates harsh penalties for minor drug use, resulting in 20-year jail terms for the cultivation or sale of marijuana. The 'three strikes and you're out' rule in California and elsewhere has meant many people have been incarcerated for 25 years for minor offences. In 2019, there were 2.3 million people incarcerated in the US,[9] equivalent to 0.7 per cent of the entire population. Of these people, over 540,000 are locked up without a conviction. Worse, two per cent of the population is under some form of correctional supervision, either in custody or out on parole.[10] A report from the Prison Policy Initiative estimated that mass incarceration cost the United States almost $120 billion a year, even without taking the costs of policing into

8 Haagerup, p. 9

9 W. Sawyer and P. Wagner, 'Mass incarceration', Prison Policy Initiative, 19 March 2019, accessed at www.prisonpolicy.org/reports/pie2019.html

10 D. Kaeble, et al., 'Correctional Populations in the United States, 2014', U.S. Department of Justice, revised 21 January 2016, accessed at www.bjs.gov/content/pub/pdf/cpus14.pdf

account.[11] A pro-rehabilitation policy as a mainstay of treatment would have been cheaper. It also would have improved the country's human capital and increased GDP because the individuals involved would have been working.

It is a sad fact that media outlets are unlikely to display the same interest in positive stories as they do in violence. Positive Peace suffers from the additional handicap that it tends to be slow moving, a phenomenon that does not lend itself to the urgency of the 24/7 news cycle. The news media's short-term focus is antipathetic to developing a sound understanding of what is needed for a society to flourish. The headline 'Nation makes improvement in overall peacefulness, continuing five-year trend' is not likely to be the lead news story any time soon.

The problem is not just that the media is disinclined to look at good news, or to appeal to audiences' more positive instincts. They are also highly selective about what kinds of stories they choose to focus on. What especially attracts the media's attention are extraordinary events that startle audiences, or when readers or viewers think these events might affect them. Commonplace violence – the quotidian murders, suicides and muggings that shatter lives by the thousands – is mostly ignored unless it is particularly gruesome or particularly local. The most damaging forms of violence in a society rarely get sufficient media coverage precisely because they happen so regularly. Terrorism, on the other hand, both is startling and can be portrayed as a potential threat to almost anyone.

Media reports of violence can contribute to more violence, in effect contributing to a vicious cycle. This can be seen in the form of copycat terrorist acts, such as driving a truck down a crowded street, or in suicides. In Australia, journalists are actively discouraged from reporting on suicides because of the fear that it will cause more suicides: there are a number of studies that indicate increased rates of suicide in the months following front-page newspaper articles of celebrity suicides. Higher rates of suicide by a particular method have been found to follow the appearance

11 P. Wagner and B. Rabuy, 'Following the Money of Mass incarceration', Prison Policy Initiative, 25 January 2017, accessed at www.prisonpolicy.org/reports/money.html

of newspaper stories on a suicide highlighting the same method. Studies also indicate a relationship between the method of suicide portrayed in a fictional film or television program and increased rates of suicide attempts using this method.

If this connection is true then it is easy to draw the same conclusions from too much coverage of terrorism, particularly as one of the key aims of a terrorist act is to garner publicity that will instil fear. This creates a moral dilemma as the public has a right to know, but what is the appropriate level of coverage?

The media challenge

It quickly became obvious to us that there is little point in uncovering new insights and perspectives without making them available to a broader audience. I wanted the work to have a positive impact on humanity. Therefore, publicising the most interesting parts of our research became central to actually creating the impact we wanted.

We have seen the massive media impact of information about global warming and the need to reduce carbon emissions. Yet even with all the coverage, humans have struggled to reach consensus on how the problem should be tackled, let alone agree on common action. Peace is of even greater importance. It is not just one single issue, like pollution, or the loss of species. It is the underlying issue.

Because I had the funds, I could undertake a global publicity campaign; this is much harder for many peace organisations that struggle with limited budgets. It's interesting how much easier it is to raise money to support those who are affected by violence or crime, especially children, than it is to fund research into peace.

We planned a global public relations launch for the first Index in 2007. We chose London, a global media capital, and started to put a launch team together. I worked alongside Stuart Smith, then the CEO of Edelman UK, a creative genius whose interests are as wide as they are deep: he studied quantum physics at Oxford. We became good friends in the ensuing years.

It was 2007, and as people witnessed the incompetent execution of the Iraq War and the appalling cost, there was a major shift of sentiment in relation to the legitimacy of the war. This changed the prevailing attitude towards peace. Many, including myself, had seen the Vietnam War as an abnormality, a conflict caught up in the complexities of fighting communism. Other conflicts, such as the Gulf War, were fought on the basis of a solid rationale. However, by 2007 it was obvious to most informed observers that the Iraq War was little more than blatant aggression. It led many who had not been especially interested in peace to start to ask basic questions about how the war had come about.

Thus the timing was right for a publicity campaign. There was widespread interest in a closer examination of violence, but we had a difficult choice to make. One of the obvious ways to gain traction with the media was to focus on the high-profile nations at the bottom of the Index. But rather than asking why those countries were at the bottom, we wanted to ask why other countries were at the top of the Index, and how more countries could join them.

We chose to launch a week before the G8 summit in Germany to give the report extra topicality. We were lucky enough to win the endorsement of over 100 eminent people, including the Dalai Lama, Bishop Desmond Tutu and eight other Nobel laureates. On the day of the launch, backed by tailored media releases for each of the 121 countries in the Index, the Global Peace Index was the most-covered story on Google and went on to generate 1,500 articles in the first few days.

Edelman justifiably won the prize for the best International Communication Strategy at the 2007 European Excellence Awards for its campaign for the launch. It was an exceptional accolade and it was highly motivational for us all. The impact of the Global Peace Index had been so great it was clear that there was a media appetite for covering peace.

As well as an excellent marketing campaign and a solid budget, another reason for the extraordinary appeal was that the results of the Global Peace Index were released in the form of a league table. Indexes and rankings have immediate appeal; they seem to excite in people an innate competitiveness, or perhaps a sporting instinct. Often, the difference in measurement between countries are very small, and the question is often asked: 'Why should we put one country at the top? Why not have seven countries equal winners?' But that is not the way human nature works: people are looking for winners.

Having rankings turned out to be an excellent way to get attention, to motivate people and to trigger a debate about the concept of peace. A list comparing nations inspires people to think of peace in new ways, and about why their country is where it is and why peaceful countries are peaceful. If people pay attention to the subject of peace, then it might be expected they will also start to think more about how to increase peace.

The other great challenge was to create positive stories about peace. It was another reason why using a list was a good approach. Rarely do you see a negative story on an athlete who won the marathon; people are naturally attracted to a winner.

Getting the media to talk constructively about peace involves overcoming their interest in fear. But fear is not all that people want. As a society we must work out how to tap into more positive emotions such as hope, trust and the desire to cooperate, the instincts that made human society and development possible in the first place. The question is how to amplify these stories so they become a much larger proportion of media coverage.

It may be true that fear is easier to 'sell' in the media and politics, but it does not follow that this is the only emotion that motivates humans, or that there are not more effective ways of motivating people. If you want to create positive change, your best way of doing it is to create positive motivation. You can do this by appealing to the universal aspiration for an improved life. Peace needs to be rebranded as an achievable phenomenon that makes the quality of our lives better – Positive Peace creates an optimal environment for human potential to flourish.

Raising awareness

We launched the first Global Peace Index in London, Washington and at the United Nations in New York. The media interest was intense, with interview requests from CNN, the BBC, Fox News and CBC, among others.

This would be my first experience with live television and, despite the careful training, the prospect was somewhat daunting. There is no room for a retake when speaking to a live global audience potentially measured in the tens of millions.

Pleasingly on the day it all went smoothly, and now I find I have little to no nerves when speaking on live television, even when it is simultaneously translated. I was recently at the BBC doing a live interview for its Persian news program, which involved simultaneous translation, and my earpiece kept slipping out. I kept stuffing it back in, so I was only hearing half of the question. At the time it seemed more amusing than anything else, which is a far cry from how I would have felt a decade ago.

The Global Peace Index also captured the interest of many organisations and individuals. For example, Enrico Giovannini, the Chief Statistician of the OECD, who was on the lookout for new alternatives to GDP, invited me to be one of the two keynote speakers at its biennial international statistical conference. I would be speaking alongside the prime minister of Bhutan, Jigmi Thinley, who was developing the concept of the Gross National Happiness Index.

It was quite an occasion. It had an audience of over 2,000 people, and I had never spoken to such a large number of people before. As with many other aspects of working on the Global Peace Index launch, it was an extraordinary growth experience for me. At the time, it was a high-pressure performance. However, I managed to meet expectations. Now, I can give talks to over 15,000 people without any nerves, but in the early stages it was not without its challenges.

Enrico's interest in the Global Peace Index was an important validation for me of its originality and relevance.

The media impact

I was amazed by the scale of the coverage that first launch achieved; it was well beyond my best expectations.

Not only was the Global Peace Index the most covered story on Google News on the day of its launch; the interest continued, with over 472,000 search items appearing for 'Global Peace Index' over the following month.

The potential media reach for news articles, radio and television programs was estimated at roughly one billion people globally. There were more than a thousand global mainstream media hits within the first 24 hours, and more than 1,500 articles within five days. Since then, the level of coverage has consistently stayed high. After the launch of the 2019 Global Peace Index there were over two billion media impressions in the first month, with articles in over 100 countries.

It was not just a matter of quantity; the coverage was positive across all platforms, and global. It was gratifying to read reports in Western media giants such as *The Wall Street Journal*, the BBC and *The Guardian*, but I was particularly pleased to see that it had sparked debate on the frontlines of peace, with reports in outlets such as the Islamic Republic News Agency, The Middle East Online, ColomboPage Sri Lanka and Pakistan Link and others.

The budget was tight, but the impact was stunning, and the launch has been used as a case study of PR excellence.

CHAPTER 9

Global and national peace indexes

Understanding how nation-states operate is an extremely complex task. This complexity can be best exemplified by the repeated failure to forecast which countries are likely to fall into conflict, or even to predict the next economic recession. Just to highlight the point, many of the main conflict-forecasting tools have less than 30 per cent accuracy.

Governments are little better at understanding how their countries function. They attempt to develop policies they believe will satisfy the needs and aspirations of their constituents, with the main aim of winning the next election. The turnover of governments in democracies testifies to how difficult it is.

Through the development of peace indexes, it is possible to better understand and explain the dynamics of national social systems.

The individual indicators in the Global Peace Index can be used to measure change. This can give insights into the changing nature and patterns of various types of violence; for example, in 2015, the biggest improvements occurred in the homicide rate. Another indicator, and again contrary to public perception, that had substantially improved in the prior decade was state-sponsored terror. This indicator measures the level of extra-judicial killings, torture and imprisonment without trial. This in some ways would indicate that the world has become slightly more civilised.

Regional and national insights from the Global Peace Index

By arranging the information contained in the Global Peace Index in different ways it is possible to derive valuable insights into various regions and countries, and into areas such as geopolitics, international relations and development aid. This is important because often trends occur globally, with some countries being more affected than others.

At the time of the 2015 Index's release, Greece was in the midst of a financial crisis that threatened to result in the country exiting from the Euro, but our research indicated that Greece's peace rating had shown a significant improvement. This provided an important counter perspective to the nation's travails. It suggested that since Greece had become more peaceful, it would not implode as the doomsayers were predicting and would probably muddle its way through, as noted in the IEP's, Global Peace Index 2015:

> Greece was the region's greatest improver, jumping 22 places in the global rankings. The country experienced an improvement in a host of indicators, including reduced *violent crime* and *political terror*. In spite of a still economically problematic situation, the country has stabilised, particularly for indicators in the social safety and security domain.

Developing national peace indexes

To gain a better understanding of the dynamics of particular states, the Institute has developed indexes for a number of countries, including the US, the UK, Mexico and Germany. The countries are selected on the basis of the availability of good data, importance and funding.

These indexes are more than using the data out of the Global Peace Index. We created new measures and adjusted the selection and weighting of individual indicators depending on their relevance to the country concerned. For example, an organised crime indicator is highly applicable to Mexico but not to the UK.

The advantage of national indexes is that they provide information and context that can be applied directly to government policy. The focus is on internal peace, with a comparative analysis including trendlines; the ranking of major metropolitan areas; a study of economic costs; and an analysis of the socio-economic conditions associated with peace. The last teases out the conditions that are most pertinent to improving peace in their respective countries.

These indexes show that each country has its own unique peace challenges. Although many of the correlations tend to be similar, there are also many subtle and at times major differences. When taken in conjunction with measures of Positive Peace, the national indexes can also be used as leading indicators of future improvements or deteriorations in peace, and although they cannot predict shocks, they do measure resilience.

When a country ranks higher in its Positive Peace scores than its actual peace it has a higher likelihood of improvements in its score. It is indicative that the higher levels of institutional capacity will support lower levels of violence. Conversely, countries that rank higher in their actual peace than their Positive Peace scores are more vulnerable to shocks and run a higher risk of increased levels of violence.

The United States

Few developed countries would benefit more from higher levels of peace than America. In 2011, and then again in 2012, the Institute produced a United States Peace Index. Although some time has passed since then, the results of these indexes are still pertinent today.

The United States is the world's largest economy, with a GDP of $20.5 trillion in 2018. At a conservative estimate, violence and violence containment cost the US economy $2.8 trillion in 2018 – 13 per cent of GDP, or roughly $8,664 per head of population. If the nation's violence-containment spending was represented as a discrete national economic entity, it would be the sixth largest economy in the world in terms of purchasing power. The economic cost of violence is truly significant to the US economy and is expressed in many ways, such as higher sunk costs from investing in security systems or purchasing insurance, both of which carry significant opportunity costs.

If the cost of violence containment could be reduced by ten per cent, it would equate to almost $300 billion annually, enough to constitute a significant economic stimulus. Given that the US economy generates a little under 10,000 jobs per billion dollars of GDP,[1] a ten per cent reduction in violence is equivalent to almost three million jobs.

It is hard to escape the conclusion that if its policymakers had a clearer understanding of the economic burden of non-productive violence-containment spending and its associated opportunity costs, they would be in a better position to implement the sort of long-term structural, economic and societal reforms that would set the stage for a new era of peace and growth.

We chose to focus on the United States in part because of its high levels of crime and incarceration, and in part because of the size of the economy, but also because the accounting procedures used by the US government are excellent, which makes it easier to get accurate statistics compared to most other countries. That made it an excellent testbed for some of the theories of Positive Peace and systems thinking that we were developing. The study only focused on the internal peacefulness of the country and did not include militarisation or external conflicts, or take account of the risk of exogenous shocks. The report was mostly well received and uncovered some interesting results.

The first United States Peace Index included a map of America according to its level of peacefulness. It showed, for example, that Maine was the most peaceful state and Louisiana the least. Interestingly, the large states of New York and California had the largest improvements in peace since 1991, while North and South Dakota had the largest deteriorations.

One of the more remarkable facts was that in 2012 the homicide rate had halved since 1991, with similar reductions recorded in the rate of assaults, rapes and robberies. Violent crime decreased every year except one in the 20 years to 2012, although the trend may be changing as the US homicide rate did rise in 2015 and 2016, before declining again in 2017 and 2018, with preliminary data pointing to a decrease in 2019.[2]

It is hard to understand exactly why the crime rate has been falling. Over the last decade there has been a widening of inequality in America,

---

1 J. Brauer and J. Tepper Marlin, *Defining Peace Industries and Calculating the Potential Size of a Peace Gross World Product by Country and by Economic Sector*, Report for Economists for Peace and Security and for the Institute for Economics and Peace, 2009.

2 J. Lartey and W. Li, 'New FBI Data: Violent Crime Still Falling', The Marshall Project, 9 March 2019, accessed at www.themarshallproject.org/2019/09/30/new-fbi-data-violent-crime-still-falling

but the country is on average much wealthier than it was in the postwar era. An improvement in social services is another factor, as is the ageing of the population and widening access to contraception and abortion. Improvements in crime detection, particularly advances in DNA testing and other forensic techniques, are also having an influence as the likelihood of being caught acts as a deterrent to many forms of criminal activity.

However, the drop in officially recorded violence has been partially offset by increases in prison violence. The explosive growth of the prison population has resulted in a reported epidemic of prison assault and rape.

The economic cost of internal violence to the US economy falls into three categories.

- The first is the expenditure borne by state governments to maintain law and order through the police and the justice and prison systems.
- A second category is the direct lost productivity from crime, which can include time off work from injuries, or lost earning capacity from early death or time spent in jail.
- The third category is indirect: the lost productivity and job creation that would have occurred had alternative investments been made in reducing the factors associated with violence.

If all the states in the US had the same level of peacefulness as the most peaceful state, Maine, it would release over $300 billion each year for more productive use in 2012.

However, just examining the financial numbers ignores qualities that are less easily quantifiable but still have a significant impact on the broader system. There is also what might be called a quality-of-life effect. Peace in the US is linked to economic opportunity, health, education and social capital. More peaceful states tend to have more economic opportunities, better basic services and higher levels of educational attainment. They also tend to have more social capital, a better sense of community and higher rates of volunteerism.

What emerged from the US Peace Index was a variety of perspectives that could inform political strategies and government policies. Pursuing peace as a political aim can bring together many elements of policy that at the moment appear to be discrete.

The government's policy on crime is not usually seen as an economic issue except to the extent that there may be budgetary constraints on violent-containment expenditure. Interestingly, as the IEP analysis demonstrates, economic performance and crime reduction are linked. If the aim is to enhance peace, they should both be seen as part of one continuum.

Peace, when it is defined and assessed impartially and empirically, is politically neutral; it is entirely consistent with the intentions of parties at both ends of the political spectrum. From the perspective of the right, peace is good for business and is aligned with reducing crime. From the perspective of the left, high levels of peace can be correlated with social equity. Moreover, when high levels of peace are present, governments are better able to deal with issues such as the environment, poverty reduction and business development.

To get a sense of how these peace insights could be applied most effectively to government policy, the US results were correlated with secondary datasets in five areas: education, health, economic opportunity, civics and demographics, and community and social capital. This provided insights into the likely effectiveness of different strategies and emphases.

In the educational area the strongest correlation with peace is high-school completion rates: both the percentage of students who graduate in a certain year and the percentage of the state population as a whole with a high-school qualification. Another measure that correlates significantly is educational opportunity. However, average annual teacher salary and average per-pupil spending did not correlate, suggesting that increased educational funding would not automatically result in increased peacefulness.

Health outcomes also consistently track the level of violence. Levels of infant mortality, teenage pregnancy, teenage death rate, and life expectancy at birth are all strongly correlated with the level of violence. Poverty and labour-force participation are also factors that seem to track violence levels. The lower the poverty in a state, the more peaceful that state tends to be. Perceptions of access to basic needs is another critical factor. The strongest 'economic conditions' correlation is between the United States Peace Index and Gallup's 'Basic Access' measure. It looks at perceptions of access to, and affordability of, basic services such as water, medicine and fresh food. This is very similar to a multidimensional poverty measure that in the UK has the strongest correlation in the UK Peace Index.

High levels of economic opportunity are also strongly associated with peace. None of the ten most peaceful American states has more than ten per cent of families living in poverty. The number of children living in single-parent families is also correlated with levels of peacefulness, as is civic engagement and trust. More peaceful states tend to have higher levels of volunteerism, and higher percentages of people attending town or school meetings.

Country indicators can be used to make more detailed comparisons with other nations, although it is important to compare like with like. In the case of the United States, Canada provides a useful benchmark, given its geographical proximity and cultural similarities. The total violent crime rate in the United States was approximately 397 incidents per 100,000 people in 2012. If America managed to reduce its crime, policing and incarceration rates to those of Canada, it would free up $361 billion each year for more productive investment in the economy.

An examination of peace in the Unites States would be incomplete without a deeper analysis of the nation's approach to imprisonment. It has the largest prison population in the world, with about 2.3 million incarcerated in 2017,[3] and more than seven million or two per cent of the population under some kind of correctional supervision. It is one of only six countries to score a maximum 5 on the Global Peace Index's prison indicator, alongside Cuba, Eritrea, North Korea, El Salvador and Turkmenistan.

Although the United States' incarceration rates are the highest in the world, there had been a modest decrease in these rates in the two years prior to the production of the Index. The trend has been gaining momentum in the subsequent years to 2019. It is now the lowest it has been in 20 years. In 2018, the US incarceration rate was 830 persons per 100,000 compared to 147 in the United Kingdom, 118 in Canada, and 73 in Denmark.[4]

In 2016, when it was costing more than $80 billion a year to keep 2.2 million Americans behind bars, President Barack Obama argued

3 Peter Wagner and Bernadette Rabuy, 'Mass Incarceration: The Whole Pie 2017', Prison Policy Initiative, 14 March 2017, accessed at www.prisonpolicy.org/reports/pie2017.html

4 'States of Incarceration: The Global Context', Prison Policy Initiative, accessed at www.prisonpolicy.org/global/

for penal reform by stating that the country's encoded norms were being bent out of shape. He said in a 20,000-word commentary in the *Harvard Law Review*:

> How we treat citizens who make mistakes, even serious mistakes, who pay their debt to society, and deserve a second chance reflects who we are as a people and reveals a lot about our character and commitment to our founding principles.
>
> There is a growing consensus across the U.S. political spectrum that the extent of incarceration in the United States is not just unnecessary but also unsustainable. And it is not making our communities safer.[5]

There is bipartisan political support as both sides of politics look to reducing costs. This is evidence of the system attempting to reset its encoded norms around sentencing to reduce incarceration rates.

Has getting tough on crime reduced crime? The picture was far from straightforward. In the 1990s there was a strong relationship between the drop in crime and the increase in the incarceration rate, but since 2000 the correlation has faded and at the time of our 2012 report was non-existent. Twenty-seven states have cut their incarceration rates while simultaneously experiencing reductions in violent crime rates. For instance, between 2000 and 2010, New York experienced a fall in violent crime and incarceration every year, as well as falls in its homicide and policing rates.

There are two ways to consider the economic costs to the country. The first is to assess the costs and benefits of removing violent criminals from the streets: whether the cost of policing and incarcerating some individuals is less than the cost of the damage these individuals will inflict. This simple, linear trade-off is usually the approach taken in America.

A better approach is to take a system-wide view by analysing the broader social costs associated with various crimes versus the costs, both direct and

5 B. Obama, 'The President's Role in Advancing Criminal Justice Reform', *Harvard Law Review*, vol. 130, no. 3, January 2017, accessed at www.harvardlawreview.org/wp-content/uploads/2017/01/811-866-Online-Rev-vf.pdf

indirect, of incarcerating individuals. Many nonviolent crimes would have a negative trade-off – the social and economic costs would be higher than the benefits.

The tough-on-crime laws that were enacted from the late 1980s filled the jails. In the early 1990s states began passing habitual offender laws, better known as the three-strikes laws, which mandated life sentences for those convicted of a serious violent felony and any two other convictions. One man was sentenced to 25 years to life after stealing a pair of socks worth $2.50, having previously committed two other crimes; another got 50 years to life when he was caught shoplifting $153 worth of videotapes, also after having offended twice before.[6]

According to the US Government's Bureau of Justice Statistics, the federal and state prison population grew by almost 400 per cent between 1980 and its peak in 2009.[7]

Just under 60 per cent of convicted adults in the US prison system in 2017 were classed as nonviolent offenders, most of them sentenced for drug offences.[8] There is evidence that rehabilitation is more cost-effective than incarceration. It is clear that with better programs and more appropriate laws further cost reductions could be made.

The economic costs of incarceration are often underestimated because the opportunity costs are ignored. The Urban Institute released a study in 2008[9] that found that 70 per cent of people entering prison had held a job for the year prior to their sentencing: if they had not been incarcerated, they would presumably still have economically productive employment.

As states incarcerate more individuals, a greater proportion of discretionary spending is committed to judicial costs and correctional services, instead of going into education, health and basic services that help to alleviate

---

6 M. Taibbi, 'Cruel and Unusual Punishment: The Shame of the Three Strike Laws', *Rolling Stone*, 27 March 2013, accessed at www.rollingstone.com/politics/news/cruel-and-unusual-punishment-the-shame-of-three-strikes-laws-20130327

7 C.B. Kalish, 'Prisoners in 1980', Bureau of Justice Statistics, 1 May 1981, accessed at www.bjs.gov/index.cfm?ty=pbdetail&iid=3365; and H.C. West et al., 'Prisoners in 2009', Bureau of Justice Statistics, December 2010, accessed at www.bjs.gov/content/pub/pdf/p09.pdf

8 Peter Wagner and Bernadette Rabuy, 'Mass Incarceration: The Whole Pie 2017', Prison Policy Initiative, 14 March 2017.

9 Christy Visher, et al., 'Employment after Prison: A Longitudinal Study of Releasees in Three States', Urban Institute Justice Policy Centre, October 2008.

the underlying environments that feed the antisocial behaviour in the first place. This can lead to a vicious cycle, as there are fewer possibilities for improvement. For example, poorer educational attainment potentially leads to more criminality in later years. The effect is seen in states such as California, which spends more on its prison system than it does on its higher education system.

There are many ways to deal with illegal behaviour, and the key question is: Which approach has the least negative impact on society and the economy? What is striking about this approach is the simplicity of the logic. Yet governments seldom consider the trade-offs.

The inaugural US Peace Index was positively received among national, state-level and regional media. Reuters, *The Washington Times* and CBS Radio produced stories on the US Peace Index the day of the launch. The Reuters story, which focused on how the top ten states fared, was picked up by dozens of outlets. Subsequently, CBS News and USA Today each published unique stories, which were then picked up by hundreds of additional online outlets.

Articles and opinion pieces appeared in outlets ranging from the *Portland Press Herald* to *The Washington Times*. The US Peace Index was featured on the front page of local newspapers including the *Des Moines Register* and the *Sun Journal* in Maine. A post on Yahoo's 'The Lookout' blog was featured on the homepage of Yahoo.com for three days. *The Huffington Post* produced two unique posts with photo slideshows on US Peace Index rankings – highlighting the most violent and most peaceful states.

We estimate that the reach was well over 550 million impressions. The economic cost of violence to the United States resonated across the board, and there was minimal negative coverage.

More partisan America

The American political debate is becoming increasingly partisan; however this trend is not new and was occurring at the time we did the US peace indexes. According to research by the Pew Research Center,[10] in 2014 the

10 C. Doherty, '7 Things to Know About Polarisation in America', Pew Research Center, 12 June 2014, accessed at www.pewresearch.org/fact-tank/2014/06/12/7-things-to-know-about-polarization-in-america/

number of Americans who express consistently conservative or consistently liberal opinions has doubled over the past two decades: from ten per cent to 21 per cent, and this trend has increased since. This has reduced the amount of ideological overlap between the two parties. In 2014, the typical Republican was more conservative than 94 per cent of Democrats. Twenty years earlier, this figure was 70 per cent, indicating an increasing degree of polarisation. The typical Democrat was more liberal than 92 per cent of Republicans, up from 64 per cent two decades earlier. Polling by Pew has also found that in 2018 only seven per cent of Americans considered themselves politically neutral.[11]

There is also growing animosity between the two 'sides'. The share of Republicans who have *very* unfavourable opinions of the Democratic Party has jumped from 17 per cent to 43 per cent in the last 20 years. The share of Democrats with very negative opinions of Republicans has likewise more than doubled in the same period, from 16 per cent to 38 per cent. Worse, of the Republicans and Democrats who have a highly unfavourable impression of the other party, the great majority say the opposing party's policies represent a *threat* to the nation's wellbeing. Meanwhile, the political centre – as defined by the number of Americans who have a roughly equal number of liberal and conservative positions – has shrunk from about half the voting population in 1994 and 2004, to 39 per cent in 2014. After the July 2018 meeting between President Putin and President Trump, over 75 per cent of Republicans supported the way President Trump handled the meeting while the majority of Democrats viewed the comments as possibly being treasonous.

Donald Trump and Bernie Sanders ran on radically different policy platforms in the 2016 presidential election, but their central appeal to voters was almost identical: they both promised to upend the political status quo. Underlying all of this is the fact that the United States has seen a fall in its Positive Peace rating in the last 15 years. It clearly points to policy areas that need to be rectified. The main areas of Positive Peace that deteriorated in the United States were the *Low Levels of Corruption*, *Acceptance of the Rights of*

11 J. Gramlich, '19 Striking Findings from 2019', Pew Research Center, 13 December 2019, accessed at www.pewresearch.org/fact-tank/2019/12/13/19-striking-findings-from-2019/

Others, and *Well-Functioning Government.* Runaway mutual feedback loops are only compounding the problems. Some of the more important negative feedback loops are rising income inequality, a failing education system and poor health. All of these feed into a less productive society which in turn affects business.

In this era of increasingly acrimonious polarisation, Positive Peace with its potential for both a stronger economy and greater happiness – to name just two benefits – could be a potential area of consensus. It is a universal human desire to live in a peaceful society, irrespective of one's political orientation. Applying the information from national peace indexes creates the common ground for a more constructive debate. This has direct relevance for conventional politics, not least because it could help overcome increasing scepticism about the ability of existing institutions to solve the problems facing their country.

The United Kingdom

Our second country index focused on the United Kingdom. As with the US Peace Index, we only measured internal peace. It came out in 2013, and it was serendipitous that the release coincided with a national debate about whether the official crime figures were real. We pulled together other ways of analysing the official crime data to determine its level of veracity and were able to show conclusively that crime in the UK was falling. This went against the prevailing view shared by many people in the UK that their society was becoming more dangerous.

Although the Index was produced in 2013 the economic costings and findings are relevant to the 2020s, as both the crime rates and the economic impact associated with them change gradually over time.

Because we could provide a sense of context about crime, we received exceptionally good publicity. On the day the report was published it was the leading story in Britain. Given the good news contained in it and the topicality of the subject, Prime Minister David Cameron tweeted about our results, and Boris Johnson, then the Mayor of London, sang about it on television, 'Oh what a beautiful day'.

The media coverage of the report reflected the focus of the different outlets. The newspaper *The Independent* focused on comparing locations. The *Daily Mail* looked at murder rates and where crime was falling in Britain, adding a patriotic touch with a headline that the rate of murders and violent crime was falling faster than anywhere in Western Europe. *The Huffington Post* pursued a cultural angle, asking if 'Binge Drinking Britain is a Myth'.

The design of the UK Peace Index was similar to the US Peace Index; however, we were able to get much finer granularity on the data, allowing us to measure down to the borough level – 32 in London alone. The report gave a comparative analysis of 343 boroughs, including historical trends, a study of economic costs, and an analysis of the socio-economic factors associated with peace.

From that we were able to come up with a range of different conclusions.

The United Kingdom had become significantly more peaceful since 2003. Violent crime peaked in 2006 and had been declining since. However, violent assault in the UK remained higher than the OECD average. Between 2008 and 2013, total homicides fell by 28 per cent, violent crime dropped by 21 per cent, weapons crime fell by 34 per cent, public disorder offences were down by 29 per cent, and the number of police officers fell by 5.5 per cent. Taken together, it indicated that Britain was becoming considerably less violent.

Britons did not necessarily see the situation this way, though. Surveys on perceptions of crime showed that people felt that crime was falling locally but increasing nationally. This is not an uncommon finding: a similar finding is true in Mexico. People live and work in particular areas, so they have direct experience of what is happening around them, but for places further afield they rely on media reports to gauge the level of safety. In reality, the fall in crime rates appears to be equally distributed geographically, with reductions across all regions of the UK.

To determine the extent to which the decrease in crime was a distinctively British phenomenon, we looked at whether the trend was similar in other countries in Europe. We found that the majority of European countries had also recorded drops in total recorded crime over the period. Of the countries where crime increased, three – Spain, Portugal and Italy – were high-debt countries that suffered from economic turmoil in the wake of the Global Financial Crisis. The UK, however, recorded the largest total drop in crime of all European countries covered.

Why had crime fallen so significantly in Britain? There were several possible reasons proposed: they included factors such as rising wages, particularly among the poorest members of society, combined with improved deterrence such as better electronic surveillance, better sharing of information between law-enforcement agencies, use of computers, better DNA profiling, and better electronic security systems. All of these are similar to the United States. There had also been a drop in drinking outside the home, which would have affected alcohol-related violence. But it is hard to infer the cause of the decrease in violence by examining the data on violence alone.

Sir Ian Blair, a former commissioner of the Metropolitan Police, thinks there is a growing aversion to violence. He told the BBC:

> When I started as a young officer, the Friday night pub fight was an extraordinarily common phenomenon. Everybody swung a chair, got a few black eyes and went home satisfied. That is not happening in the same way anymore. Domestic violence is being targeted. Football hooliganism, with the exception of the occasional incident, is dying away.[12]

If our analysis could not conclusively nail down the causes of the fall-off in violent crime, we could definitely locate what was not having an effect. Reductions in police numbers did not seem to play a role in either reducing or increasing crime. Changes in the youth demographic did not appear to be of significance either.

One of the more interesting findings was that poverty is important. In the 32 London boroughs it was shown that poverty, or low income, showed a strong correlation with levels of peacefulness. It is interesting to note that analysis of real wages by the UK's Office of National Statistics shows the lowest earners in the bottom ten per cent, who received £15,565 a year or

12 'UK Peace Index highlights rate of fall in violent crime', BBC News, 24 April 2013, accessed at www.bbc.com/news/uk-22275280

less, had a 51 per cent real pay rise since 1998. The improvement in peace, in other words, had coincided with improvements in the minimum wage.

Looking more deeply into multidimensional poverty yielded more insights. The correlation between peace and multidimensional poverty was among the highest we discovered. Multidimensional poverty, which goes beyond income-based poverty, affects standards of health, the fostering of human capital and many other factors considered vital to well-performing societies. We looked at six dimensions: income, employment, health and disabilities, education, housing, and living environment. What was truly significant was that as the number of dimensions of deprivation increased so did the strength of the correlation.

We found that long-term employment opportunities had a particularly strong correlation with peace. As well as providing income, employment is also important to social cohesion and an individual's sense of self-worth. Poor employment prospects have direct and indirect impacts on a person's health.

It should be emphasised that it is employment opportunity, not just having a job, which is critical. Employment is important, but for it to have an impact on peace there must be opportunities for advancement and improving economic outcomes. The report found that outside of London, certain types of occupations in a region are linked to peace. In areas with more professional occupations or larger employers with more clearly defined career structures, the more peaceful the region tends to be. Areas that require a qualified and managerial workforce will tend to be more economically active, have higher incomes, and will produce more employment opportunities for their residents. This lowers unemployment, which in turn has a strong impact on peace.

In the UK, high levels of health deprivation and teenage pregnancies seem to be correlated with low levels of peace, as they are in the United States. Once again, there seems to be a tipping point. Past a certain level of general health, further improvements do not correlate with similar increases in the peacefulness of a region.

Just after the launch of the UK Index I attended a meeting at Scotland Yard: the police had also found the report interesting. They recommended that I meet with the commander of Tottenham Police Station in northwest

London. Tottenham is one of the toughest areas in London and some months later it became the starting point for the London riots. I was apprehensive about how to build the bridge between our statistical research and practical on-the-ground policing, but I was encouraged by Thomas Morgan. He was one of our more brilliant researchers, who was based at Oxford University at the time. So I decided to take up the invitation.

The station itself looked battered, overcrowded and had no real area for visitors. It felt like a fortress, but in a place like Tottenham, aesthetics take second place to security. The commander was a gentleman in his late forties. He was bright, had an engaging personality and was eager to discuss our findings.

What we arrived at was truly transformational. He could clearly identify how the six dimensions of deprivation associated with multidimensional poverty fed into crime, based on his own experiences. However, what really blew me away was that for each of the dimensions we could brainstorm place-specific solutions for Tottenham. I marvelled how Thom would display scatter diagrams, interpret them and the commander would have an idea for a solution.

One of the catalysts for social rejuvenation is employment. It may be more efficient to build government offices elsewhere, but the total benefit to Tottenham would be better if some offices were located in the borough, with an emphasis on hiring locals. More money would be spent in the area by people living there, thereby improving the economic flow-on effects through Tottenham and decreasing poverty. Government work would also give better opportunities for career progression.

Deprivation in education and health can be measured by the distance needed to travel to medical facilities or to a school. These can be addressed by better city planning. Although it might be cheaper and more efficient to centralise hospital care outside the borough, the broader effects of keeping a local hospital may outweigh the additional overhead.

Although the UK is not a violent country by global standards, the cost of violence is still large. The study estimated that the total economic impact of violence and crime on the British economy was £124 billion in 2012. That is, £1,875 per person per year. Reducing crime by nine per cent would release

£11 billion, the equivalent of the total cost of the London Olympics, for more productive investment every year.

While America and Britain share many characteristics, one of the more interesting differences is in the composition of violent crime. Britain's homicide rate is one-fifth of America's, but the United States' overall violent crime rate was much less than in Britain.

It seems the main reason for the difference in homicides is the gun policies of the two countries. The situation in the United States regarding weapons is deeply problematic. Ordinary citizens can buy military-grade weapons. One of the findings that has consistently emerged from the peace indexes is that, with few exceptions, the more guns there are in a society, the more people get killed by them. One of the interesting effects of COVID-19 was that in the US gun sales dramatically increased. Some stores saw their monthly sales increase by over 300 percent. When in fear Americans seem to turn to their guns.

I have a South African friend who emigrated from Johannesburg to live in Australia. One day when we were playing golf, he told me why he had moved. Johannesburg is a violent city and he would put a handgun under his bed each night in case the house was broken into. Then he would dutifully put it away each morning before breakfast. One morning he forgot to put the gun away and only realised when he got to work. All day the thought that kept running through his head was that his three- and five-year-old sons had found the gun and were playing with it. The anxiety was so strong that it prompted him to emigrate with his family. More people are shot accidently with guns than deliberately. This incident also highlights in a small way how a violent environment impacts productivity. It's hard to work at full capacity when you're worried about your children being shot.

However, Britain does have a problem with violent crime. Despite recent gains the rate is still over 800 per 100,000 people, one of the highest in the developed world. On average, violent crime costs the UK around £3,700 per incident in direct medical costs. A further £50,000 is taken from the economy in lost productivity and emotional trauma for the average violent crime. There is also a flow-on factor through the economy, which is estimated at the same amount as the lost productivity. The total impact from violent crime is nearly £19 billion. In aggregate this means that violent crime diverts a potential £47 billion from the UK economy in medical costs and lost output alone.

If the UK could reduce its violent crime rate by half, making it comparable to that of the United States, it would potentially free up £23 billion to the economy in realised productivity and saved medical costs. Conversely, if the United States could lower its homicide rate to that of the UK's, it would potentially release US$34 billion for more productive investment.

The UK Peace Index has some political implications. Its insights into poverty is a good example. The impact of multidimensional poverty can inform the discussion about public infrastructure and development. The information about inequality and peace may also inform political debate about wage and salary levels.

Mexico

The IEP's longest-running series of in-depth country reports has focused on Mexico, a nation with some daunting internal challenges. The indexes were initially underwritten by Alberto Coppel, a wealthy Mexican with a strong interest in peace. Our aim has been to highlight the underlying causes and extent of the nation's difficulties and to bring publicity to the problem and possible solutions. We have now completed six Mexico reports. When they were released each of them was the major news story of the day and was positively received.

The first Mexico Index was published in 2013. The results reflected what some of the more observant people in Mexico suspected: that, although there were still unacceptably high levels of violence, peace had improved slightly. When we completed the second Mexico Index in March 2015, it was clear that the general trend had continued, despite a number of high-profile incidents during the previous year, including the abduction and murder of 43 student teachers in September 2014. However, the 2019 report found that the trend had reversed with homicides rising 80 per cent from 2015 to 2019. These cycles of improvement and then deterioration are not uncommon in high-violence societies.

When we analysed the socio-economic factors associated with violence in Mexico, it became evident that they were different from what typically occurs globally. It was markedly different from the picture in the United States and the UK. The violence follows the lines of the drug routes, rather than reflecting normal socio-economic patterns that show a close correlation between crime and poverty. Frequently, violence would erupt in the wealthier parts of Mexico, particularly in states that were on drug transport routes. States that bordered the United States, the destination for most of the drugs, were particularly vulnerable. As these states did not have abnormally high crime rates prior to the drug war, it provided a unique opportunity to analyse the effects of violence on these states' economies.

We did this by using 2000 as the baseline year and looked at the GDP growth for the five most peaceful states and the five least peaceful states through to 2014. Both groups had similar per capita income in 2000, but by 2014 the most violent states had 30 per cent lower income, highlighting the effects of violence on the economy. See figure 9.

Former President Felipe Calderón did not like calling it a drug war. He always called it a war on organised crime. On reflection his description was more accurate – the cartels have diversified a long way beyond drugs.

Mexico is the least peaceful country in Central America and the Caribbean. In the international rankings, it fell 34 places in the Global Peace Index between 2008 and 2019 to be ranked 140th. The last decade has seen significant upheaval as the cartels competed with each other and the government for control over smuggling routes and civil influence. The homicide rate reached 27 per 100,000 people in 2019. By comparison, it was 4.8 per 100,000 in the US in the same year. This rate was the worst for any country in the OECD and one of the worst in the world. Other crimes related to organised criminal activity also soared, with violent crime, kidnapping and extortion all following the homicide trend.

From 2011 to 2014 it looked like the government had managed to turn the tide on violence, with the Peace Index improving by 18 per cent. However, it has been deteriorating every year since then.

For the first release, civil organisations questioned the reliability of government data. So to check the accuracy of the official figures, we

FIGURE 9

Mexico peace and income

Mexico's more peaceful states have had higher GDP growth than the least peaceful states.

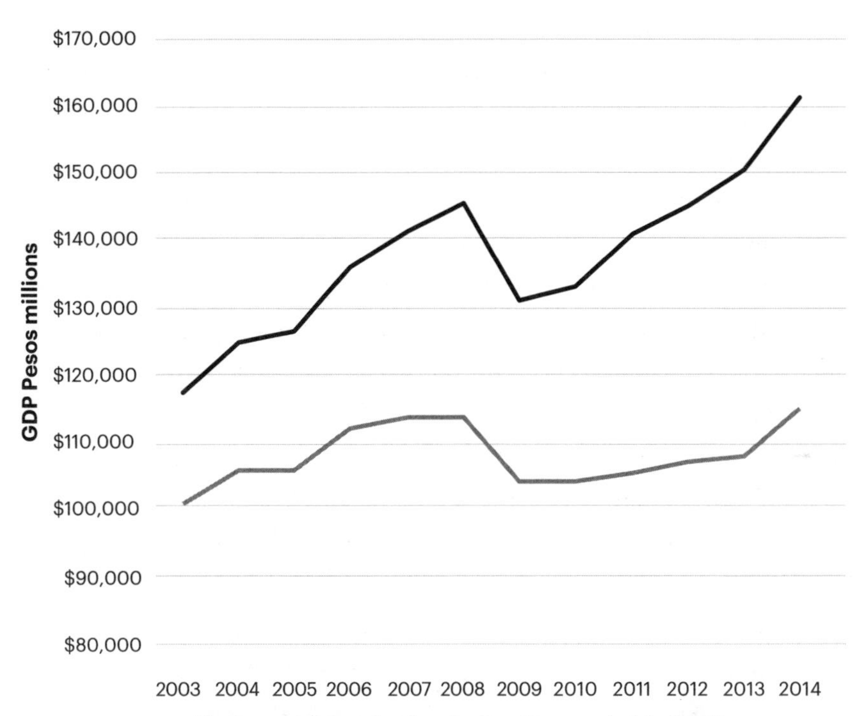

SOURCE: IEP, MEXICO PEACE INDEX

compared multiple datasets for homicides and established that the trend was real. These datasets include both hospital-recorded deaths and police statistics. But some questions linger. A substantial number of people have 'disappeared' in Mexico since 2007. Indeed, the number of recorded disappearances has increased substantially. Although not every one of these missing people will have been murdered, given the number of mass graves that have been uncovered, it is highly probable that a percentage of those missing have been killed and should have been included in the homicide figures. Even allowing for this, and if all the missing persons are assumed to have been killed, the homicide rate would not have substantially changed.

The size of the drop and then increase in homicides was substantial but where was it coming from? The improvement from 20 homicides per 100,000 people in 2011 to 13 per 100,000 in 2014 represented a 34.5 per cent improvement, which is very high. Similarly, the increase in homicides after 2015 was just as dramatic. To examine this further, the IEP looked at the different rate of change in the Mexican states with high levels of homicides and high levels of organised crime, compared with states that had low levels of homicides and low levels of organised crime. We also examined changes in homicide rates by gender.

Both approaches pointed to the reduction being due to a drop in organised-crime-related violence. In 2011, several of the states that had the highest rates of homicides also had high levels of organised crime. They were also the states that had the largest decreases in their total homicide rates after 2011. An example from the report follows.

> Analysing the gender balance of victims highlighted that both men and women experience high rates of violence in Mexico, but typically for different reasons. Although women are involved in drug-trade-related crime and violence, they are more likely to die from other types of violence, such as domestic violence. Mexican men are more likely to be victims of homicides related to organised crime. The data showed us that violence related to organised crime was declining while interpersonal violence is not. Using the same analysis from 2015 onwards highlighted that the upward movement in the homicide rate was linked to increases in organised crime. Since 2015 only two states, Coahuila and Durango, recorded improvements in their homicide rates. The effect of President Calderón's war on the cartels had been to break the bigger ones up. As the leadership were either captured or killed it caused the cartels to fracture. This led to increased competition between the splintered groups for control of the trafficking routes and the 'plazas', which is the reference used to refer to the places where drugs are traded. In 2006 there were three major cartels, the Gulf cartel, Sinaloa cartel

and the Tijuana cartel. By the beginning of 2020 there were 18 crime groups vying for control.

Coinciding with the increased homicide rate was an increase in the use of firearms by an astronomical 119 per cent since 2015. Highlighting the deadly effect of this increase, homicides committed with a firearm increased to 69 per cent in 2018, which is 12 percentage points higher than three years earlier. Baja California recorded the largest deterioration, with an increase of over 200 per cent in its assault with a firearm rate.

The research from the first Mexico Peace Index in 2013 found that Mexico had one of the highest potentials of any country to improve its peacefulness. One method of assessing this was to compare the levels of Positive Peace to the levels of actual peace as measured through the Global Peace Index. Mexico's Positive Peace ranking was 67 places higher than its Global Peace Index ranking in 2019, indicating a large potential for improvement.

On a deeper dive into Positive Peace, corruption stood out as the Pillar that needed to improve the most, but not all types of corruption. Although the overall measure was worse than the global average, it was not a long way behind. However, the levels of perceived corruption in the police and the judiciary were among the worst in the world.

Mexico ranked the worst of the 35 OECD countries for corruption in Transparency International's Corruption Perception Index. In 2018, nearly 70 per cent of citizens thought that the police were corrupt, compared to much smaller percentages for the military and business. Highlighting the extent of the lack of trust in the police, some 97 per cent of extortion cases and 95 per cent of rape cases are not reported or investigated.[13]

Political violence is also on the rise. In the year to the end of August 2018, 850 events were classified as political violence, with most related to the Mexican elections of that year. Of these events, 75 per cent targeted municipal political figures, while 18 per cent were targeted at state officials and seven per cent federally.

---

13 Institute for Economics and Peace, *2020 Mexico Peace Index.*

The story of Joaquín 'El Chapo' Guzmán, head of the Sinaloa drug cartel, highlights the issues with corruption. El Chapo – Shorty – Guzmán was captured in 1993 in Guatemala, extradited and sentenced to 20 years in a maximum-security prison for murder and drug trafficking. Eight years later, when he was facing possible extradition to the United States, he bribed prison guards to allow him to escape, hidden in a laundry cart. He went on to become the world's most powerful drug lord, according to the US administration. Between 2009 and 2011 *Forbes* magazine rated El Chapo as one of the most powerful people in the world, ranking 41st, 60th and 55th respectively. It is not unreasonable to say he was the second most powerful man in Mexico, after the magnate Carlos Slim.

In 2014, Guzman was recaptured and placed in a maximum-security prison. Bizarrely, he was able to escape again. This time an industrial-strength tunnel was built into the prison with a railway track, lighting, fresh air and reinforced walls. It ran for 1.5 kilometres into a house that was under construction. Guzman simply slipped from his cell into the tunnel, which had been connected to a grate in the shower area of his cell. Guards did not see anything despite the fact he was incarcerated in what was supposed to be Mexico's most secure prison. He has since been recaptured, and this time he has been extradited to the US to stand trial. However, after his capture his two sons, Alfredo Guzmán Salazar and Ivan Archivaldo Guzmán Salazar, took over the cartel along with Ismael Zambada García, highlighting that a lot more is needed than just capturing the head of the organisation.

El Chapo's exploits highlighted other problems, particularly with the country's penal system and impunity rates. Impunity is typically measured using the percentage of homicides that go unpunished. Alarmingly, in many of the worst-performing states the number of prison inmates is falling while impunity is increasing. In the worst-performing states, fewer than five per cent of homicides are solved and the perpetrator convicted. Nationally the figure is not much better: in 2019, 90 per cent of homicides did not result in a trial.

There is a relationship between the overcrowding of prisons and the underfunding of the prison and judicial system. A 2016 report by the Mexican National Human Rights Commission found that in some cases

30 inmates were living in cells built to hold four people.[14] There is an urgent need to improve facilities as there may be a reluctance to sentence prisoners if they can't be housed. The report found the higher the levels of overcrowding, the higher the impunity rates.

Even without the overcrowding, Mexico has an impunity problem. On 26 September 2014, about 100 students from a teachers' college in the southern state of Guerrero commandeered some buses. As they had in years past, the students planned to take the buses to Mexico City to attend a march to commemorate the 1968 massacre of hundreds of students, and then return them. This was a tradition both the bus companies and the authorities typically tolerated.

However, the police opened fire on the buses, leaving six dead and many more wounded. The police reportedly detained 43 of the remaining students, and they were never seen again. This caused massive protests throughout Mexico and became a symbol of the corruption of the police and the government. So much so that the government was forced to allow an Inter-American investigative commission to be formed to investigate the disappearances as a Mexican commission couldn't be trusted.

The commission was granted diplomatic immunity so that its investigation would not be impeded. But within a few months, the relationship between the government and the investigators began to sour. The government maintained that local police officers, along with the drug gang they worked for, kidnapped the students, killed them and incinerated the bodies in a nearby dump, even though there was no clear motive. As soon as it became clear that the investigators would challenge that narrative, pro-government newspapers turned against the commission, while the Mexican government opened a criminal investigation against it, based on unsubstantiated claims about the misuse of funds. Finally, it emerged that the government had been using sophisticated spy software to target the commission.[15] The commission claimed that the government stonewalled and blocked it. Eventually the

---

14 Maria Verza, 'Report: Most Mexican prisons overcrowded, dirty, dangerous', AP News, 13 April 2016, accessed at apnews.com/7b1f29a8cf0f4ad89e772e6ca473f029/report-most-mexican-prisons-overcrowded-dirty-dangerous

15 Azam Ahmed, 'Spyware in Mexico Targeted Investigators Seeking Students', *The New York Times*, 10 July 2017, accessed at www.nytimes.com/2017/07/10/world/americas/mexico-missing-students-pegasus-spyware.html

commission gave up. In their final report, the commissioners were damning of the authorities. 'The delays in obtaining evidence that could be of use to figure out possible lines of investigation translates into a decision [to allow] impunity,' it said.[16] The exact fate of the missing students is still not known.

The rise in violence related to organised crime in Mexico was swift, but could have only happened on the back of entrenched corruption. In 2003, violence in Mexico was correlated with measures of deprivation.

In particular, it was more likely to occur in regions where education was low and housing was poor. In areas where there was violence, the business sector was weaker, confidence in the government and the judiciary was lower, and corruption was more prevalent. This is similar to global trends and also corresponds to national trends in the United States and the United Kingdom.

By 2014, however, violence was higher in more affluent places where ordinarily better living conditions would have predicted the opposite effect. The higher a state performed on income, health and housing, the less peaceful it tended to be, which is both counter-intuitive and contrary to development theory. The pattern highlighted the distorting effect of organised crime on the distribution of violence throughout Mexico. The drug cartels follow the best distribution routes, which have generally been in areas of higher socio-economic status, next to the US border, or near suitable distribution points on the coast.

Unsurprisingly in a country deeply affected by drug-related violence, the Pillars of Peace that matter the most in Mexico are *Well-Functioning Government*, *Low Levels of Corruption* and *Good Relations with Neighbours.* The violence is not statistically linked to inequalities in health, education or wealth.

Corruption is the overriding problem, but the difficulty in fixing it cannot be overemphasised. It explains why the level of violence in Mexico exploded suddenly rather than increasing in a steady, linear fashion. If Mexico can act aggressively against corruption it will not only lead to less violence; it will also have a strong and positive effect on economic wellbeing and

---

16 D. Leveille and M. Campbell, 'Investigators release a damning report on Mexico's 43 missing students', PRI, 25 April 2016, www.pri.org/stories/2016-04-25/investigators-release-damning-report-mexicos-missing-43-students

development. This fits neatly with the systems concept of tipping points. A runaway feedback loop had become established: as corruption was not being addressed this created the conditions for more corruption. But the shock that caused the system to rebalance for the worse was when the power structures changed within the international drug cartels as Mexico became the premier transit route to the US. The change then became fast and unstoppable.

But there is some hope. Elections held on 1 July 2018 heralded the arrival of a new political party, the National Regeneration Movement (MORENA Party). The presidential election was won by the MORENA candidate Andrés Manuel López Obrador. The party stood on a strong anti-corruption platform. However, it was the most violent campaign Mexico has experienced in recent history, with 130 political figures killed from September 2017 to the day of the election.[17] Time will tell whether MORENA can make the necessary inroads into corruption.

Violence comes with a price tag and in Mexico it was assessed using the same methodology as used in UK and US peace indexes. This was the first attempt at a systematic calculation of the holistic cost of violence in Mexico. The IEP analysis found that the cost of containing and dealing with the consequences of violence in 2017 reached $4.3 trillion pesos (US$249 billion), equivalent to 21 per cent of Mexican GDP or a little over $33,118 pesos (US$1,948) for every Mexican citizen. That is nearly three times the amount the Mexican government spends on health. Violent crime accounted for almost 80 per cent of the costs: homicides were 32 per cent of the total, and rape, robbery and assault 47 per cent.

Our 2018 Mexico Peace Index found that the cost of violence was up 15 per cent from the prior year. Isolating the effect on the overall economy is difficult, given the myriad domestic and international variables. However, a good method for understanding this is by comparing the country's contribution to global economic growth at different stages of a cycle of violence. Between 1990 and 1999, before the sudden deterioration in peace, Mexico was the ninth largest contributor to global economic growth. Between 2000 and 2009, when the violence was ramping up, it dropped

17 Benjamin Sveen, ABC News, Australia, 2 July 2018.

to fifteenth. It then recovered to twelfth, from 2010 to 2014, when Mexico was beginning to experience lower levels of violence. From this it can be seen that Mexico's comparative economic performance matched the different phases of violence in the country.

The Index also studied Mexico's 76 major cities to create a Metropolitan Peace Index. It consisted of two indicators: homicide rate and violent crime rate. From this we created a more nuanced picture of violence at the city level and it was possible to identify which cities were more successful at maintaining peace. Such information can be useful when developing local policies.

To launch the first Index, I held a breakfast in Mexico City for 45 journalists. All the major current affairs programs were represented. The questions on the subject of violence in Mexico were as intelligent as any questions I have had anywhere else in the world. Good questions do not have to be detailed; they just have to be the right line of inquiry to create insight. That was what I experienced with the local journalists.

I realised, a day or so later, that for the media this was personal. In the preceding 12 months, 20 journalists were killed covering the drug wars, and the carnage has continued. The attacks on journalists has continued through the ensuing years and in the first nine months of 2019 at least 12 journalists had been murdered. That had really concentrated their attention on questions of violence and peace; it was something to which they were empathetically and emotionally connected. According to the press freedom organisation Article 19, 'Mexico is the most dangerous country in the world to practise journalism.' However, prosecutions are proving to be difficult. Mexico has a special prosecutor dedicated to pursuing crimes committed against the press, but nearly all of the 544 attacks against journalists in 2018 remained unsolved, according to the NGO Article 19.[18]

18 Informe Anual 2018, 'Ante El Silencio, Ni Borron Ni Cuenta Nueva', Article 19, 17 April 2019 (article in English), accessed at www.article19.org/resources/mexico-report-shows-silencing-of-journalists-and-media-freedom/

The IEP's activities in Mexico

The upshot of the Mexican peace indexes is that there is growing demand for the IEP's work in Mexico, and in 2017 we established an office to help promote the work and to engage with parties interested in improving Mexico's situation. As well as advising governments, the Positive Peace workshops have been of particular interest, with many training sessions conducted in conjunction with state officials, Rotary and the Mexican Armed Forces.

Members of the Armed Forces found the Positive Peace approach to be more holistic and effective than just considering peace as the deployment of security forces to reduce direct violence. This perspective lets them realise that violence cannot be tackled by one single actor and enables them to consider themselves not only as providers, but also beneficiaries of the peace that Mexico longs for. By the end of 2019, we had given training to 1,800 Armed Forces members and 500 police officers, with more training to come.

The IEP has also provided workshops to more than 500 municipal officials in all of the regions of the State of Jalisco. This resulted in officials realising there are many things that a municipal administration can do to build peace within their communities.

Africa

To date the IEP has not done any indexes for African countries but hopefully in the near future we will. I have seen vast changes across the continent, mainly for the better, and it would be helpful to get some good granular data into the public domain to counter the overwhelming narrative, held by many, that Africa is beyond help.

Africa is a continent in transition. I spent some time with a group of young Maasai men in Samburu, in northern Kenya. We had taken a break from reviewing our projects to go trekking in the bush, and the young men were our guides. At the end of a long day, we sat and drank beer, while the men taught me how to use their traditional weapons such as spears and bows. We were throwing spears and shooting arrows into a dry riverbed as the sun went down and we talked about our worlds. It was a magical experience.

The men use tracking skills handed down through countless generations to glean a narrative from a few swirls in the dust made by animals. While walking up a dry riverbed they would point to these markings. 'That's from a hyena. See how it has sat down on the sand and see how the dirt has been pushed in a sweeping circle. He was sitting on his rump and scratching his head, which has caused the movement in the sand as his body rotated. His body moves around because of the force of the scratching,' one guide explained to me. They call this 'the storybook of the night before'.

The fathers of these men were semi-nomadic, illiterate herders. Unlike their parents, the men I met had the benefit of schooling. Their world view has consequently been shaped by modern Western educational concepts. As well as using ancestral skills to read the storybook of the past, they also use modern tools to write the storybook of the future. They take their bookings by mobile phone and use the internet.

Violence in the area is declining – cattle raids, an old source of bloodshed, are less common, but are still a major source of death. Also, domestic violence is still endemic in many communities. The women prefer to marry educated men because they are less violent, and both men and women are abandoning the traditional practice of letting their elders choose their partners and marrying for love instead.

Parents can play an important role in peace within the family home. They are responsible for disciplining the children and many Africans are fond of the saying 'Spare the rod, spoil the child'. When viewing family dynamics systemically we can see that feedback loops are critical – discipline is itself a feedback loop that sets the ground for appropriate social behaviour. Beat the children and the message is that physical violence is justified. Education is the key to breaking the cycle, probably more so than law enforcement.

The importance of the eight Pillars is clear in the African context. For example, their prioritisation of education reflects a striving for a high level of human capital. The guide's father had many wives but the guide himself only wanted one. He would talk about the expense of feeding and educating his children properly. As education and food have improved in Africa, more children are growing up healthy and without the stunted cognitive development inflicted by early childhood malnutrition. As the health system improves more children survive and the birth rate tends to fall, leading to better provisioning and more parental attention for those children. This will greatly improve the future human capital of the continent.

These men understand the corrosive effects of corruption. All too often in Africa the law and legal systems are corrupt and clash with tribal customs, and the police are regarded with suspicion, if not seen as a source of outright oppression.

The future

What emerges from the national and subnational indexes is that a more refined understanding of how each country's and region's peace can be created. It will cast a light on their unique challenges and provide information that can help to aid policy and development. Our goal is to cover as much of the world as possible, and to take the data down to as granular a level as is feasible. This is a vast undertaking, but I do believe over time it will happen.

The lesson from the country indexes is that if you can measure something, it is possible, through statistical analysis, to better understand the underlying dynamics of the system. Nations function differently depending on their unique path, and the more detail that is available, the more likely it is that interventions will be appropriate and successful. At a very basic level, just understanding whether things are improving or deteriorating is useful in itself. If you cannot measure it, then understanding it is difficult.

CHAPTER 10

Measuring and understanding terrorism

If there is one area relating to violence that captivates global attention it is terrorism. General Martin Dempsey, former chairman of the US Joint Chiefs of Staff, has said that 'the world is more dangerous than it has ever been', believing there is an 'aggregate' threat from Islamic extremist networks that stretches from Asia to Europe to Africa.[1]

Others have very different views. John J. Mearsheimer, a professor of political science at the University of Chicago, argues that the threat from the Middle East is over-hyped: as a number of observers have pointed out, Americans are more likely to die slipping in the bathtub than from a foreign terrorist attack. At its height, Islamic State had no more than 40,000 troops, which is equivalent to just two infantry divisions. 'The idea that Islamic State is going to develop the power projection capability to go on a rampage outside the Middle East is a laughable argument,' says Mearsheimer.[2]

As usual, the truth lies somewhere in between the two positions. The forces that have come into play since 9/11 involve geopolitical, religious and territorial disputes. The disturbing negative trend in terrorism can be mainly attributed to just four groups: Boko Haram, the Taliban, Islamic State, and al-Qaeda and their affiliates. These four groups all follow similar forms of radical Sunni Islam known as Salafi Jihadism, based on many of the same precepts as Saudi Arabian Wahhabism. Unlike the relationship between religion and conflict where the relation is weak, the modern wave of terrorism has distinctive religious overtones. Although there is a new rising trend in the West of far-right terrorism, globally it still pales into insignificance compared to Islamic-inspired attacks.

---

1 C. Preble, 'The Most Dangerous World Ever?' *Cato Policy Report*, September–October 2014.

2 Interview on 'Between the Lines' ABC Radio National, 'Is American Foreign Policy Misdirected?' 6 August 2015, accessed at www.abc.net.au/radionational/programs/betweenthelines/is-american-foreign-policy-misdirected3f/6671670

Over the last decade no area of violence has been as fluid or fast changing as terrorism. Even during the period of writing this book the face of terrorism has changed dramatically. It is a complex picture with many unknowns, but what is not in any doubt is the emotional impact of terrorist acts.

The emotional ramifications of terrorism are felt strongly through those societies that are affected and this is one of the key goals of terrorists. This high level of societal angst has many flow-on effects, not least because it clouds clear thinking. Contrary to much public perception, the number of fatalities from terrorism has been falling in recent years. It peaked in 2014 at 32,775, before falling by 75 per cent in 2019 to over 8,000 deaths and is likely to keep on falling in the near future. It should be noted that these numbers exclude battlefield deaths.

The largest improvements occurred in Iraq, Nigeria and Syria. These countries still suffer large losses from terrorism, highlighting that eradicating terrorism is a difficult and lengthy process once it becomes established.

Figure 10 shows the steep rise in terrorism. Interestingly, after 9/11 deaths from terrorism actually decreased for the next two years. The lowest point for terrorism in the last 50 years was 2003.

There are two main inflection points on the graph below. The first sharp upturn came with the start of the Iraq War and kept rising until the US-led troop surge in 2007. Terrorism then fell by 40 per cent in the ensuing years till 2010. This success was brought about through US military muscle, combined with the buying off of the Sunni militias with cash and weapons. But this short-term tactical success turned into a long-term strategic loss. It, along with the Obama administration's decision to pull out of Iraq, created the backdrop for the growth of Islamic State. More importantly the Iraqi government failed to build on its tactical success by creating a viable and inclusive administration, creating the perfect conditions for the rise of Islamic State.

Initially, Europe escaped the worst of the fallout from the terrorism raging through the Middle East. This changed in early 2014 with a series of large-scale assaults, including the March attacks on the airport and metro in Brussels (32 dead) and a series of bombings in Turkey, including an attack on a Kurdish rally in October, resulting in 102 dead. The upward trend continued in Europe in 2015, notably the November 2015 attacks

FIGURE 10

Deaths from terrorism, 1998–2018

Deaths from terrorism have decreased 52 per cent since their peak in 2014.

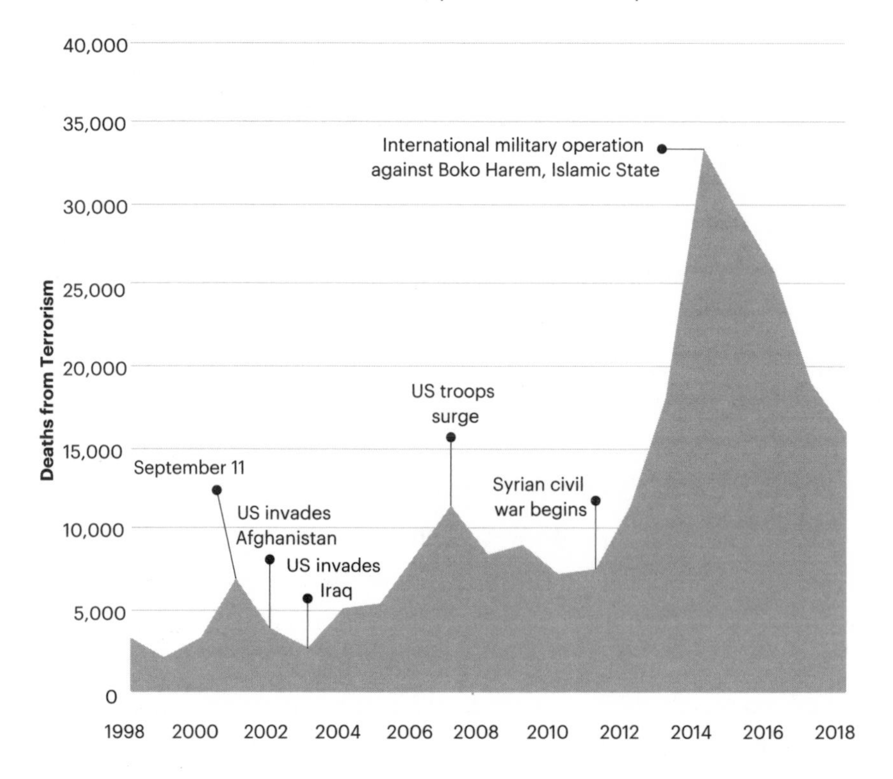

SOURCE: START GTD, IEP CALCULATIONS

in Paris, which killed 136 people. In 2015, deaths in the OECD jumped by a staggering 650 per cent when compared to the prior year, with over 600 people being killed. The emotional impact on Europeans was profound.

This was graphically underlined during the launch of the 2015 Global Terrorism Index, which unfortunately coincided with the November 13 Paris attacks.

This single event shaped the messaging for the release. All Western media paths led back to Paris and the outpouring of grief and anger it provoked. Too often the bigger picture got lost. It meant many issues could not be broached, such as the underlying conditions of Muslims in France.

The Paris attacks

The Paris attacks were dreadful, but when considered in the wider context they were only a small fraction of the overall number of people killed by terrorism. In 2015, there were 15 attacks that killed over 100 people. The Paris attacks ranked 11th in terms of lethality, with 136 killed and almost 100 seriously injured. The attack on the Bataclan theatre alone killed 92 people. In total, nearly 30,000 people were killed by terrorist attacks in 2015.

The week prior to the Paris attacks two bombs went off in Beirut, killing over 50 people. This got only a minor mention in the Western press. My media friends made an interesting observation about the way we emotionally identify and connect with situations and people. The media reported the Lebanese attacks, but because there is little Western media infrastructure in Beirut, there were no interviews with survivors, or narratives around the lives of those who died.

Paris is saturated with Western media, so these personal stories and narratives were easily obtained, many of the survivors spoke English and many Europeans speak French. These vivid, emotionally charged images saturated the psyche of Western audiences.

What my friends also said was that it is the personal stories and narratives that create the emotional identification, driving the striking level of empathy felt towards the Parisians. If this same level of empathy could be generated by the media for other violent conflicts, then the world would be a more peaceful place.

I cannot help thinking that most societies put a greater value on the lives of those who we perceive to be similar. Otherwise, why would we tolerate the grinding poverty that occurs in many parts of the world? Or why would we tolerate the suffering and misery that have become Iraq and Syria? In those countries, nearly 10,000 people died from terrorism in 2015.

The Western media coverage of personal narratives underlines the fact that everyone is vulnerable: it could have been any of their viewers at the Stade de France, or sipping an after-dinner coffee at the Café Bonne Bière when the attackers hit. When I think globally and view society through the Pillar of Peace *Acceptance of the Rights of Others*.

The post-Bataclan rage made it impossible to raise key topics such as the quality of life for Muslims within France. Yet some stark observations can be made. As of 2016, France had more foreign fighters entering Syria than any other OECD nation except for Turkey, and the sixth highest number globally. Mid-range estimates indicate that some 1,800 foreign fighters have travelled there since 2011. This is believed to be roughly five per cent of all the foreign fighters who have gone to the country, including those from neighbouring Muslim countries. It immediately poses the question: Why? Yet this was not a question that could be asked, let alone answered, in the blistering emotions that ensued in the days and weeks after the attacks.

The sobering reality is that there is deep discrimination towards Muslims within French society, although this is not well known, and, more staggeringly, it goes largely unmeasured. The French government does not classify people by their religion because France views itself as a secular society. Therefore, there are no official records that count Muslim unemployment, or the percentage of Muslims who live in slums or below the poverty line. Neither is there an official count of the number of Muslims in jails. Some estimates put the number as high as 50 per cent of the prison population.[3] This is far higher than Black incarceration rates in the United States or Aboriginal incarceration in Australia. It is a reminder of the point from which my journey began: without accurate statistics how do we know whether our actions are helping or hindering us in achieving our goals?

The reactions of Western governments and Western societies in the days and weeks following the Paris tragedy were predictable and understandable. How do we find the enemy within before they hit us again? Such an instinctive reaction is natural and needed, but long-term strategic reflection on our instinct to fight violence with more violence is also needed. The invasions of Iraq, the destabilisation of Syria and the occupation of Afghanistan have all contributed to the rise of modern terrorism in the Middle East. The more fundamental questions are: Were any of these wars avoidable? What should have happened? How to create a peaceful environment in these countries so that invasion wouldn't need to be contemplated?

3 Sam Bowman, 'Are 70% of France's Prison Inmates Muslims?', Adam Smith Institute, 29 March 2017, accessed at www.adamsmith.org/blog/are-70-of-frances-prison-inmates-muslims

Iraq

Iraq was invaded on a false premise and, within weeks, victory was declared. In hindsight, this turned out to be more of a marketing ploy than anything else. A misguided program of 'de-Ba'athification' removed the country's ruling elite from power, the army was disbanded, and untested leaders were brought in to fill the vacuum. Little thought was given to what would make for a cohesive and competent government moving forward, and no lessons were learnt from the Marshall Plan at the end of World War II, where European elites were largely left intact. Iraq's new leaders had spent their time in exile in Tehran and shared many of Iran's feelings towards the United States. It created the conditions for distrust right from the beginning. The forerunners of Islamic State started to take territory, using terror as one of their core tactics. Terrorism was on the rise again, and this time it would reach new heights of destructiveness.

One of the primary reasons for Islamic State's success in Iraq was that Iraq's military had become dysfunctional and highly corrupt. As Islamic State advanced, the Iraqi army collapsed, mainly because of its inability to provide logistical support, so degraded had it become as a fighting force – despite tens of billions of dollars having been spent on equipping and training its personnel. In response, the US army launched another program to improve the training and incorporate Sunnis into the military. The aim was to train 5,000 Sunni soldiers in 18 months. That training was abandoned because there were not enough Sunnis willing to fight, highlighting the divide between the Sunnis and the Shias.

By the time Islamic State started to advance, the Sunni–Shia coalition government had collapsed. Arrest warrants for treason were issued for Vice-President Tariq al-Hashimi, the head of a major Sunni faction. He was later tried in absentia and sentenced to death. Without a unified government and given the high availability of guns, how could it have ever worked?

As a result of these and other policy failures, Iraq could scarcely be called a coherent country, and it is unclear what will happen next. The current challenge in Iraq remains the same as it was in 2003: to create a legitimate government that commands loyalty across ethnic, tribal and sectarian lines. More recently, in 2019, millions of people took to the streets to demonstrate against corruption, Iran's control of the government and the lack of responsiveness to the people's needs. They wanted a fundamental overhaul of the government structures that have been in place since the US invasion in 2003. These demonstrations were violent, with nearly 700 people being killed. In early 2020 the United States assassinated the head of Iran's special forces, General Qassem Soleimani, further destabilising the region. What the future holds is difficult to predict, but more violence is certain.

Calls for renewed large-scale foreign military intervention are problematic. Large numbers of Western troops would likely be seen as occupiers and then targeted, and there is little appetite among the Western public for the casualities and cost of another war.

The situation is further complicated by the unresolved question of the Kurds, an ethnic group that lives in a swathe of territory that straddles parts of Iraq, Syria, Turkey and Iran. Kurdish forces have been given weapons to fight Islamic State, but they are just as likely to use them to fight for independence. The Kurds in Iraq have already carved out a de facto autonomous region in the north, and fighters associated with the Turkish-based Kurdistan Workers' Party, better known by its Kurdish initials PKK, have resumed attacks on the Turkish government. In 2019 Turkey attacked border towns in the northeast of Syria held by the Syrian Democratic Forces, a Kurdish militia that fought against Islamic State. Both Russia and the United States responded, exerting diplomatic pressure on Turkey, resulting in a truce, but hardly a stable situation for either Syria or Turkey.

Iran is becoming a more assertive power. It is looking to play a larger role in regional affairs and is the most influential country in Iraq. The re-imposing of punitive sanctions by the United States on Iran, its leaders and businesses, especially the oil industry, has caused consternation from the United States' allies. Also, the possibility of further conflict has been heightened by the proxy wars between Iran and Saudi Arabia that are springing up in places such as Yemen. New fault lines are appearing, with Saudi Arabia, the United Arab Emirates (UAE) and Turkey having placed sanctions on Qatar, with the aim of making the state more accommodating of Saudi interests.

It is clear that we are witnessing a tectonic realignment of the power structures in the Middle East, but how these dynamics will play out is difficult to ascertain. Given the low levels of Positive Peace and resilience across the region, the long-term prognosis is not good.

Afghanistan

Afghanistan is in similar straits to Iraq. Despite the vast sums of money spent trying to develop the country, it has failed. The US Department of Defense estimated that by mid-2014, United States appropriations for the reconstruction of Afghanistan had totalled $109 billion, more than the entire Marshall Plan even after adjusting for inflation.[4]

Figure 11 depicts how the country is spinning out of control, and when viewed through the lens of Positive Peace it is easy to see why. In Afghanistan the West partnered with the Karzais, who did not have the moral authority to pull the nation together. What's worse, according to numerous reports, the family was highly corrupt. Opium, which had been suppressed when the Taliban ran the country, became the crop of choice in many regions. And when the family and associates defaulted on loans, the national bank was bankrupted. These are just some of the governance tragedies plaguing Afghanistan.

The US has finally given up and at the time of writing this book it was attempting to arrange a peace deal with the Taliban. It is in the process of drawing down its troops. How this ends is difficult to see but does highlight the limit of military power and a significant loss of US prestige. Over time it appears that the Taliban will gain control of the government. How it views the West and who its strategic partners will be will shape the geo-politics of the region for many decades.

From a Positive Peace perspective, for conflict to stop there need to be improvements in the domains of a *Well-Functioning Government*, combined with *Low Levels of Corruption* and an *Equitable Distribution of Resources*. That was not the case in Afghanistan and underscores the flaws of relying on a military solution alone, and the blindness of those who led the reconstruction effort. Without stronger US military support Ashraf Ghani's

4 'Quarterly Report to the United States Congress', SIGAR (Special Inspector General for Afghanistan Reconstruction), 30 July 2014, accessed at www.sigar.mil/pdf/quarterlyreports/2014-07-30qr.pdf

FIGURE 11

Afghanistan – Deaths from terrorism and conflict, 2003–2018

Terrorism and armed conflict deaths moved in tandem in the countries most affected by terrorism.

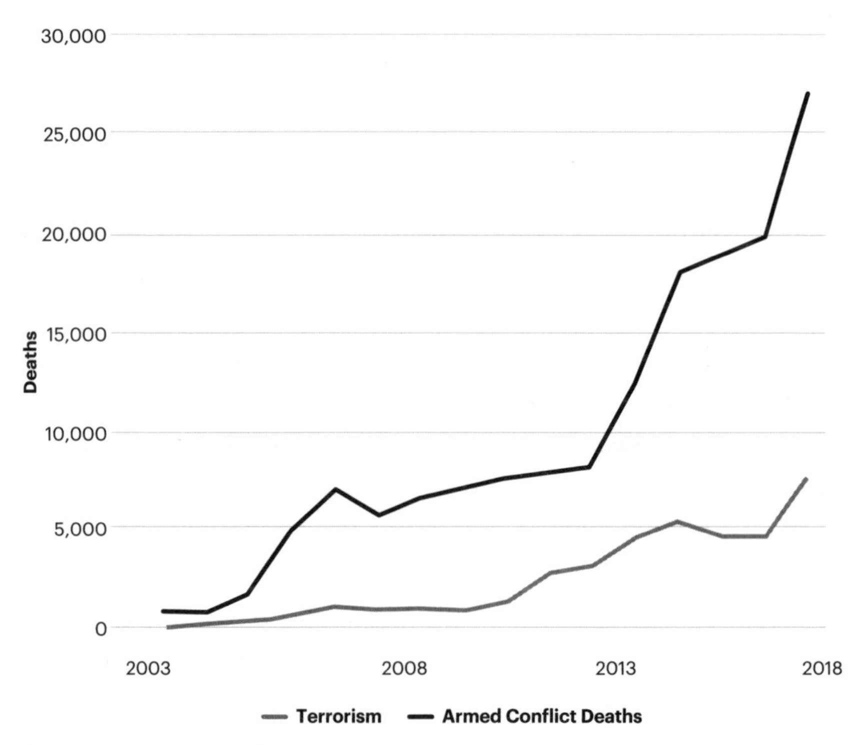

SOURCE: UCDP, START GTD, IEP CALCULATIONS

government will also fall. A future Taliban government is hardly likely to be friendly to US interests in the region.

Make-up of modern terrorism

The *Global Terrorism Index 2019* highlighted a complex and rapidly changing set of dynamics. The global picture had improved, with the number of people killed by terrorist activity decreasing in each of the prior four years, but the improvement was not uniform. The number of deaths in Nigeria, the epicentre of the Boko Haram movement, declined by a staggering 80 per cent during the year, and there were significant improvements in

Syria and Pakistan on the back of a successful military operation against Islamic State. However, Afghanistan continued to deteriorate, reflecting the worsening situation in the war against the Taliban. Afghanistan has now replaced Iraq as the country most affected by terrorism. Deaths caused by terrorism in Afghanistan increased by 71 per cent in 2018.

The vast majority of terrorist activity is in the belt stretching from North Africa to Central Asia, reflecting the fact that those most impacted by Salafi Jihadi movements are other Muslims. In 2016, Islamic State, Boko Haram, al-Qaeda and the Taliban between them accounted for 59 per cent of all terrorist deaths, while 75 per cent of all terrorism-related fatalities occurred in five predominantly Muslim countries – Iraq, Afghanistan, Nigeria, Syria and Pakistan. In 2018, three of these four groups were still among the four deadliest, only with al-Qaeda being replaced by the Khorasan chapter of Islamic State. All four are Islamic-based groups.

The global decline in the number of deaths is encouraging, and with the end of Islamic State's control of territory and the revenue generated from it, the trend is likely to continue. However, the problem is that many of the battle-hardened fighters will move on to other conflict areas. The number of countries experiencing at least one death from terrorism increased to 71 in 2018, up from 69 countries in 2017, while 103 countries – two-thirds of the Index – experienced at least one terrorist attack in 2018.

This spread is troubling, but not surprising. Islamic State has been encouraging fighters to open up new fronts for some years and with their loss of territory many have joined other groups, such as the Khorasan chapter of Islamic State in Afghanistan.

The physical disintegration of Islamic State has translated into a substantial decrease in attacks in Western democracies. In Europe the number of deaths from terrorism fell for the second successive year, from over 200 in 2017 to 62 in 2018. Only two attacks killed five or more people, compared to 11 in 2015. Although this trend is positive, it would be unwise to be complacent. Lone actors inspired by Islamic State are still initiating terrorist attacks and far-right terrorism is on the rise, although from a very low base.

Radical jihadi groups have shown a consistent ability to reinvent themselves, frequently in a more virulent form. Even before it started losing territory, Islamic State was calling for some of its overseas followers to remain in their home countries and mount domestic attacks, and ever since its arrival Islamic State has been looking to lower the technical barriers to carnage. This has given rise to low-tech, lone-actor attacks, such as the spate of incidents that have used rental cars as a murder weapon. They are much cheaper to set up and difficult to detect ahead of time, and they are deadly.

The new wave of terrorist violence needs to be seen in context: although Salafi Jihadi violence is a relatively new phenomenon, the developed world has a long experience of terrorism. Since 1970, there have been some 10,000 deaths from terrorism in the OECD. Islamic State is only the fourth deadliest organisation in the last 50 years, accounting for just 4.7 per cent of deaths in the OECD. Al-Qaeda is the deadliest, with 31 per cent, the majority on 9/11; the Irish Republican Army (IRA) and its affiliates accounted for 19 per cent, and the Basque separatist group Euskadi Ta Askatasuna (ETA) seven per cent. If the 9/11 deaths were subtracted, then al-Qaeda would be behind the IRA and ETA. Even after the destruction of Islamic State other groups will arise. What's needed are programs and policies that alleviate the underlying conditions that give rise to terrorism in the first place.

Far-right terrorism

One of the more worrying trends is the surge in far-right political terrorism in the West over the past five years, although the absolute number of far-right attacks remains low when compared to other forms of terrorism. In 2018, far-right terrorist attacks accounted for 17 per cent of terrorist incidents in the West. In the past five years, in North America, Western Europe and Oceania, far-right attacks have increased by 320 per cent. This trend has continued into 2019, with 77 deaths attributed to far-right terrorists to September 2019. The number of arrests linked to right-wing terrorism in Europe in 2019 increased for the third year in a row. However, the level of political terrorism in the West has been much higher in the past. In the last ten years there have been 322 terrorist attacks classified as either far left or far right, compared to 1,677 attacks between 1970 and 1980.

Far-right terrorism is more likely to be carried out by individuals unaffiliated with a specific terrorist group. None of the attackers in the last two years has been affiliated with a group, making it difficult for the police to isolate beforehand.

The rise in politically motivated attacks by unaffiliated individuals comes at a time when Positive Peace is declining across the West. Declines in Positive Peace are usually associated with higher levels of social disorder.

Factors associated with terrorism

Statistical analysis of the drivers of terrorist activity show there are two distinct sets of factors associated with terrorism, depending on whether the country is developing or developed.

In oppressive countries, the factors most closely linked to terrorist activity are political violence committed by the state, and the presence of a broader conflict within the country. The research finds that 99 per cent of all terrorist attacks between 1989 and 2019 occurred in countries in conflict or with high levels of state-sponsored terror, which is defined as extra-judicial killing, torture, and imprisonment without trial. The relationship between oppression and terror seems to be a classic systems feedback loop: terrorism leads governments to implement stricter, more authoritarian controls on their citizens through torture or state violence, and the repression leads to more people being alienated, resulting in retaliatory terrorist attacks, thereby creating a vicious cycle of violence. Over 90 per cent of all terrorist deaths occurred in countries already mired in internal violent conflicts.

Only one per cent of terrorist attacks occurred in countries that did not suffer from an ongoing conflict or where the state did not practise political terror. This underlines the close link between existing conflicts, group grievances and political violence and terrorist activity.[5]

In developing countries, the history of conflict, levels of corruption, human rights abuses and group-based grievances show the strongest correlations to terrorist activity. Other socio-economic influences, such as poverty, are at best only indirectly connected. Also, in developing countries the data finds no direct link between terrorism and human development,

5 Institute for Economics and Peace, *Global Terrorism Index 2018*.

such as schooling or life expectancy. Nor do economic indicators correlate to the level of terrorism. To highlight this point, both Syria and Iraq were middle-income countries before becoming engulfed in conflict. However, both were racked by ethnic and religious tensions and contained high levels of *Group Grievances* and low Positive Peace.

The factors that are especially prominent in developing countries suffering from high levels of terrorism are those that point to a lack of political and social cohesion. They include hostility between different ethnic, religious and linguistic groups, a lack of intergroup cohesion, corruption and the presence of *Group Grievances*. Indications that provide the clearest signs of the likelihood of terrorism include:

- Governments with little legitimacy and high levels of corruption
- Extremist ideologies
- Inequality of power
- Discrimination based on ethnic or religious origin
- A failure to integrate dissident groups or emerging social classes.

If we look at who is becoming radicalised it is not necessarily the dispossessed or poor, but rather groups that are socially excluded. Quite often the terrorists are better educated but with lower earning potential. Factors such as poor life expectancy, educational attainment and lower per capita income may be common in areas with increased levels of terrorism. However, they are not unique to them and cannot be considered root causes of terrorism.

What is particularly noteworthy and underscores the effect of group grievances is the disparity between the educational attainment of recruits joining Islamic State compared to the jobs they held (see Figure 12). They tend to have held jobs of much lower status than their educational attainment suggests they deserve. A study by the Brookings Institution estimated that the unemployment rate of Muslim immigrants in France is twice that of the overall population.[6]

---

6 Jonathan Laurence and Justin Vaisse, *Integrating Islam: Political and Religious Challenges in Contemporary France*, Brookings Institution Press, 2006, p. 33, accessed at www.brookings.edu/wp-content/uploads/2016/07/integratingislam_chapter.pdf

FIGURE 12

Education level and occupation status of foreign Islamic State recruits

There is a significant mismatch between levels of education and occupational status for Islamic State recruits with high and medium levels of education.

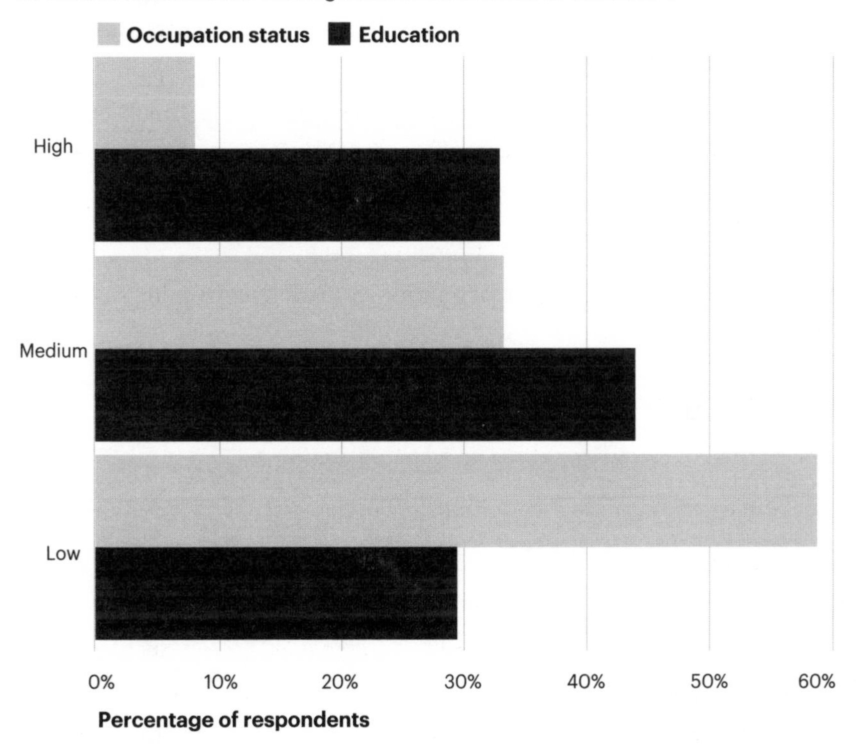

SOURCE: COMBATING TERRORISM CENTRE, IEP CALCULATIONS

David Keen, a political economist and Professor of Complex Emergencies at the London School of Economics, has suggested several measures that should be taken to counteract terrorism effectively.[7] For example, avoiding the reinforcement of poor governance is critical. This makes the aggrieved feel more aggrieved.

> Governance deficits are perhaps the single most significant factor in driving conflict. This means that support for repressive and corrupt

7 L. Attree and D. Keen, 'Envisaging more Constructive Alternatives to the Counter-Terror Paradigm', *Global Terrorism Index Report*, 2014.

actors and regimes needs to be avoided because of its potential to lessen accountability and worsen governance deficits.[8]

In developed OECD countries the drivers appear to be different. Socio-economic factors such as youth unemployment, militarisation, levels of criminality, access to weapons, less belief in the electoral process and distrust of the media are the most statistically significant factors correlating with terrorism. This reinforces some of the well-known drivers of radicalisation and extremism.

Importantly, net migration has no statistical link to terrorism.

The predominant types of terrorism, and their extent, are changing. The religious radicalisation of large-scale terrorist groups following Sunni Wahhabi philosophies is a new phenomenon. These groups use religion as a driving ideology for terrorism and propose global theocracy as an antidote to the breakdown of effective government, as seen in Iraq and Afghanistan. In the past, most terrorist organisations had nationalist separatist agendas. Such groups still exist, but their activities have not greatly increased this century, while radical forms of Wahhabism and Salafi Jihadism have generally grown in intensity. Perversely, success breeds success in terrorism as elsewhere. This can be seen from the number of groups that pledged allegiance to Islamic State as it rose in strength.

Research shows that religiously inspired terrorist groups are among the most difficult to defeat. Analysis by Khusrav Gaibulloev and Todd Sandler spanning terror groups active between 1970 and 2007 found that of the 122 religiously inspired groups they studied, 64 per cent survived and only 12 per cent had been defeated by military or police action. By comparison, of the 464 left-wing, right-wing and nationalist groups studied, 29 per cent survived and 20 per cent were defeated by military and police action.[9]

Gaibulloev and Sandler also noted that religiously based terrorist groups were significantly less likely to join the political process.

8 Attree and Keen.

9 K. Gaibulloev and T. Sandler, 'An Empirical Analysis of Alternative Ways that Terrorist Groups End', *Public Choice*, vol. 160, nos 1–2, 2014, pp. 25–44, accessed at doi.org/10.1007/s11127-013-0136-0

Looking more broadly at the groups that had ceased to be a threat, the analysis found that about a third had been defeated, a third had succumbed to internal splintering and the last third had either won or entered the political process.

This research built on earlier findings by the RAND Corporation,[10] which found among other things that the narrower the goals, the more likely the group was to achieve them through a politically negotiated settlement. The RAND survey also concluded that when a terrorist group had more than 10,000 fighters, it was too powerful for the police; it couldn't be stopped without military force. The degree of force brought to bear on Islamic State and Boko Haram seems to confirm this, and it should be noted that Islamic State, Boko Haram and the Taliban all have more than 10,000 members.

Defeating them on the battlefield is only the first step. The key to long-term success will be the way the peace is handled in the aftermath. The lessons of the failures in Afghanistan and Iraq need to be learnt. The future peace must be perceived as just, inclusive and providing opportunity for all religions and ethnicities to thrive.

Religion and peace

No discussion of peace and conflict in the modern era can afford to ignore the broader issue of religion. When analysing violent conflicts, religion is only a minor factor in most conflicts. It is different for terrorism.

Religious identities run deep, and according to survey data many more people claim to follow some form of spiritual belief than not. Of all the countries covered by the Global Peace Index, there were only 11 where more than 20 per cent of the citizens would classify themselves as atheists.

Reading the headlines, one is tempted to conclude that much of the violence we see around us has its roots in religion, but the data does not support this. We were surprised when we did the analysis to find that there was no statistical link between levels of atheism and peace or its inverse, between religiosity and violence. Even at the extremes, the least peaceful

10 S.G. Jones and M.C. Libicki, 'How Terrorist Groups End', RAND Corporation, 2008, accessed at www.rand.org/pubs/research_briefs/RB9351.html

countries are not necessarily the most religious or vice versa. When looking at the ten most peaceful countries in the GPI, three would be described as highly religious. When looking at the ten least peaceful nations, two would be described as the least religious. When reviewing countries that are highly peaceful, many rank low on atheism. At the other end of the scale there are many unpeaceful countries that have high rates of atheism – North Korea, for example – while other countries riddled with conflict have low levels of atheism – Syria for example.

But this is different from saying that religion has no role in violence. In a review of terrorist killings in 2018, 62 per cent were attributable to four groups – Islamic State, Boko Haram, the Taliban and the Khorasan chapter of Islamic State – all of which follow radical fundamentalist interpretations of Sunni Islam. In this case there is a significant relationship to religion. This only helps to underline the complexity of attempting to draw broad-based conclusions about the relationship between conflict and religion.

An IEP report investigating the relationship between religion and violence found that, although religion was prominent in many conflicts, it was not the fundamental driver. Other aggravating factors need to be present, such as political dominance of one religious group, an inequitable system, gross group grievances or religious suppression.[11] Olivier Roy, a French academic who has done extensive research on Salafi Jihadism, concludes that in most cases what we are seeing is a specific interpretation of Islam becoming a lightning rod for a range of grievances: not the radicalisation of Islam, but the Islamicisation of radicalism, as he puts it. This is another example of why, in order to understand the situational context in which peace is either improving or deteriorating, we have to look at the whole system, not focus on specific causes.

IEP's 2014 *Peace and Religion* report proved to be highly controversial. Discussion of religion provokes strong emotions, with the results running against many people's perceived ideas. While religion has evidently been a factor in many conflicts throughout history it is far from the only reason for conflict.

---

11 Institute of Economics and Peace, *Five Key Questions Answered on the Link Between Peace and Religion*, October 2014.

So is Islam the problem? We found no connection. Despite the apparent role that Sunni and Shia sectarian violence plays in the Middle East, when we look at the global situation, countries with high proportions of both Sunni and Shia Muslims do not necessarily have correspondingly high levels of violence. Countries that have lower corruption, a well-functioning government and better relations with neighbours are more peaceful, regardless of the particular levels of Sunni and Shia affiliation.

Qatar was the most peaceful country in the Middle East and North African region in 2019. It has the same balance of Sunni and Shia as Afghanistan, one of the least peaceful countries. Similarly, there are differing levels of peace for countries where the proportions of Sunni and Shia are similar. Bahrain is significantly more peaceful than other war-torn countries that have similar Sunni–Shia splits, including Iraq, Lebanon and Yemen. Many relatively peaceful countries have a significant proportion of both Sunni and Shia. In other words, although religion is the rallying cry, other factors form the ground from which religious extremism can spring.

There are many interfaith organisations working on peace; the two largest are Religions for Peace and United Religions Initiative, and both have adopted Positive Peace. The United Religions Initiative and the IEP recently signed a memorandum of understanding. The organisation consists of 1,000 community circles that work with grassroots programs to bring religious understanding into conflict areas. Positive Peace provides a practical framework for building peace, one that fits neatly with the moral constructs of all major religions.

It can be said that countries without a dominant religious group are, on average, more peaceful and have less restrictions or social hostility around religion than countries with a dominant religious group. However, government type has greater explanatory power than religion in understanding differing levels of peace.

Sheikh bin Bayyah is a leading Sunni theologian and renowned scholar. Speaking at the 2014 conference on our *Peace and Religion* paper he highlighted how classical Islam had been distorted by opportunistic new terror movements by focusing on a particular *fatwa*, or religious ruling, used by the mullahs associated with Islamic State to justify their carnage.

The *fatwa* ostensibly declared: 'If your ruler is not following the laws of Islam, you have the right to destroy him.' But the Sheikh did not believe this reading was accurate. He scoured the old manuscripts and was eventually able to trace the mistake to a transcription error made over 120 years ago. Two critical dots over a word had been dropped, fundamentally changing the meaning. The correct sentence was: 'If your ruler is not following the laws of Islam you have the right to correct him.' One is a civil conversation; the other is murder.

Concerned about the error, the consequences of which are profound because it legitimises terror attacks on governments, Sheikh bin Bayyah contacted some of the radical clerics to point out what he had discovered. They replied: 'Well, you may be right, but we don't care.' Religion, unfortunately, often becomes a tool for more sinister agendas.

We know that certain conditions need to be present to fuel terrorism: strong group grievances, lack of political legitimacy, state acts of extra judicial killings and torture. A sense of disenfranchisement or other grievances can then easily be attached to religion. Many conflicts acquire a religious gloss, not least because it allows leaders to invoke divine approval for acts of violence. The mixing of conflict with religion is not unique to the Middle East. Northern Ireland's civil war, which originated in disenfranchisement of Catholics by Protestants, became defined by religious labels and involved many acts of terrorism targeting Britain. Although religious terrorism is not unique to the Middle East, it certainly is where it is most virulent today.

Economics and terrorism

One of the cities I have been closely involved with over the years is Brussels. It has suffered directly and indirectly from Islamic State's campaign in Europe. Watching the effects terrorism had on that city has helped me understand some of its wider psychological and economic ramifications.

As I mentioned, the launch of the 2015 Global Terrorism Index coincided with the Paris terrorist attacks. Watching the events unfold, I could see the impact these events had on the economy. Five days after the launch I was in Brussels for a launch event at Belgium's Royal Military Academy.

Due to credible intelligence that pointed to a series of attacks similar to those in Paris, Brussels was shut down for many days. The presentation I had been going to give was cancelled on the morning, all schools were closed and many of my meetings were cancelled because people were not going to work. One Belgian television program calculated that the shutdown cost the city €51.7 million a day, or over €300 million in total. There was also a lot of discussion about restricting free movement of people through the EU Schengen zone.

Five months later, I was in Berlin waiting to return to Brussels on an early morning flight; it was one of those uneventful mornings, slightly cold and overcast with little wind. I was up early, starting to prepare for the next couple of days of meetings; I had no thought that I would not get there. The plane taxied onto the runway, then started to take off, rapidly gaining speed. Then aborted, decelerating very quickly and pushing everyone forwards, caught by their seatbelts. I thought it was a mechanical fault.

Just as we reached the terminal it was announced over the PA system that there was an incident at Brussels airport. A bomb had exploded and all flights were cancelled. Once back in the terminal, I quickly phoned my travel agent to attempt to rearrange things, and in his fast and faultless style he found that I could get a flight to Amsterdam and then catch the train up to Brussels. This meant that I would only miss my first two meetings.

I was back in the air literally within 90 minutes. During my flight, the terrorists also bombed the railway station just outside of the European headquarters in Brussels, which meant that all trains were cancelled. Once in the Amsterdam terminal I rearranged my itinerary and stayed in The Hague for the next three days before finally getting to Brussels.

In Brussels a media frenzy erupted. Our representative there, Serge Stroobants, must have done about 20 interviews for the international media. When I did finally arrive, the hotel where I would stay, The Amigo, had an armed vehicle in front of it along with a group of armed guards. It was thought that the hotel could be a target. Inside, despite the tension, the staff greeted me in a very friendly manner as we had built up a rapport over the many years that I had been staying there. The Grande Place, one of the great squares of Europe, only 50 metres away, was also a target.

The hotel was deserted, the Grande Place was deserted, and for a week after the attacks the schools and many government buildings were closed. This was a clear example of the damage that terrorism caused to the normal functioning of society and the consequential economic losses that go with it. Again, many of my scheduled meetings had to be cancelled because people could not return to work.

It would be three months before my next trip. When I arrived again at The Amigo the staff greeted me in their usual friendly manner. The place still looked emptier than I remembered so I asked what was happening. The staff commented that the number of guests was about half of what it usually was.

As I contemplated the economic impact of the attacks, I realised how vulnerable the European economy was at that time. GDP growth rates were estimated to be 1.8 per cent, the government debt–to-GDP ratio in the Euro area had increased 5 percentage points over the year to 93 per cent,[12] and productivity was expected to increase by just one per cent. The impact of the shutdown on the economy must have been significant, and if restrictions were placed on the free flow of people through the Schengen zone it was likely that the impacts would have caused the evaporation of the weak productivity growth and further depress GDP. If this did happen then the long-term effects on peace could have been dramatic. Falling productivity, flat growth and higher unemployment would create the conditions for considerable social unrest, yet there was little discussion on what impact this may have on the economy.

The effects of terrorism were clearly highlighted by a small research study the IEP undertook for the World Travel and Tourism Council, an organisation that very much understands the value of peace. The analysis found that it can take up to eight years before tourism returns to normal after a major terrorist attack on a tourist destination. To highlight just how strong the effect can be we decided to take two sets of similar countries, one set from the developed world and one set from the developing world. From each set one country had a terrorist attack on a tourist destination

12 Eurostat, news release, 22 July 2015, accessed at ec.europa.eu/eurostat/documents/2995521/6923259/2-22072015-AP-EN.pdf/bf173a0e-0eba-4ab9-878c-6db8d1f6452b

FIGURE 13

Change in tourism revenue in 2015

Tourism revenues drop after terrorist attacks. Italy and Morocco didn't experience major terrorist attacks while France and Tunisia did.

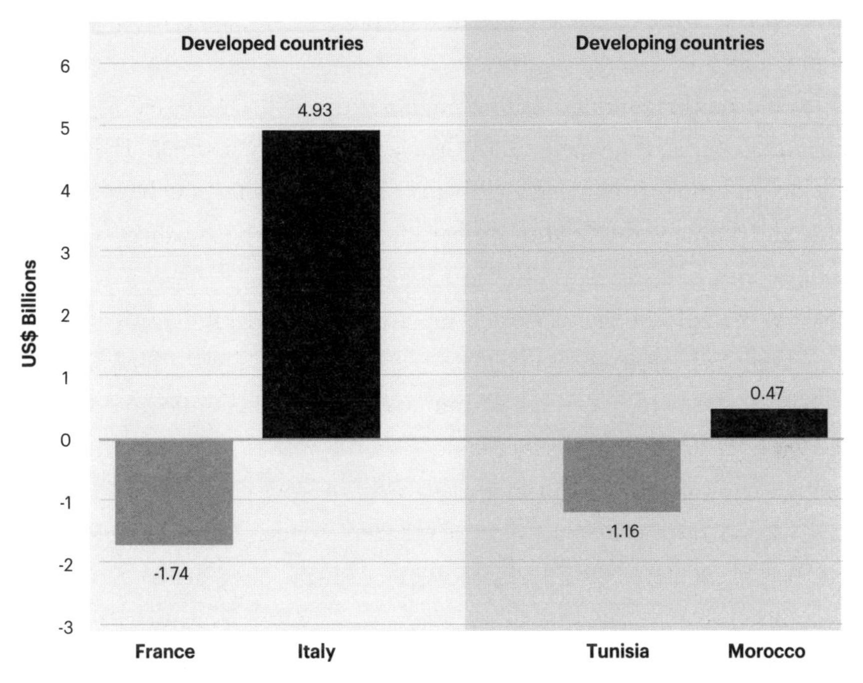

SOURCE: WTTC, START GTD, IEP CALCULATIONS

and the other did not. As can be understood from Figure 13, the effects are substantial.[13] Tourism revenue in France and Tunisia dropped in the year after they suffered terrorist attacks, while revenue in two similar nearby countries, Italy and Morocco, increased.

Tourism is a microcosm of the much broader damage that terrorism can do to an economy. Direct costs from the 9/11 attacks in New York and Washington are estimated at $65 billion, but when the indirect costs are included that rises to $190 billion or 0.7 per cent of US GDP.[14]

---

13 'Tourism as a Driver of Peace', World Travel and Tourism Council, 2016, accessed at www.wttc.org/research/other-research/tourism-as-a-driver-of-peace/

14 J.E. Mueller and M.G. Stewart, *Chasing Ghosts: The Policing of Terrorism*, Oxford University Press, 2016, accessed at global.oup.com/academic/product/chasing-ghosts-9780190237318?cc=ap&lang=en&

Our research has shown that small and less diversified economies are particularly vulnerable to the economic impact of terrorism. Advanced diversified economies with high levels of Positive Peace are economically and socially more resilient and have shorter recovery periods from incidents of terrorism. These effects are mainly explained by the ability of diversified economies to reallocate resources, such as labour and capital, to other areas of the economy that are not as badly affected.

The Global Terrorism Index

The origins of the Global Terrorism Index lay in the Global Peace Index. The Global Peace Index used to include an indicator called the *Likelihood of Terrorism*, which was subjectively scored by a group of independent experts. What we realised after a number of years was that the risk assessment estimates were somewhat haphazard.

Attempting to qualitatively predict the likelihood of terrorism was fraught with difficulty: sometimes the estimates were strikingly accurate but at other times they were very much off the mark. Instead we searched for a new source that counted the actual occurrences of terrorism. This meant that the indicator changed from a forward estimate to be trailing and factually based. We found a number of sources but concluded that the National Consortium for the Study of Terrorism and Responses to Terrorism (START) database from the University of Maryland, which contains over 140,000 terrorist incidents going back over 20 years, was the most accurate, detailed and comprehensive.

Some years later, as the pace of attacks started to rise with the ascension of the groups that would eventually become Islamic State, it became clear that the way we were constructing the indicator could be used to build another index. In 2013, I decided that the timing was right to launch our first Global Terrorism Index.

In many ways, it was a daunting prospect as our background knowledge of terrorism was sparse. The approach we adopted was similar to the Global Peace Index. We would build the Index, set up an expert panel to advise us and then use statistical analyses to discover the patterns associated with terrorism, as well as drawing on other studies to form a more fully rounded picture.

As with all the indexes, identifying the starting point was critical. There is no single, internationally accepted definition of what constitutes terrorism. Rather, there are a number of competing approaches and typologies reflecting differing political perspectives. Studies of political terrorism have found over 100 definitions of the word, covering over 20 separate elements.[15] Defining who is, and who is not, a terrorist depends heavily on which narrative is found to be persuasive – 'One man's terrorist is another's freedom fighter', as the phrase goes. Mandela went to jail for terrorism. Senior members of the IRA are now the leaders of Sinn Féin, a legitimate political party. Such ambiguity has hindered clarity about the term's use.

In the 1970s and 1980s, the United Nations attempted to define terrorism but failed because of the differences of opinion between various member states about conflicts of national liberation and self-determination.[16]

The linguistic origin of the word is the French *terrorisme*, which referred specifically to state terrorism practised by the French government in the 1793–1794 Reign of Terror. Nevertheless, in contemporary parlance we mostly use the word 'terror' to describe acts that threaten the state and its citizens, and which require a response by the instruments of the state: the police or the military.

The definition START uses is: 'The threatened or actual use of illegal force and violence by a non-state actor to attain a political, economic, religious, or social goal through violence, fear, coercion, or intimidation.' One benefit of using this definition is that it is clear and simple to convey. We decided to run with the definition used by START because it meant that we didn't need to combine other datasets or subtract from theirs.

Several criteria have to be met in order for a violent event to be counted as a terrorist act. It must be intentional, the result of a conscious calculation by the perpetrator. It must involve some level of violence, or threat of violence. It must be a non-state actor because state terrorism is excluded.

---

15 A. Schmid, 'The problems of defining terrorism', *Encyclopedia of World Terrorism*, vol. 1, Armonk, 1997.

16 M. Angus, 'The Right of Self-Defence under International Law – the Response to the Terrorist Attacks of September 11', Australian Law and Bills Digest Group, 12 February 2002, Parliament of Australia website.

The omission of state terrorism against its citizens, such as extrajudicial killings or the use of drones to carry out assassinations, from the Global Terrorism Index has drawn some criticism. In Syria, both the Assad government and Islamic State have a history of brutalising their own citizens. Omitting state terrorism allows us to differentiate between these two forms of terror. State-sponsored terrorism is captured in the Global Peace Index as a separate indicator. One of the problems with including state-sponsored terrorism is what to include. Does the use of US drone strikes for targeted assassinations of terrorist leaders count? The dividing line between what is a legitimate military objective and what is a state terrorist act can be difficult to identify.

The Index itself is comparatively simple. It counts the number of people killed by terrorism, the number of injuries, the number of attacks, and the amount of property damage. It then puts a weighting on each one of these.

Quite often property damage has a comparatively small overall economic value. If a suicide bomber walks into an Iraqi restaurant and blows it up, it might cost between $40,000 and $400,000 to build a new one. Yet if that terrorist kills ten people, that is 40 years of lifetime earnings lost for each person. Assuming they could have been expected to make about $20,000 a year, it equates to $800,000 in lost lifetime income. That is without taking into account the lost productivity of family and friends from grieving, the post-traumatic impact on bystanders, or the impact on investment. The long-term indirect costs of terrorism are typically ten to 20 times larger than the direct costs.

The Global Terrorism Index has been a resounding success. Probably the aspect that most surprised me was how well it has been received by the global intelligence community. Although they are far more skilled in counter-terrorism activities than the IEP, the Index provided an integrated and reliable international coverage of terrorism with hard facts, trends and other factors associated with terrorism. Most intelligence organisations focus on the areas of importance for their own countries rather than a global overview of terrorism. It seems the very process of developing an index takes on a more holistic approach as diverse sets of data are collated and analysed, thereby creating an integrated, top-down view.

The media have also embraced the Index. We held launch events for the 2019 report in 22 locations across four continents, and it was estimated that the media reach was over 2.4 billion impressions, the highest we have had for any launch. There were over 800 individual news reports spanning the globe and embracing the full political spectrum, from *The Guardian* to Fox News, and from Al Jazeera and Al Arabia to the *Daily Mail*, illustrating the broad acceptance of our fact-based methodology.

Terrorism and Positive Peace

Terrorism has been the most prominent violence containment issue of the last decade. The rise of Islamic State and its ability to project operations into Europe created a new sense of urgency. The Western response has been to improve intelligence-gathering capabilities, to fund and support the movement's opponents, and to use airstrikes against Islamic State positions in Syria and Iraq.

In the past the West has supported governments perceived as friendly, regardless of how unpopular they may be with their citizens. The emphasis on stability at all costs is fragile and can be prone to catastrophic failures, such as the Arab Spring or the civil war in Syria. These societies lacked the resilience to deal with substantive shocks.

Corruption is a useful barometer of fragility. It happens to be high in all of the ten countries suffering the most from terrorism. Countries that are high in corruption are more likely to sustain group grievances and practise state-sponsored terror. They are also more likely to be more poorly perceived by their citizens.

Positive Peace provides a different lens through which to approach national development, and it is the starting point for improving resilience. It is holistic and systemic in its approach and takes into account the path or trajectory of the society, rather than attempting to rip it apart to create something new. Positive Peace creates the conditions under which the informal social contracts that hold societies together can develop and then evolve. This creates an optimal environment for human potential to flourish.

Positive Peace is just as applicable to fighting homegrown terrorists in the West as it is in the Middle East and North Africa. When analysing OECD countries, the factors associated with higher levels of terrorism are higher rates of unemployment, less belief in the political system, higher crime, higher drug taking and poverty. While these factors do give clear insight into the environment surrounding terrorism, they also point to other social challenges. Yet what is most telling, as has already been discussed, is that Positive Peace in the United States and many European countries is in decline. Both the United States and Europe have suffered drops in media freedoms and rising perceptions of corruption, particularly in politics. It is easy to see the polarisation that is occurring is the United States and Europe through the current rise of anti-establishment political parties.

Understanding these critical issues through single points of reference, such as too much immigration, too much accumulation of wealth by a few, too many Muslims or jobs going overseas, will miss the point. Nations are functioning systems: there is a need to truly understand the system and then nudge it towards higher levels of Positive Peace.

CHAPTER 11

Lessons learnt

The IEP's work has generated more interest than I could have ever imagined. Given the events of the last decade there is a global yearning for a more peaceful world. This has largely been brought about by the rise of terrorism and the intractable conflicts in the Middle East, coupled with growing scepticism towards Western political systems, especially their inability to tackle ecological and sustainability issues, such as climate change. The geo-political effects of COVID-19 will only increase this yearning.

Our success can be measured in many ways. The ever-increasing global media coverage of our products is a good gauge. It is hard to put a price on media coverage, but one example relates to the launch of the Mexico Peace Index. Every year the launch is one of the major news stories in Mexico, dominating news coverage. The 2016 report was covered extensively on Televisa, one of Mexico's most popular television channels. The coverage lasted seven minutes. If we had wanted to advertise on the program it would have cost us hundreds of thousands of dollars per minute.

The first launch of the Global Terrorism Index followed in a similar vein and was also a great success. According to Google, it was one of the three most read news stories globally for two days.

Since those first launches the IEP has come a long way. Our social media reach is still growing quickly and had a billion impressions in 2019. We currently average 150,000 unique visitors per month to our website, Vision of Humanity. Likewise, our following on Facebook and Twitter is strong, and growing. The number of Twitter impressions in the first six months of 2019 grew at a rate of 35 per cent. But probably the statistic that amazes me the most is the number of media impressions we receive and in 2019 there 16 billion of them.

Our peace message is finding resonance in all parts of the world. However, simply creating content for media consumption is not enough. Media articles in many ways are stories, or a single narrative. The aim has to be to move beyond stories, which are almost always partial. If we are to attain a systemic understanding of peace – a necessity to manage the challenges of the Anthropocene – then stories are, in a sense, a hurdle to be overcome because they are a single narrative rather than a complete view that incorporates many stories.

Consider the situation in Ukraine.

This is what it looks like from a Western perspective. A post-Soviet republic holds a presidential election in 2004, which a candidate from the east of the country, Viktor Yanukovych, steals with criminal backing. This provokes a peaceful popular uprising known as the Orange Revolution, resulting in a re-run of the election and the victory of his opponent. Six years later, Yanukovych wins back the presidency, jails his main opponent on trumped-up charges, and amasses a huge fortune through corruption. Under Russian pressure, the new president betrays an election promise to sign an agreement with the European Union, provoking demonstrations. Yanukovych then pushes through draconian laws against the demonstrators with the aim of shutting down the protests, leading to the police killing more than 100 people. The president flees; a new government is elected. The Russians use the departure of the president and the appointment of the new government as an excuse to annex one part of the country and to invade another.

This is how Russia and the separatists see it. Following a disputed election result in 2004, a planned uprising backed by Western intelligence forces the judiciary to re-run the election. The winner presides over a factious and sectarian administration every bit as corrupt as its predecessor. It's no surprise that the previously ousted winner, Viktor Yanukovych, is properly re-elected six years later. He refuses to sign an agreement with the Western powers that would have impoverished swathes of the population. In response to this decision, protesters, again backed by Western intelligence agencies, occupy the central square, paralysing the capital. Sniper fire from the protesters leads to a counterattack, resulting in 100 deaths. Following the collapse of police resistance, a junta is imposed by forces backed by Western interests. For their own protection, one part of the country votes overwhelmingly to join Russia, while in another a popular uprising against the Western-backed junta leads to the creation of two independent people's republics. They are attacked by fascist militias, and volunteers from Russia come to their aid.

What I'm describing are two mutually exclusive accounts of what happened in Ukraine.[1] The problem with these opposing accounts – and most opposing accounts – is that both can be 'right', based on the interpretation of some selected facts. Yet they flatly contradict each other. This is what happens whenever there is an attempt to use narratives alone to explain the complexities of peace and violence.

Stories typically have heroes and villains and routinely imply that some form of punishment – inevitably violent – should be visited upon the villains. In war, the heroes are those who fight for our side and the villains are those who fight against us; there is little attempt to be dispassionate.

Narratives in many ways underpin a causal view of the world. They have a beginning, a middle and an end. They move in a linear way, linking the selected facts together. Narratives can, therefore, run counter to understanding the truth; what's needed are many narratives to understand the picture.

If we want to achieve peace in the Anthropocene, creating a binary moral world of good and evil will only make it harder. We must move beyond narratives and divisive moral judgements. This is not to suggest that there is no such thing as good and evil behaviour, only the need to transcend these narratives if we are to find peaceful solutions that encompass all.

The Global Peace Index helps us to move beyond mere stories and leads instead to a fuller, more verifiable and rigorous picture: a collection of morally neutral facts that can be used as a starting point to build a shared vision of what needs to be addressed. The Index opens the door to a more factual approach to understanding the dynamics of global peace.

---

1 David Edgar, 'What did happen?', *London Review of Books*, vol. 38, no. 2, January 2016, pp. 9–12.

The IEP's approach to data

The foundation of the IEP's work is its empirical data. Our rankings in the Global Peace Index are deduced from the facts that we have assembled. This bottom-up approach is designed to eliminate research bias as best we can, a necessity if our research is to provide a starting point for an empirical discussion of how to achieve peace in a world of competing views.

We did not start out with a theory we wanted to prove, but let the facts lead us to their own conclusions. This is the difference between induction and deduction. Induction starts with a premise and attempts to prove the premise, whereas deduction lets facts guide the outcome. The IEP's approach is deductive.

One of the offshoots of the high levels of visibility of the Index is that more studies are being undertaken that use quantitative approaches to understanding peace. This is particularly noticeable in some areas of academia and with NGOs that are developing measures in local contexts.

In other ways, the impact of the Global Peace Index has been subtler. One of these influences came from the approach taken in developing the methodology. For example, one of the unique aspects of the Global Peace Index is the grouping of the three domains to create the Index. Many experts have said to me that they had never considered grouping criminal violence and conflict together. One of our basic assumptions was that a broad definition of peace and violence was necessary to fully understand peace. Once this was done it could then be sliced in multiple ways: by internal or external peace, or, alternatively, by the dimensions of ongoing conflict, militarisation or domestic safety and security.

Another original element is the idea that peace and violence within a society can be considered similar to peace and violence between societies. Lives lost in war, or through domestic violence, are treated as having the same value. In terms of a person's experience, this seems reasonable. There is no fundamental difference between being a victim of violence – or fearing becoming a victim of violence – as a result of war or as a result of crime; they are both devastating. Likewise, the peace that results from not being subjected to an external threat is much the same as being free from a threat from fellow citizens.

To achieve a high level of rigour we have to understand the necessary boundaries of the endeavour. As the 19th-century British historian Lord Acton commented, mastery is acquired through resolved limitation. What are the limits with the Index? One is that, as with any empirical approach, it is positivist: it can only include what can be and is being positively measured. It is also dependent on the quality and breadth of the input data.

Another limitation arises when we start to consider the subjective experience of peace, which is difficult to measure objectively. To help balance this, one of the measures used is the level of 'perceived violence in society', which captures the fear of crime among the general public and is measured via expert assessment. There can be a disconnect between the perception of the level of crime and its actual occurrence.

Measuring perceptions can become problematic because at the individual level, it's a subjective experience. Acts that would be perceived as unacceptable violence in one country might be considered acceptable in another. An example is corporal punishment in schools. Measuring perceptions can be riddled with cultural complexities. However, fear of violence is a perception that we did consider valid across all societies because this affects behaviour. If people are fearful for their personal safety, they change their habits, which can affect many things, including economic activity.

Another limit with the definition is that it does not include measures of people's intentions in relation to maintaining peace or descending into violence, especially the choice of leaders.

When looking at the entire system, it can be argued that the vicious and virtuous cycles of peace shape citizens' choices, and therefore intentions. However, in many cases, especially in authoritarian states, the intentions of individuals, especially of political leaders, can have a dramatic effect on future peace.

An example would be Germany in the lead-up to World War II. It may have been possible to anticipate that the vicious cycle plaguing Weimar Germany had increased the risk of violence, and perhaps war, but it was far from inevitable. It was the particular intentions of one person, Adolf Hitler, which led to the conflagration that ensued. That is not an area that can be easily covered by empirical analysis.

The approach in the peace indexes is very different from the usual methods of understanding peace, which tend to lean heavily on the narrative of what the leaders intend to do. A political leader's will, even when dominant, is only one among many.

This is where understanding Positive Peace is critical because it represents a systemic measure of the resilience of a society: its ability to withstand shocks, including those initiated by its own political leadership. Who and what arises is dependent on the state of the broader system: its history, its encoded norms and the strength of *the attitudes, institutions, and structures that create and sustain peace*. In the example of Germany, if the French had not made Germany make such exorbitant payments following its defeat in the World War I, the economic depression in Germany would not have been as severe and the conditions may not have allowed a Hitler to arise.

Tolstoy observed the problems with this kind of analysis in his masterpiece *War and Peace*. He criticised the limitation of the usual war narratives, noting that 'the march of humanity, springing as it does from an infinite multitude of individual wills, is continuous'.

Tolstoy talked of the 'continuous movement of history', a similar notion to the idea of systems that sees societies as moving along a path. He wrote that most historians try to depict this movement by selecting, at random, a series of successive events, spinning them into a story, with a beginning, a middle and an end. The problem, he argued, is that 'there is and can be no beginning to any event, for one event flows without any break in continuity from another'.[2]

An aspect of Tolstoy's genius was his ability to depict the wider panoply of war and peace, which he contrasted with the narratives and inner lives of his heroines and heroes. This wider perspective is the novelistic equivalent of taking a systems perspective.

Tolstoy criticised the 'Great Man' theory of history.

> The study of the actions of one man – a king or a commander – as though their actions represented the sum of many individual wills to

2 L. Tolstoy, *War and Peace*, Part 3, Penguin Classics, 1957, p. 975.

> assume a *beginning* to any phenomenon, or to say that the volitions of all men are expressed in the actions of one historical character, is false *per se.*[3]

Much is currently being made of President Trump and how one man is upending 80 years of global alliances and conventions. However, he arose in the context of a system that is straining under immense internal pressures and fighting within and against itself. This has arisen because of the background conditions in the country and is as much a symptom of longer term dysfunction. The American electorate is looking for change in the system.

Insights from the last decade of the Global Peace Index

The 2019 Global Peace Index was a major milestone for the IEP. It was an opportunity to pause and look back over the past decade to gain a better understanding of the changing dynamics of peace over that time. There were many trends, some positive, some negative, but probably the most interesting outcome was the realisation that it was possible to develop multiple stories or narratives from the same data. Again this drove home how multifaceted and complex the nature of peace is and the integral position systems thinking plays in understanding it.

We found that the improving trend of the prior 50 years has reversed. The world had become less peaceful over the prior decade. Surprisingly, the domain covering *Militarisation* had improved, which was in stark contrast to what most people thought. Even though conflict was increasing, more countries were decreasing the size of their militaries than increasing them.

However, the domains for *Ongoing conflict* and *Societal safety and security* both deteriorated significantly over the last decade, because of three main factors: battlefield deaths increased substantially; the number of deaths from terrorism increased from 11,000 in 2007 to peak at 32,765 in 2014, before falling to 8,000 in 2019; and the number of internally displaced persons

---

3 L. Tolstoy, *War and Peace*, Part 3, Penguin Classics, 1957.

(IDPs) and refugees was at a 60-year high, increasing to 70 million in 2019. Much of the deterioration was the result of the wars in the Middle East. If nothing else this points to both the stupidity of fighting wars that were not needed and the West's inability to understand how to transit countries to post-conflict and then to rebuild peaceful societies.

What became apparent was that the global headlines only partly reflected the reality of what had happened. There were three different views that could be taken on the progress of world peace over the prior decade.

The first is based on the facts above. It is perfectly logical and factually based. Over the last decade the world has become less peaceful, with more countries decreasing in peace than increasing. This has been driven by higher numbers of battlefield deaths, record refugee flows and record levels of terrorism.

The second is that in many ways, peace is progressing and it's only the situation in the Middle East and the knock-on effects from those conflicts that are bringing the level of global peacefulness down. In fact, if the conflicts in the Middle East and North Africa and their knock-on effects were removed from the world, then it would on average have actually become more peaceful. The overall score would have improved, but more importantly, over the last decade, more countries would have improved their scores than deteriorated. Therefore, it can be argued that the most pressing issue is solving the wars in Afghanistan, Syria, Libya and Yemen. If this is done, then the world will probably continue on its path to greater peacefulness, creating the bandwidth to work on solving violence in places such as Nigeria, Venezuela and South Sudan, to name just three.

The third scenario is that there are two worlds of peace and this can be coined by the phrase 'The growing inequality in global peace'. The countries at the top and those at the bottom are moving further apart. The most peaceful countries on the Index have recorded the highest levels of peace in their history. For many of these countries the percentage of GDP spent on the military and their long-term homicide and violent crime rates are at historic lows. However, the countries at the bottom of the Index have kept steadily deteriorating over the past decade. This highlights the growing inequality in global peace.

The data supports any of these three interpretations, each one suggesting a non-exclusive way to view the challenges we face when trying to build a peaceful world. This multiplicity of interpretations also bolsters the argument for approaching the problem through systems thinking, which is better able to accommodate multiple entry points when it comes to enhancing peace.

The conflict in Syria was responsible for the vast majority of the increase in the number of refugees over the last decade. In 2007, just 0.1 per cent of the Syrian population was classified as refugees or IDPs.[4] This figure rose to an extraordinary 63 per cent or 13 million people in 2015, highlighting the devastating flow-on effects from failed military interventions in Iraq and attempted regime change in Syria. The majority of these people were internally displaced.

While no other country comes close to having as many refugees and IDPs as a percentage of its population as Syria, there are eight other countries with more than ten per cent of their population displaced in some form. Somalia and South Sudan both have more than 20 per cent displaced.

State failure, conflict and terrorism were the major drivers, with the largest increases coming in countries engaged in protracted civil conflict. Outside of Syria, conflicts in Yemen, Libya, the Democratic Republic of the Congo, and Ukraine led to large increases in the number of displaced people. All of these countries had between three and nine per cent of their population displaced.

The flow of refugees into Europe has also created unforeseen political disruptions. Long-standing fears about competition for jobs and cultural pushback have been amplified by new worries about 'Trojan terrorists' slipping into countries along with genuine refugees. This, in part, is what lies behind the rise of new political parties across the European continent. Fear is a powerful force.

Warnings of large refugee flows swamping the capacities and cultures of European nations became commonplace. An illustration of this was Germany. It was estimated that a million refugees would arrive in Germany in 2015 – a

4 For a definition of the term 'refugee' see Article 1(A)(2) of the 1951 Refugee Convention, UNHCR, accessed at www.unhcr.org/3b66c2aa10. 'Internally displaced persons (IDPs) ... have not crossed an international frontier, but have ... also fled their homes', quoted from 'Refugees and displaced persons under international humanitarian law', International Committee of the Red Cross (ICRC), 29 October 2010, accessed at www.icrc.org/en/document/protected-persons/refugees-displaced-persons

one-off addition of about 1.2 per cent of the total population. However, a more nuanced analysis finds that the problem could have been managed. The numbers are large but they could have been supported and integrated.

What's more, 45 per cent of the population in Germany is aged 55 or over, compared with just six per cent of the refugees, with the majority being under 21 years of age. To maintain economic growth, the country needs to replace its ageing workforce. Germany also took in over 400,000 people after the Balkan wars. This was shortly after reunification with East Germany, when there were far fewer resources available than today. The 2015 resistance to the refugees in Germany was rooted in political appeals to fear rather than logic. Australia has taken in one per cent of its population as immigrants every year for the last 50 years and integrated them successfully. It's estimated that three out of every four Australians either were born overseas or have an overseas-born parent.

If the size of today's refugee flows is worrying, it pales into insignificance when compared to the potential scale of displacement from climate change, degradation of the water tables or a depleted ecosystem. There may be hundreds of millions of people on the move in the future. The World Bank estimates that 343 million people worldwide live within 5 metres of sea level, 13 million in Bangladesh alone. How we react to today's refugee challenges will be critical in determining future responses and future global peace.

Uganda, Colombia, Chad, India and Sri Lanka were the five countries with the largest reductions in the number of deaths from internal conflict. Conversely, 16 countries had increases of over 1,000 deaths, with the largest increases occurring in Syria, Afghanistan, Mexico, Iraq and Yemen.

The high number of deaths from conflict in Mexico resulted from an explosion of violence following President Calderón's crackdown on cartel activity that began in 2007. The conflict claimed over 35,000 lives lost in homicides in 2019 alone.

One of the positive offshoots of the increased intensity of conflict has been a marked improvement in the international commitment to peacekeeping, as measured by the timeliness of payments for UN peacekeeping operations. This has shown the biggest improvement in the decade to 2019 of any indicator in the Index. Each country is charged a levy for each peacekeeping operation undertaken by the UN, according to their percentage of levies of UN general funding. Some countries pay all their fees, others only pay for the peacekeeping operations they agree with, and others pay nothing or pay very late. Over the 13 years this indicator has improved by 12 per cent. Corresponding with this improvement in funding has been a large increase in the number of UN peacekeeping forces being deployed, jumping from 40,000 in 2003 to over 100,000 in 2015 (see Figure 14). As the economic impact of COVID-19 takes hold governments may direct funds away from supporting peacekeeping operations and towards propping up their local economies. This would have a negative impact on the world's ability to control and contain conflict.

Long-term improvements in peace

The last decade has been bad for peace, but if we go back further it is clear that over the last 60 years, the world has become more peaceful. Since the end of World War II, conflict and war, particularly colonial and interstate conflicts, have decreased consistently, as has the number of people killed in conflicts. Both sub-Saharan Africa and South America, other than a few exceptions, are now almost free of interstate armed conflicts. These improvements mainly occurred after the end of the Cold War. Internally, over the last 30 years, developed countries have experienced large drops in the rates of homicide, assault and robbery.

These improvements in peace have not been linear. The deterioration in overall peace in recent times highlights the uneven pace of change, sometimes improving dramatically and at other times deteriorating. This is consistent with the idea that countries and regions can enter vicious or virtuous cycles, and these cycles can run for decades – even centuries – and underscores that the world does not move uniformly or even in the same direction. At the end of the Napoleonic Wars, Europe thought that it had put war behind it, only to erupt 100 years later into the worst violence in its history.

But even if the arc of history does seem to bend towards greater peace, it would be unwise to be complacent. Future improvements are not assured.

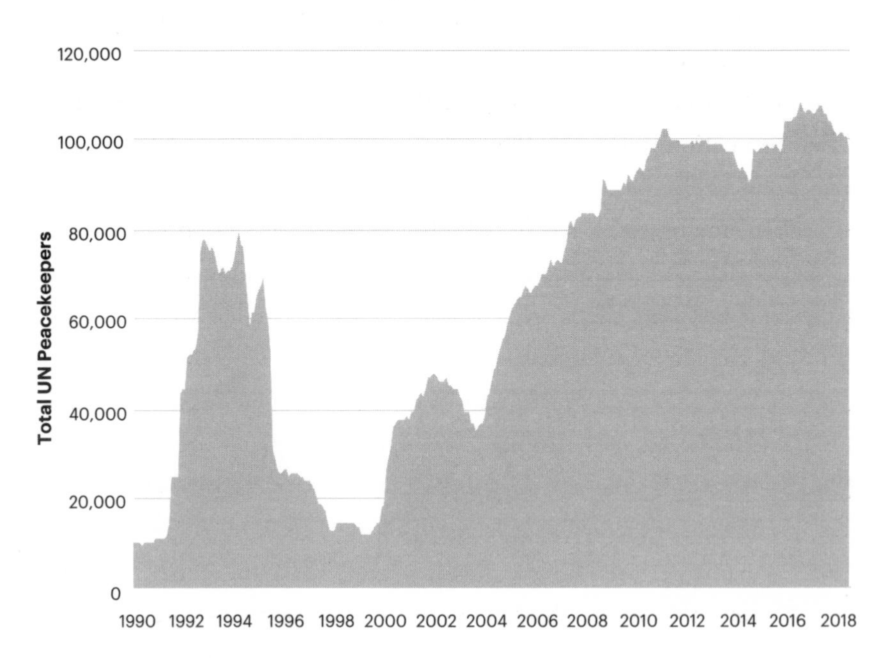

SOURCE: IEP GLOBAL TERRORISM INDEX 2019

The re-emergence of China as a major global power after more than 300 years of eclipse by the West is challenging the status quo in unpredictable ways. Similar problems could arise from the reassertion of Russian power over its neighbouring states, or an erratic and aggressive foreign policy by the United States. Ecological threats are rising, driven by over-population, lack of fresh water and climate change, to name some.

Technology – from cheap and reliable small arms, to nuclear intercontinental ballistic missiles – is changing the nature of conflict, amplifying both the ability to kill and the potential to expand the theatre of conflict to encompass the globe. Guerilla movements have become more lethal, and terrorism more effective. There may not necessarily be more terrorists, but they have found more effective ways of extending their reach with more effective tools at their disposal. Similarly, the issue for the modern army is not the invasion, but how to build peace afterwards. Iraq, Libya and Afghanistan are testaments to this. The nature of conflict is being redefined in ways that make it potentially far more deadly but also more difficult to win. Armed conflicts are increasingly targeting civilians. General Sir Rupert Smith describes this 'war amongst the people' as the next step after war between nation-states, which arguably reached its zenith in World War II:

> War amongst the people is both a graphic description of modern war-like situations, and also a conceptual framework: it reflects the hard fact that there is no secluded battlefield upon which armies engage, nor are there necessarily armies, definitely not on all sides. To be clear this is not asymmetric warfare ... War amongst the people is different: it is the reality in which the people in the streets and houses and fields – all the people, anywhere – are in the battlefield. Military engagements can take place anywhere: in the presence of civilians, against civilians, in defense of civilians. Civilians are the targets, objectives to be won, as much as an opposing force. Nation states, especially Western ones and Russia, but others too, all send in their armies, their conventionally formulated military forces to do battle – to have a war – in these battlefields, and they do not succeed.[5]

The haunting images of cities such as Mosul and Raqqa after the fall of Islamic State – the destruction of homes, and families trapped as human shields to slow advancing troops – are testament this.

Corruption and peace

The IEP's analysis has uncovered some crucial but little-understood relationships. The correlations between peace and corruption are particularly interesting.

---

5 R. Smith, *The Utility of Force*, Penguin Books, 2005, p. 3.

Corruption can be defined as the abuse of a position to gain an undue advantage. This might occur through a range of channels, such as government, business or community relationships. Corruption may also result in the generation of wider community tensions, undermining peaceful relations. Corruption creates a highly inefficient economy, as resources do not go to the most efficient companies, the best people are not hired, and bad projects will get the green light ahead of the good projects. It is impossible to miss the substantial impact of corruption on the lives of ordinary people.

Some of my earliest experiences with development aid underscored the devastating effects that corruption can have on peace and development. We would regularly hear stories of police who would only work on a crime if the victim paid them, of judicial systems run as Dutch auctions or worse, where the police were the organised crime syndicate. Many years ago in Myanmar, one of the staff working on one of our projects had his bicycle stolen. He knew who'd taken it but the police wanted a certain amount of money to work on the case. He paid it. The police then told him to go and collect the bicycle from the thief. The thief then paid the police to avoid charges. For the thief it was a cost of doing business, for the police theft was a business. Their wages were so poor they needed to supplement their income. I have learnt that what is considered corruption varies greatly between societies.

Corruption is a relative phenomenon. If anyone thinks that the West is free of corruption, they need look no further than the electoral system and how many election campaigns are funded by big business or unions. If anyone thinks commercial political donors do not expect a return on their investment, they are naive. The issue of corruption is complex and inherently layered with moral values and judgements. In many countries, tax revenue is far less than what is needed to fund basic government services such as education and the healthcare system, so teachers and doctors go into business for themselves. They need to so as to feed their families.

In Kenya in the early 1990s, we were looking at improving the buildings in a school. I like funding infrastructure because the result is tangible and leakage can be kept to a minimum. In this case, I couldn't understand why the headmaster was being paid over ten times what the teachers were receiving. The teachers were only getting $100 per month, which was hardly enough to live on.

When I asked about it, no matter what angle I came at it from, I would always be deflected. It was only many years later that I realised why it had happened. School principals had less opportunity to charge for their services. The types of charges teachers would make would vary from country to country and school to school. In one school that I came across, students had to buy their desk when they started, and they did not get the desk back when they left. In some schools, teachers had monopolies on selling pencils, pens and workbooks to students. In others they would give private tuition to help students get high grades. These deals are known as 'facility payments'. The moral dilemma is: What level of service is a community willing to go without to avoid corruption and how compromised are the services through these facility payments?

The primary problem is that students from the richer families, who can afford the tuition, get better marks – and so become eligible for good jobs with the government and industry – while bright but poorer kids struggle. It is easy to see the loss of national productivity from these practices and their potential to fuel anger. This puts ordinary Africans in a Shakespearean dilemma: they must decide whether to pay the facility payments, or to fight against a sea of corruption. For most there isn't much choice: the strength of the encoded norms protecting this kind of corruption makes it all but impossible for an individual to change the system, and refusing to participate denies one's children what better education offers.

Another common practice in many developing countries is 'Cha money', which is most commonly a charge placed by the police on motorists. This is where the police stop cars at random and fine them. What they ask can be as blatant as: 'Will you help me feed my family today?' The money is then taken back to the police station and divided up among the officers. From one angle this could be seen as a middle-class tax, but in most developing countries it causes a lot aggravation because of its unfairness.

The customs of societies are far from universal and the ways people relate to each other differ greatly. This is especially true for Africa: if a person in authority does not give to family, relatives and clan, especially when it comes to jobs, they are considered a bad person and run the risk of being cut off from their families. The emphasis of the social structure is on looking after those you are closest to. In the West we call it nepotism, and the more blatant forms are frowned upon, but think of the number of second- and third-generation family politicians our systems support. We don't see too many second- and third-generation CEOs in publicly listed companies. But in Africa it is simply how things must be done. This creates a distinct dynamic in the society, albeit an extremely inefficient one.

What this suggests is that making moral judgements about petty corruption can be counterproductive. If there is some moral ambiguity in a teacher or a police officer supplementing their inadequate salary, it becomes significantly clearer where corruption drives violence.

Corruption within the police, the judiciary and the military is especially bad for peace. After a certain point police become so corrupt, they become enablers of violence, rather than preventers, and from there it is a short step to becoming perpetrators.

Corruption within the military can be particularly destabilising, causing conflicts to last longer than necessary and turning killing into a profit centre for corrupt generals and their suppliers.

Iraq provides a useful example, with the corruption within the military being one of the key reasons for the ineffectiveness of the Iraq military in fighting Islamic State in 2011 and 2012. Supplies disappeared, pay was stolen and commanders got their promotions through bribes, leaving an army that was literally and metaphorically ill-equipped to fight. This quote from a November 2014 *New York Times* article underscores the extent of the problems:

> One Iraqi general is known as the 'chicken guy' because of his reputation for selling his soldiers' poultry provisions. Another is the 'arak guy,' for his habit of enjoying that anise-flavoured liquor on the job. A third is named after Iraq's 10,000-dinar bills, 'General Deftar,' and is infamous for selling officer commissions. They are just a few of the faces of the entrenched corruption of the Iraqi security forces. The

> Iraqi military and police forces had been so thoroughly pillaged by their own corrupt leadership they all but collapsed in the face of the advancing militants of the Islamic State – despite receiving roughly $25 billion worth of American training and equipment over the prior 10 years and far more from the Iraqi treasury.[6]

This highlights the devastation that corruption can have on the military, and the devastation a corrupt military can have on peace.

However, the relationship between corruption and peace is not linear. Rather, after a certain threshold is reached, the institutional degeneration is such that society starts to break down more rapidly, resulting in a collapse of legal frameworks and formal and informal codes of conduct. On reflection, this should not come as a surprise. Once police corruption passes a certain point, law enforcement activities become more likely to increase crime rather than decrease it. This is because the police start committing crimes. They become involved in organised crime, for example, joining the drug gangs in Mexico, or are simply uninterested in solving crimes and are only focused on enriching themselves. In some Mexican towns and cities, organised criminals have taken over the local police departments, subordinating them to servicing their illegal business interests.[7]

Our research has shown that there is a distinct tipping point (see Figure 15). At first, increases in corruption result in only a minor impact on peace. But that effect gathers momentum rapidly once a certain level of corruption has been reached, after which small additional increases in corruption tend to have a disproportionately harmful effect on peace.

About 64 countries, approximately one-third of the countries in the Global Peace Index, are at, or near, the tipping point. Although there is no strict empirical definition of what constitutes the tipping point, it is possible to make a generalisation based on the data as depicted in Figure 15. There is a closer relationship between internal peace and corruption than external

6 David Kirkpatrick, 'Graft hobbles Iraq's military in fighting ISIS', *The New York Times*, 23 November 2014.

7 Jan Martinez Ahrens, 'Mexican president dissolves municipal police forces in bid to stop drug gangs', *El Pais*, 28 November 2014, accessed at elpais.com/elpais/2014/11/28/inenglish/1417180109_334639.html

FIGURE 15

Corruption and peace

Increases in corruption have a small impact on peace until a tipping point, after which small increases in corruption result in substantial falls in peace.

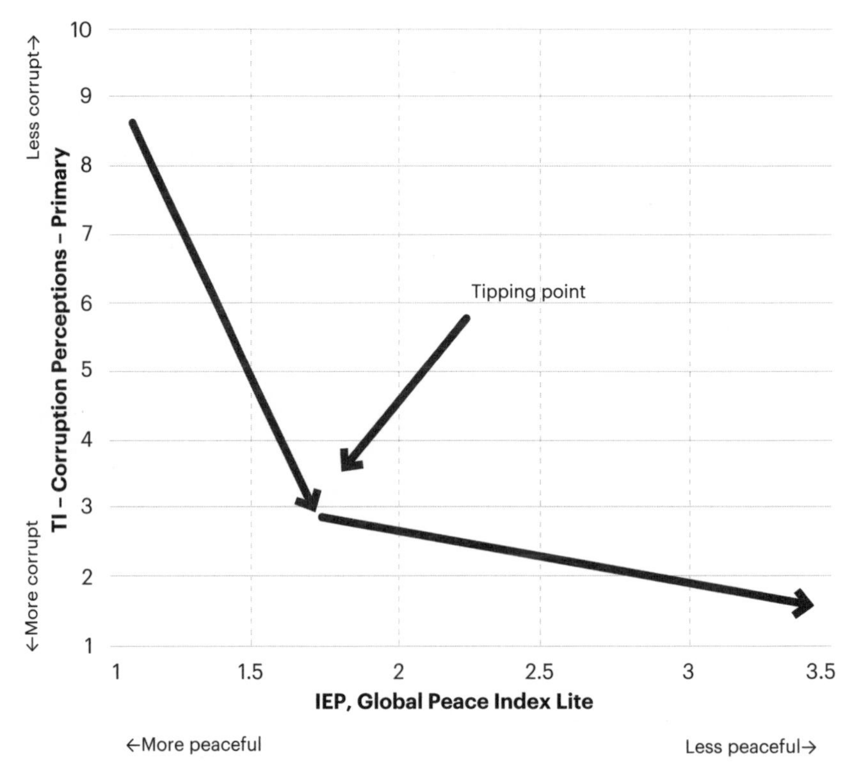

SOURCE: IEP; TRANSPARENCY INTERNATIONAL

peace, which suggests that corruption is more corrosive to the internal working of a country than its external relations.

Our research has found that eight internal indicators from the Global Peace Index deteriorate dramatically once a country moves through the tipping point. These indicators are political terror, political instability, the violent crime rate, violent demonstrations, organised conflict, access to small arms and light weapons, the homicide rate, and the level of perceived criminality in society.[8]

8 Institute for Economics and Peace, *Peace and Corruption*, 2015.

An example is Mexico, which has high levels of perceived corruption. In 2019, roughly 70 per cent of Mexicans thought the police were corrupt, and a similar percentage thought the judiciary was corrupt. This leaves Mexico alongside such countries as Kyrgyzstan, Myanmar and Mali.

High levels of police corruption result in the significant under-reporting of offences because of the distrust of law enforcement. In Mexico it is estimated that only three per cent of extortion and five per cent of rape cases were reported and investigated in 2019.[9] Similar patterns are seen in Colombia and the Central African Republic, where high levels of police corruption correlate directly with some of the world's highest homicide rates. As the perceptions of police and judicial corruption increase, trust in these institutions decreases. The level of safety worsens, and criminals are able to operate with impunity.

Corruption problems are widespread. The IEP's 2015 *Peace and Corruption* Report used Transparency International's 2013 Global Corruption Barometer and found that 60 per cent of those interviewed globally believed that the police are corrupt or highly corrupt. This was highest in African countries such as Malawi (95 per cent) and Liberia (94 per cent). Latin American and Caribbean countries do not fare well either. Some of the more problematic countries were Mexico, Jamaica and Venezuela. All have high homicide rates and high levels of violent crime. At the other end of the scale are European countries such as Finland (five per cent), Denmark (nine per cent) and Switzerland (13 per cent). All have strong levels of internal peace and very low homicide rates.

When countries become more peaceful and less corrupt, a virtuous cycle comes into effect. As the percentage of crimes solved increases, the trust in police also increases. If police forces improve their capacity to prosecute crimes, then trust in both the police and the judiciary improves. Conversely, a lack of trust in legal frameworks will lead to citizens not feeling safe and modifying their behaviour accordingly.

Although not as highly correlated, judicial corruption is also statistically significantly associated with higher crime. Its effects can be pernicious when

9 Institute for Economics and Peace, *Mexico Peace Index 2020.*

it is widespread because it increases the opportunity for violent offences to go unpunished, and those with money are free to commit what crimes they like. This sets in train a vicious cycle, creating greater incentives for violent offenders. This in turn creates more crime, which leads to more bribery.

Some lessons can be drawn from our research about the best political system for building internal peace and containing corruption, but there are exceptions. Democracies seem to perform best: there are no full democracies within or below the tipping point, although some in Europe are approaching it. At the same time, a number of countries, such as Singapore, Qatar and the UAE, are classed as authoritarian, yet score well on both peace and corruption.[10] No political system on average performs better than democracies. For countries near the tipping point there is a mixture, with 20 authoritarian regimes, 25 hybrid regimes (authoritarian regimes with some democratic processes) and 19 flawed democracies.

The relationship between tax revenue and corruption is key. One of the most effective ways of tackling corruption and enhancing internal peace is to increase the efficiency of the tax revenue in the country to levels where it is possible to pay civil servants a living wage.

The most corrosive type of corruption is grand corruption. This is where senior members of government grant concessions in return for bribes. One clear example is the building of roads. If a company bribes a government official to build a road it significantly inflates the cost and the company can use whatever materials it likes. Rather than creating a road with a 20-year life it builds one that needs continuous repairs and has to be replaced early.

'Purchasing' a monopoly through bribes reduces free-market competition, thereby reducing supply and increasing the cost of goods, as well as materially impacting the nation's productivity. There is little difference in the West when governments sell off assets that are effective monopolies. Just check the price of a coffee in a privatised airport compared to a shop outside the perimeter. Monopolies control prices.

Probably the best example from my own experience was in a north Asian country which is still recovering from the Vietnam War and its legacy

10 Institute for Economics and Peace, *Peace and Corruption,* 2015.

of landmines and unexploded ordnance. We were offered a project to clear landmines in the vicinity of a long stretch of dusty rural road. On reflection we decided the project was not cost-effective. However, a European charity did decide to do it. The minister in charge asked for ten per cent of the project's value. Naively, the charity paid the sum. Once the project was complete the government surveyor came back and apologised, saying that he had given them the wrong road. The charity, even more naively, said, 'OK, we will do the right road.' Then the minister said that he wanted yet another ten per cent. At this point the charity declared, 'No, it's your mistake, not ours, why should we pay you again?' The following week all the funds in the charity were seized by the government for tax irregularities. The road was never cleared. Such is the nature of systemic corruption. My approach with my charitable affairs has been never to pay a bribe and never to let the government get control of the money.

Still, in relation to facility payments and social customs, it makes little sense to approach them from a Western moral perspective. The encoded norms around corruption are difficult to change, are built into the social fabric, and are only understood when approached in a systemic way. We cannot, or should not, make universal pronouncements about morality. What we can say is that such practices are not good for efficiency or fairness.

A hypothetical example I use regularly to highlight the moral dilemma of corruption is that of emergency aid for feeding people in conflict situations, such as Syria. If, for example, 50 per cent of the food was taken by war lords along the way, most people would say that was unacceptable and would not to do the project. It costs about 30 cents a day to keep someone alive, and with a reasonable level of nutrition. However, if I said that I could keep people from starving for 60 cents a day most would consider it a reasonable investment.

Peace and urbanisation

The Global Peace Index can shed light on mega-trends, one of which is urbanisation. It will be one of our biggest challenges over the next 50 years.

Half the world's population already lives in cities, and that is expected to climb to two-thirds by 2050.[11]

One of the more interesting findings of the Index is that the higher the level of urbanisation, the more peaceful a country is likely to be. This is contrary to many people's perception because in most countries crime rates are higher in the city than in rural areas, leading to the understandable assumption that the more people who live in cities, the higher the per capita crime rate. One only needs to think of the favelas in Brazil or the slums of Nairobi.

Cities can be beneficial for development, especially when it comes to improving economic opportunities. Our research suggested that the transition to higher levels of peace seems to be a by-product of industrialisation and that the process of wealth creation and improved governance dampened violence in both cities and the countryside. As people move to cities crime does increase, but the offsetting effect from the increase in wealth is a reduction in overall violence. Prosperous cities tend to offer higher levels of safety and security. There is a statistically significant correlation between the percentage of a country's population living in urban areas and that country's societal safety and security score.

But cities can also be places where there is heightened interpersonal and collective violence. Rates of homicide and violent crime are typically higher in large cities than in rural areas. In Central and South America, the majority of homicides take place in cities of greater than 50,000 people.

To understand these contradictions, the IEP set out to define the relationship between a country's level of urbanisation and how it affects its levels of safety and security. The results are an object lesson on why focusing on a single factor, in this case urbanisation, as a possible cause of a high or low level of peace can be misleading. Instead, it is necessary to understand the system, and how various factors interplay.

We found that high levels of urbanisation are associated with more violence when scores on the rule of law, intergroup grievance and income inequality are poor.

---

11 'World's population increasingly urban with more than half living in urban areas', United Nations, 10 July 2014, accessed at www.un.org/en/development/desa/news/population/world-urbanization-prospects-2014.html

Countries with stronger measures of Positive Peace can manage increasing urbanisation better. By contrast, countries with lower Positive Peace measures of rule of law, intergroup grievance and income inequality risk a deterioration in their societal safety and security scores as their levels of urbanisation increase. The quality of the rule of law has the largest effect on safety and security scores.

Many assume that violence in cities is largely due to social stratification, but the data does not necessarily support this assumption. There are many things that do not prove to be statistically significantly associated with safety and security in the context of urbanisation. These include: the rate of urbanisation, the level of trust in a society, discrepancies in occupational outcomes or educational levels between ethnic groups, uneven economic development between groups, the quality of the infrastructure, adult literacy, gender inequality and youthfulness.

This is an important insight for development policy. If maintaining peace is the number one priority, then knowing what is not likely to be a challenge to peacefulness can help give policymakers a clearer guide to what they should concentrate on when attempting to create peaceful urban environments.

The findings that emerge from this are that urbanisation needs to be well managed, and that during periods of mass migration, the focus must be on addressing the underlying drivers that cause urban violence to rise as much as on economic development, including rule of law, intergroup grievances and income inequality.

The good news, especially given the momentum towards urbanisation, is that increasing the population of a city will not inevitably lead to more violence. Instead, it will very much depend on many of the factors already outlined.

Globalisation versus populism

Advanced Western democracies appear to be at a turning point, and the US may be at a tipping point. As political systems are captured more and more by powerful interest groups, the virtuous cycle of improving peace, wealth and freedom that started at the end of World War II appears to be stopping. In some cases it has moved into reverse.

Globalisation has given millions of people the opportunity to work their way out of poverty. Between 1990 and 2013, nearly 1.1 billion people moved out of extreme poverty, cutting the global poverty rate from 35 per cent to 10.7 per cent, according to the World Bank.[12] However, in the developed world the benefits of globalisation are being captured by fewer and fewer people. Political parties that historically worked to deliver broad social equality have narrowed their focus to the politics of identity, leaving many poorer citizens feeling that they have been abandoned by the political mainstream. Too often the mainstream parties now represent the values of liberal elites and have little connection with the bottom 25 per cent of society who are struggling in a world where their job security is evaporating, their income is falling, and their stress levels are rising.

Modern political campaigning is becoming increasingly expensive and the source of the funds for electioneering is coming mainly from companies and wealthy individuals. Many of these companies donate to both sides of politics to hedge their investment in furthering their own interests. This trend seems to have no end in sight. The rise of populism is a natural by-product of this divergence between the interests of the political elite and the upper middle class and the needs of ordinary people.

In many ways, 'populism' is a bad word to describe these movements as they tend to be guided by many principles. The driving forces behind Trump, Brexit or the Alternative for Germany are different; however, they do have one factor in common: they are against the established order and are seeking dramatic change.

But these populist movements will struggle to deliver on their promises. Their policies are mainly aimed at channelling displaced anger towards immigrants, big political structures such as the EU, or Muslim groups. Even if it were possible to 'solve' these issues, it would do nothing to solve the decaying living standards of the working class. Research by the Economic Policy Institute in the United States, for example, shows that real hourly

12 'Poverty', The World Bank, 2 October 2019, accessed at www.worldbank.org/en/topic/poverty/overview

rates for low-wage workers declined by five per cent between 1979 and 2013,[13] while the cost of living more than tripled.[14] There has been some improvement in the minimum hourly rate in recent years but it is not enough to make up the difference. The recent uptick in wages will be short lived. The high levels of unemployment caused by COVID-19 will depress wages for some time to come.

Looking at Denmark, Australia and the United States through the prism of the Pillars of Positive Peace gives an insight into the deteriorating dynamics of what are broadly believed to be some of the world's most successful societies. The Positive Peace score for each of these countries has deteriorated over the last decade. Gender rights have improved in all of them. However, broader measures of government effectiveness have fallen in two of these three countries, while *Group Grievances* have increased in all as well. Freedom of the press, which is the cornerstone of *Free Flow of Information*, has fallen. *Low Levels of Corruption* – another Positive Peace Pillar – has also deteriorated in all three countries, while factionalised elites, which are a measure of political tensions and political competition, have also become more prevalent in all three.

Fixing these problems will be neither easy nor simple. It requires a fundamental change in the way policy is conducted and the way society envisions itself.

Interconnected world

We live in an interconnected world: pollution on the eastern seaboard of China affects the air quality in Los Angeles. In this world, governments need to broaden their policy horizons beyond the narrowness of national interest.

Globalisation is not new. Global trade as a percentage of GDP only exceeded what it was just before World War I at the beginning of the

13 Lawrence Mishel, Elise Gould and Josh Bivens, 'Wage Stagnation in Nine Charts', Economic Policy Institute, 6 January 2015, accessed at www.epi.org/publication/charting-wage-stagnation/

14 American Institute for Economic Research, Cost of Living Calculator, accessed at www.aier.org/cost-living-calculator

21st century.[15] Nineteenth-century colonialism was a global phenomenon. But in this phase of globalisation, the degree of interconnection is considerably more intense. As Michael Spence, a Nobel Laureate in Economics and Professor of Economics at New York University's Stern School of Business, says:

> There is plenty of incentive for countries to collaborate, rather than using trade, finance, monetary policy, public-sector purchasing, tax policy, or other levers to undermine one another. After all, given the connectedness that characterises today's globalised financial and economic systems, a full recovery anywhere is virtually impossible without a broad-based recovery nearly everywhere.[16]

Many governments do acknowledge that providing aid is a moral imperative, and there is a commitment from developed countries to provide funds. However, since the end of the Global Financial Crisis, aid commitments from the developed world have fallen, and have become as much about advancing national economic interest as helping the less fortunate. Yet such aid, which is essential, tends to be narrowly focused and all too often aimed at alleviating the symptoms of poverty and distress rather than their causes. Investing in Positive Peace, by contrast, would address an underlying global set of problems as well as helping the national economic interest. It would help build an environment that addresses many of the other challenges that aid is meant to solve, thereby creating the conditions for human potential to flourish.

The global debate – changing perceptions

The growing worldwide media response is evidence of the increasing global interest in peace. However, it begs a fundamental question: If so many people are interested in peace, why is so little invested in creating sustainable peace, when compared with the massive investment in containing violence?

---

15 Ronald Finlay and Kevin O'Rourke, *Power and Plenty: Trade, War, and the World Economy in the Second Millennium*, Princeton University Press, 2007.

16 M. Spence, 'A World of Underinvestment', *Project Syndicate,* 20 May 2015.

For example, in 2016, $1.7 trillion was spent on national militaries, $1.3 trillion was spent on internal security, and only $7 billion was spent on peace-building operations. That is a ratio of $428 for every dollar spent on building peace. If peace is a global issue and a global public good, surely it is possible to find global mechanisms for proactively investing in solutions to minimise these expenses? It's almost impossible to argue with the logic that if violence could be prevented then why not make the investment?

But as obvious as the solution might seem, there are powerful and deeply ingrained political reflexes that work against it being adopted as widely as it needs to be: many politicians are unaware of the cost-benefit advantages; political leaders get more mileage out of managing problems than they do out of preventing them; and frequently there are very real difficulties in calculating the nature, timing and scope of preventative interventions.

The key to overcoming these challenges and changing the paradigm is convincing politicians that promoting peace is cost-effective, and the first step is to produce accurate estimates of cost. Most rational leaders understand an economic argument.

To help educate the public on the economic advantages of proactively building peace we decided to include our cost calculations in all our major publicity campaigns, including the many briefings given to governments and multilaterals. It has been heartening to see the take-up. Many global leaders have now quoted our research on the cost of violence, including Ban Ki-moon, the past Secretary-General of the UN, and the current Secretary-General, António Guterres. Also, it's been included in US draft legislation. This creates the basis for a more rational debate, allowing the proponents of peace to counter the emotional appeals with facts.

But the difficulty of achieving this can be seen by the attraction of law-and-order politics ('getting tough on crime'), with the inherent assumption that voters respond more reliably to fear than hope. I was dumbstruck by the Western Australian state election in 2017. It was a tight election and the Deputy Premier decided to launch a campaign to get tough on crystal methamphetamine, a highly addictive drug known as 'ice' in Australia. She wanted to spend an additional A$175 million on a 'war' against ice, including tougher penalties – she suggested 15 years minimum jail for street dealers; building more jails to house them; increasing the funding to the judiciary to cover the additional casework; and increasing the number of police specifically focused on drug crimes. Out of the $175 million, only $2 million was going to be spent on prevention programs. The desperation of this campaign became apparent on the day of the election, when the government was decisively defeated because of a range of issues.

The key question is how to create low-crime societies with less need for suppressive government actions. For true progress there needs to be a fundamental change in the way society determines the best path for its development. This brings us back to Positive Peace. In democracies, politicians usually follow what they think people want. So the key in Western democracies is to inform and encourage the general public to be truly interested in peace: to show the public that, more often than not, going to war for peace is as self-contradictory as it sounds; that peace is more than an absence of conflict; and that peace can be fostered and strengthened by policies that are within reach of any government.

To do this globally will require a significant realignment of national and international interests. If governments are to make a significant investment in peace they must expand beyond their national focus and commit themselves to the collective good. South America, for example, has largely reduced its military capacities on the back of treaties negotiated between many of the countries. Interstate conflicts in Africa are much rarer than they were 30 years ago. Peace is possible, but both the elite and the general populace must understand its benefits.

CHAPTER 12

Building resilience through peace

Positive Peace can enhance many aspects of society beyond reducing the likelihood of conflict. As mentioned, one of its foremost qualities is higher resilience by strengthening the societal factors that allow societies to adapt to change, absorb shocks and then recover from them.

Positive Peace is an excellent tool to understand and measure the adaptive capacities of a society – its resilience to most shocks – which in part is determined by how a society is structured and the way people relate to each other.

An example is resistance movements (see Figure 16). Although none of the indicators in the Positive Peace Index measures internal conflict directly, there is a clear relationship between the levels of Positive Peace and dissent. Countries with higher Positive Peace tend to have fewer civil resistance movements.

Why? Because countries with high Positive Peace environments are geared towards adaptability and this is what creates resilience. And the key to adaptability is compromise. Countries high in Positive Peace allow more avenues for discussion and change.

Such adaptive abilities can be seen with the example, already cited, of Iceland's exceptional response to the Global Financial Crisis. When the crisis hit, Iceland suffered the worst banking collapse relative to the size of its economy in economic history, effectively making the country bankrupt. However, Iceland happens to be the most peaceful country on the Global Peace Index and with very high measures of Positive Peace. It was able to make some heroic adjustments.

Greece, by contrast, is less resilient. It has a lower level of Positive Peace, and lower levels of internal peace. It was still struggling to adapt some eight years after the crisis.

The vulnerability of the world to stresses created by the financial markets will not go away. The level of debt globally was 320 per cent of global GDP in 2020. This figure has increased substantially since the Global Financial Crisis and as the economic effects of the COVID-19 crisis work their way through the system much of this debt will be unsustainable. Governments will be seeking debt relief, as will corporations and individuals. There is only a certain amount of debt relief that can be granted before banks and governments become insolvent.

It is difficult to picture just how much more the global debt will have blown out after the COVID-19 crisis, but what we do know is that the new funds and support packages being deployed by governments are massive.

Superior adaptability can also be seen in Japan's response to the devastating 2011 tsunami, when the Japanese people demonstrated an exceptional ability to work together. Many even handed in cash that they had found to the authorities after the tsunami. Japan is in the top 20 countries on Positive Peace and in the top ten of the Global Peace Index.

Compare this with Haiti, which ranks 144 in the Index. When a magnitude 7.0 earthquake destroyed the capital in 2010, killing over 300,000 people and making one and a half million people homeless, the country was unable to respond effectively. Despite $8 billion in international aid, armed criminal gangs re-emerged to prey on the victims, the health system all but collapsed, leading to a devastating cholera outbreak, and seven years after the earthquake 55,000 people were still living in camps.

This is why it is important to understand whether nations and communities are becoming more or less resilient. The countries at most risk of economic loss, violence and societal breakdown will have the lowest levels of resilience and Positive Peace factors in place. Nations with low levels of Positive Peace are less likely to remain flexible or 'pull together' and rebound in the face of crisis.

The concept of resilience and the related ideas of stress, strain and fracture are mainly derived from engineering. An object put under stress can return to its original shape. However, depending on the materials the object is made of, the type of stress and the length of time it is under stress mean that it might not return to its original position; if so, then it is suffering from strain. The material will not perform as well in the future and will become brittle. Apply further stress, and it will eventually break. The additional stress that causes the fracture may be minimal. This is analogous to a tipping point.

Something similar applies to societies. The extent to which they can bounce back is reflected by their Positive Peace rating. A country weak in Positive Peace will find it more difficult to return to its previous state than a country strong in Positive Peace. Eventually, if the stress is strong enough the system will fracture, leading to societal breakdown. All societies can break down: it depends on the level of stress. However, the stronger the resilience – Positive Peace – the lower the risk and the quicker the recovery.

An example of this kind of fracture is happening around Lake Chad in Central Africa, which provides the livelihood for some 30 million people. Years of drought – the number of rainy days in northeastern Nigeria has declined by 53 per cent since the 1970s – combined with the over-extraction of water for agriculture have led to the lake shrinking from 25,000 square kilometres to 2,500 square kilometres between 1963 and 2013. It is little surprise that the three countries dependent on it – the Central African Republic, Chad and Nigeria – are all are affected by conflict. Lukas Rüttinger writes in his report *Insurgency, Terrorism and Organised Crime in a Warming Climate*:

> Around Lake Chad climate change contributes to resource scarcities that increase local competition for land and water. This competition in turn often fuels social tensions and even violent conflict. At the same time, this resource scarcity erodes the livelihoods of many people, aggravates poverty and unemployment, and leads to population displacement. Non-state armed groups, in particular Boko Haram, thrive in this fragile environment.[1]

---

1 Lukas Rüttinger, *Insurgency, Terrorism and Organised Crime in a Warming Climate*, Adelphi, 20 April 2017, accessed in www.climate-diplomacy.org/publications/insurgency-terrorism-and-organised-crime-warming-climate

The differing effects of stress on countries becomes evident when considering resource constraints, such as lower water tables in the most populous parts of the world, the continual increase in the number of people on the planet, or the overuse of the planet's bio-resources. The impact of these challenges will not hit all parts of the world evenly. Countries such as Japan, Australia, New Zealand, North America, and much of Europe, will fare comparatively well because they are rich, not overpopulated and, with the possible exception of Europe, able to protect their borders. In countries that are overpopulated and the birth rate is high, there are likely to be very deep problems.

The relationship between stress and Positive Peace is especially evident when there is drought. In societies with high levels of Positive Peace, such as Australia, structures are in place to bring the necessary aid and assistance to farmers, and to find other food sources where needed. Economic support to primary industry also means that business recovers more quickly. In nations with weak Positive Peace, such as many in Africa, that rarely happens even when resources are available. Consequently, drought often has a more devastating impact.

Some of the countries most affected by water shortages include China and India. Parts of Africa are also affected.

It is likely that falling food production and lack of water will directly and indirectly trigger extreme levels of migration and leave more vulnerable societies with less adaptive capacity and at risk of implosion.

India has to use trains to transport water. In 2016, when the west of the country suffered the worst drought in decades, a daily tanker train travelled 340 kilometres to deliver half a million litres to the approximately 300,000 people in Latur, in Maharashtra state,[2] where summer temperatures average a sweltering 41°C.

I received an email recently from Julia Francombe, the founder of Kenyan-based Samburu Trust, which helps nomadic Samburu tribespeople, especially in the areas of ecological and water conservation, health and education. We

---

2 Atikh Rashid and Manoj Dattatrye More, 'How India's longest water train is coming to Latur', *The Indian Express*, 17 April 2016, accessed at indianexpress.com/article/india/india-news-india/how-indias-longest-water-train-is-coming-to-latur-2756820/

have been working with the Trust to build dams to supply water for Samburu cattle and for the wildlife in the region. Julia had just spent a month living in the cattle camps – each one home to some 600 warriors and up to 20,000 head of cattle – to gain a clearer picture of how the Samburu were coping. The email graphically illustrated how the Samburu people and the Trust had bolstered the coping capabilities of the Samburu to confront prolonged and severe drought.

She wrote:

> I'm just back from the north, have been out with the warriors and cattle for over a month, I needed to see and experience what was really happening for myself.
>
> These incredible young guys wake up every morning and do the best that they can do in that moment. They share what food and water they have on that day. They are well armed, well organised and doing a pretty incredible job with the cattle. They meet every evening, hours spent discussing their next move: where to go and what to do. It is incredible to experience.
>
> To see little kids – five years old responsible for 30-plus calves – whose existence depends on the cattle and they also depend on the kids. When the calves show them the way home they drink their urine as a form of appreciation. It's impossible not to get lost in a flat landscape, covered in thick bush. An incredible bond at a very young age – their survival depends on each other. The guys go to water every two days – the bush is thick and everything is thorny. The blessing is there are lots of leaves and seed pods bunched under the bushes which is what the cattle are surviving on.
>
> There has since been a little rain – enough to bring the grass up 3 or 4 inches but not really enough for the land to recover. The rain seems to have stopped – it is nowhere near enough yet. We are praying for more.
>
> Further up north in the district of Laikipia it is pretty hectic. The Pokot have moved in and are fighting. They have killed wildlife by the thousand – burnt houses – it is a level of violence no one in the

> area has experienced before. The Kenya Defence Forces (KDF) are now well established and clearing the area together with Police – every two or three days there is some sort of battle or shootout. As of two days ago the army have been rounding up and impounding cattle. Today the Pokot have begun to hand in illegal firearms and cattle have been released. Over 120 people have died.
>
> The Samburu stood down when the KDF arrived on the scene – they have been avoiding conflict and have not fought the defence forces yet.
>
> As security deteriorates the price of food increases, if they are lucky to get it at all. As an example, the price of sugar is now over 250ksh [a kilo] in the Samburu markets – (less than 100ksh in Nairobi). The bottom has fallen out of the livestock market, teachers have not returned to schools – it's a spiral. Communities are surviving by cutting sandalwood, which is illegal but fetches a high price. With everything else going on it's not a priority for security forces, they are just unable to police it. That in turn is depleting the rangeland further.

The Samburu were suffering, but they had managed to escape the worst of the fallout from the drought because they, unlike the Pokot, had improved their levels of resilience. I am always amazed by the capacity of humanity, its resilience. But the catch seems to be that in most cases it only comes out in times of peril. We don't seem to be good at planning for events that will inevitably happen. Climate change is a testament to that.

Ideas of stress, strain and fracture are, of course, only metaphors. Analogies between physics and the social world must be approached with some caution. In physics the outcome from a certain level of stress usually follows a mathematical formula. In societies the outcomes are much harder to predict, not least because people are aware of what is happening and can either adapt and minimise the problem or exacerbate it.

India's water problems could be minimised by promoting more sustainable water use, particularly reducing the use of groundwater – the water table in some countries such as India is sinking by 0.3 metre a year. There are simple solutions, such as minimising rice and sugar cane farming in drought-affected areas. The problem is seldom developing plans or even funding them. Rather, the problems are systemic and baked into society's structures – it might be dealing with powerful farming groups or the inability to get cooperation between political parties. Whose budget will the funds come from and what are the general principles defining what is considered equitable sharing of the water and how much should be charged for it?

What we do know is that in a global environment in the Anthropocene era, resilience takes on a greater significance than before. We also know that Positive Peace provides a mechanism for building resilience and a framework for approaching development so that it is tackled holistically.

Failed states

The importance of resilience as a goal has yet to be fully appreciated. The international community's approach to weaker states over the last 50 years has tended to be based on a desire to promote stability. This has often meant backing regimes that use force to maintain peace. In the end, this has proved unsustainable. At some stage, weaknesses appear in the system, after which it runs the risk of imploding.

Generally, the Western decision-making process has focused on: Who can we work with? How can we build their power? A much better option would be to aspire towards Positive Peace.

Failed, or failing, states present one of the greatest challenges to global peace. Once countries pass a certain point of failure, it becomes all but impossible to stop a vicious cycle of descent, cascading through ever-worsening levels of violence.

In these situations, our research has shown that the first priority must be to buy time by establishing security. This can be done through peacekeeping operations, internationally brokered peace treaties, power sharing, or other mechanisms. Once that is achieved, the next step should be to build resilience. Our research has shown that after security, the two most important factors to address are *Corruption* and *Group Grievances*. What is important is not to aim for perfection but just to improve on what the situation was beforehand. Once the system has been stabilised, then the focus needs to be on developing all the eight Pillars of Positive Peace.

Positive Peace offers a road map to achieving a greater degree of predictability, but it is not a linear progression. Rather, it is like a series of events affecting each other. That is because complex systems are subject to constant feedback: small inputs may have large effects, while large inputs may have only small effects. Forecasts become unreliable because systems do not always react in the same way, even when they are subject to the same forces.

Everything depends on the unique balances within the individual society.

When a country reduces its levels of violence, it creates savings that can be invested in ways that improve peace, thereby setting off a self-reinforcing virtuous cycle, providing it's invested properly. Conversely, if there is an increase in violence it will be costlier and make it even harder to prevent more violence.

Security and the state

Since the terrorist attacks of 9/11 in New York and Washington, the emphases on internal peace have changed. There is a far greater concentration in the developed world on maintaining higher levels of security, which has often led to the increasingly intrusive use of surveillance technology, as was graphically demonstrated with Edward Snowden's revelations about National Security Agency activity.

This singular focus on security, although necessary, comes at the expense of other areas of Positive Peace. It can be seen in the impact on the *Free Flow of Information*, for example. In response to the threat of terrorism, many countries are introducing laws broadening the secrecy around government intelligence operations. In Australia it is now an offence for journalists to report on 'special intelligence operations', with penalties of up to ten years in jail. The breadth of 'special intelligence' is wide, with the government being able to include many government activities under this law. There is no public interest defence available to journalists. There is nothing that would prevent the prosecution of a journalist even if they inadvertently disclosed information about such an intelligence operation in the course of their normal reporting.[3] This means that if the government so wished, it could suppress any information on, for instance, a corruption case if it decided it was in the national interest, and the facts would not see the light of day.

For many countries such developments are likely to continue. Surveillance will remain a cornerstone of their violence containment strategy, involving both national security agencies and the police. The darker side of all of this is that if and when governments take a dislike to a group, they will have enough information and power to stop the group if they so wish.

Peaceful civil resistance movements might be stopped if a government thought they was against its interests and easy to do. This could include environmental groups, anti-corruption initiatives, civil rights organisations or other groups opposed to the government policies of the day.

Allegations of governments spying on nations they consider their friends, including their leaders and their businesses, are well documented and have been extensively covered in the global media. That narrative is interpreted in many different, and often opposing, ways. The adoption of more aggressive security legislation, for example, is seen by some as a justifiable and necessary mechanism in the fight against hidden enemies, such as terrorists, while others regard it as the removal of basic citizen rights. Both sides are able to construct coherent narratives to support their position.

The prevalence of such conflicting stories reinforces the point that enhancing security can be effective, but it comes with costs that ripple through the system. Removing the underlying conditions that give rise to conflict, as best as possible, would be a much more pragmatic approach.

Positive Peace and civil resistance movements

It is worth understanding why the suppression of civil resistance movements can be particularly corrosive to peace. When viewed from a systems perspective, civil resistance movements are a response to a persistent mismatch between inputs, a government's encoded norm and its actions.

3 P. Dorling, 'Security laws bring us closer to the day when journalists will be jailed for reporting', *Sydney Morning Herald*, 17 March 2015, accessed at www.smh.com.au/federal-politics/political-opinion/security-laws-bring-us-closer-to-the-day-when-journalists-will-be-jailed-for-reporting-20150317-1m0zc6.html

The input may be complaints against the government, or protests over corruption or dissatisfaction with high food prices, or lack of action on climate change. The encoded norm may range from suppression to simply ignoring the situation, to using propaganda to attempt to change people's perceptions.

The situation will be exacerbated by the actions of the government, if the encoded norms respond like the ones mentioned here. In some cases, the encoded norms do not work to create homeostasis or balance. Instead, they create a runaway mutual feedback loop, where the government's response aggravates the situation, leading to more of the same. Think of the 2019 demonstrations in Hong Kong. As the government increased its pressure on the demonstrators the demonstrations ramped up, resulting in the government exerting even more pressure. Another example is a government imposing controls on the price of rice to keep consumers happy, provoking farmers to organise protests; or the suppression of religious identity, resulting in a backlash that could be expressed through riots, the vandalism of government buildings or the formation of new political movements.

Once a civil resistance movement has started, the system might move towards some form of self-modification. New encoded norms may be formed that suppress the input or, alternatively, integrate the civil resistance movement by addressing its main grievances. Some examples of positive change are the rise in gender equality or the Northern Ireland civil rights movement. Occasionally the encoded norms fail to manage the challenge and the system breaks.

Suppression prevents the system from self-modifying by blocking the inputs that encourage adaptation. Countries high in Positive Peace provide the formal and informal encoded norms that lessen the likelihood of movements arising in the first place. When they do, they strengthen the adaptive capacity to channel the change positively and nonviolently.

The higher the Positive Peace rating, the more likely the outcomes will be nonviolent and grievances will be reconciled. Countries with higher levels of Positive Peace, when faced with resistance movements, are less likely to experience extreme violence, and are more likely to successfully negotiate

FIGURE 16

Prevalence and nature of resistance campaigns

Countries high in Positive Peace have fewer civil resistance campaigns and are far less violent.

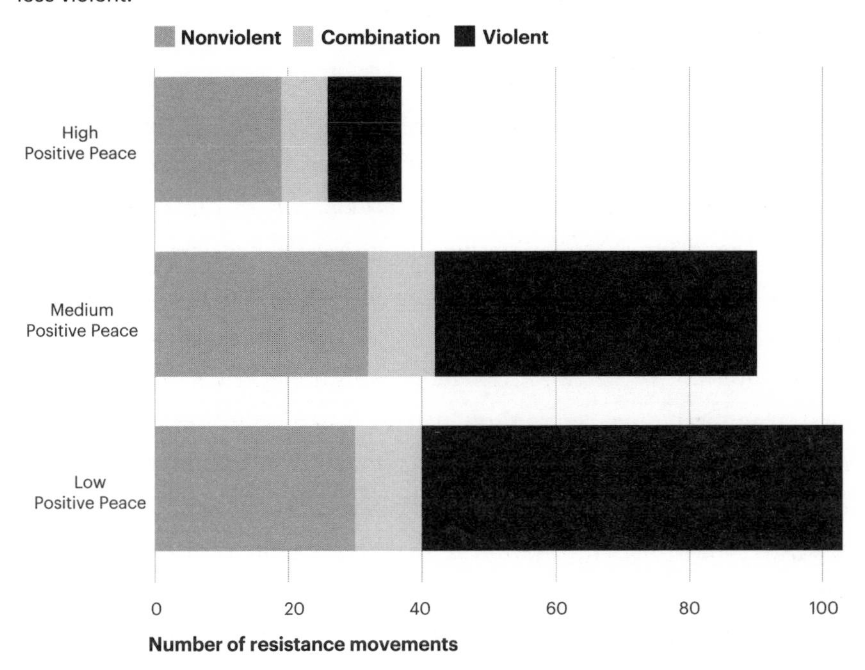

SOURCE: UNIVERSITY OF DENVER, IEP

mutually acceptable outcomes. The system rewards, and therefore creates incentives for, nonviolence. This is seen in the relative success of nonviolent campaigns in high Positive Peace countries. In addition, other coping mechanisms come into play when Positive Peace is strong.

Globalisation

The creation of worldwide systems of trade, transport and communications has sped up the transmission of ideas, goods, information, capital and people. Distance means less than it did, even when compared to 20 years ago. Developments such as greater social, political and economic activity across borders and regions, and a greater interconnectedness of trade, investment, finance, migration and culture are all clearly discernible. However, modern geopolitical phenomena, such as globalisation, cannot be adequately understood as a single, overarching narrative.

Different perspectives give rise to very different narratives: the same phenomenon can mean different things to different people, especially when they come from different cultural backgrounds. Second-generation Mexican Americans would have a different view from fifth-generation Texans, for example. The rise of China as a global power would be viewed very differently by a Chinese business executive and a local fisherman from Thailand competing against factory fishing vessels. Indeed, that is one of the features of globalisation, namely a collision of various communal or national narratives.

Globalisation has come with many positives, such as common standards and rules, but has also led to rising nationalism, especially in countries that feel they are losing their national identity, for instance the United Kingdom. This loss may be heightened by immigration, for example, or the loss of national controls through broader regional organisations, such as the EU or free trade.

To understand globalisation, therefore, we must create a picture of what is happening that is as accurate and impartial as possible. Globalisation is often viewed through an economic lens. We need to move beyond this single narrative, towards a more holistic understanding of the flows of ideas, values and technologies between cultures. We need a better understanding of the system. That is what the Positive Peace Index is designed to do. By integrating thousands of datasets – each statistic reflects many individual stories – it is statistically possible to build a more holistic and systemic picture.

Common mistakes

If there is one lesson to take from the Iraq War, it is that winning a war today requires more than just military might; it is necessary to win the peace as well. When that country, and ultimately the region, descended into extreme levels of violence, it left many in the West doing a lot of soul searching. Images from 2003 of a triumphant President George W. Bush on the deck of the aircraft carrier USS *Abraham Lincoln* with the 'Mission Accomplished' banner in the background highlight the absurdity of the view that even massively superior forces alone can bring peace in the modern era. To achieve a reasonably peaceful political outcome there has to be much more than just the application of lethal force.

The US leadership's lack of understanding of what was needed to achieve peace meant that their concentration was focused on a set of initiatives designed more for its domestic audience than on any proven framework. As it turns out, it failed. Iraq and Syria have disintegrated. First al-Qaeda in Iraq and then its successor, Islamic State, turned the entire area into a war zone.

This dire outcome should not surprise. It is difficult to create peace after a military invasion if a large proportion of the domestic population was opposed to the invasion. The Allied Coalition may have seen themselves as liberators, but many Iraqis saw them as conquerors.

As we saw in Iraq, there are usually many groups that believe they will profit through creating dysfunction. Sometimes they will have criminality in mind; sometimes it will be about trying to control territory. It is true that unless there is basic security there will be no peace. However, basic security is only the first step. The way in which it is created also has to be sustainable. It has to be crafted in a way that will enhance the factors that contribute to Positive Peace. In Iraq in 2007, the US-led coalition managed to produce a semblance of peace with a combination of more troops and buying off the Sunni militias with cash and weapons. But the peace was an illusion and quickly failed. The same weapons and money given to the militias helped to fuel the rise of Islamic State, along with the corruption that became endemic within the government.

Another perennial problem revealed by the Iraq War is the presence of influential vested interests. After the initial advances, many companies, usually with good contacts inside the Washington beltway, lobbied to get large contracts for reconstruction or violence containment. For most of them, creating peace was secondary to creating profits.

Failing to adapt to different cultures, or to understand how they work, is another persistent problem. If the government gets the military to build a girls' school in Afghanistan should anyone be surprised if the school becomes a target? This is not to say that one should not push for social evolution, but imposing social revolution can provoke massive opposition from local communities and hurt the very people the program was trying to help.

To overcome these problems local buy-in is essential. Positive Peace provides a framework from which to conceptualise change, but local people must be allowed to fill in the details of the approach. Only they possess the necessary cultural sensitivity to ensure the system adjusts along a viable path. Wherever possible, change should be incremental, as this creates the least risk. What is important is the direction and momentum of the system, as systems are self-perpetuating. Is it moving in the right direction and with enough momentum?

In conclusion

The pace of change is accelerating. It is fuelled by many factors: new technologies, scientific breakthroughs, global sustainability challenges, and a more interdependent global community. They all contribute to a bewildering sense of impermanence. With the geopolitical changes of the last few years, we now see old allies cast as unfair competitors, and many Western nations facing internal pressures unlike anything experienced in the past 40 years. The after-effects of the COVID-19 pandemic further question the readiness and structure of our systems.

In many ways we are struggling to reconcile our political and philosophical models with these changes that are being thrust upon us by the sheer scale and pace of human activity. The only real certainty is that humanity's future will not resemble its past. New approaches will be vital for humanity's adaptation to resource constraints.

Even our perception of the centrality of human existence in the universe is challenged as our knowledge of space increases. It is estimated that there are 100 octillion stars, or one with 29 zeros after it – this poses a powerful challenge to our belief systems. It is simply impossible that our species is the most important creation in such an immeasurably vast universe.

The breathtaking insights of science seem to be opening up almost limitless possibilities, but they are also deeply disconcerting. Scientific discoveries in fields such as quantum mechanics, synchronicity and entanglement are causing our basic concepts of time to break down.

At the same time as this expansion in human knowledge and capabilities is occurring, we are facing limits we never have imagined. It is becoming clear that societies built upon the exponential increase in the consumption of finite resources will not be sustainable. Where are the international, or national, initiatives funded by governments to find ways forward? Sadly, many governments seem invested in stopping change. Just look at the international response to climate change, especially in countries with large fossil fuel bases. Look at the responses to the COVID-19 pandemic – many nations moved too late, others stopped their media from commenting on it and the unpaid debt left over from the Global Financial Crisis meant kick-starting the economies became more difficult.

New ways of managing human affairs are needed, but in many ways, the system is struggling. Locked into homeostasis, where the system is unable to make the necessary modifications for meaningful change until it is forced upon it, by which time it is often too late.

This is where systemic Positive Peace gives a new philosophical approach and theory of change that can provide a practical approach to better adapt and manage change.

The Industrial Revolution went hand in hand with the Enlightenment. Natural philosophers such as David Hume, Voltaire and Adam Smith reshaped the conceptual world in ways just as profound as steam power, cotton gins and iron-rolling mills reshaped economies and society. This intellectual revolution is missing in our current age. The current economic and social system is predicated on the assumption that the principal purpose of life is to work so as to make money. This world view has limited value and even less appeal, especially when many people's living standards are shrinking. We need to embrace a new philosophical landscape. One that gives humanity meaning within the expanded universe, a framework that is sustainable, and which moves towards a culture that extends the concept of value beyond the mere monetary to embrace the whole sphere of humanity and the environment we live in and depend upon.

It is largely accepted that globalisation and rapid technological change have created the need to adopt some universal principles that can unite us. Economic and philosophical models are required that are predicated on basic human values, and that cut across different religions, cultural norms and ideologies.

Yet it is surprisingly difficult to identify what those universal values should be. Freedom is considered a universal value. But is it? All societies have limits on freedom, some more justified than others. For example, what is considered a tolerable level of nudity varies greatly between societies. Freedom from inequality may seem like a universal value, but is it equality of outcomes or equality of opportunity? We may consider certain human rights to be universal, but who decides what those rights are and how they are conferred? Justice is a legitimate universal value, but what is considered to be just in one culture could be considered unjust in another. What is considered an acceptable level of violence also varies. Think of the disciplining of children: the level of acceptable corporal punishment varies greatly from one society to another.

Peace is clearly a candidate as a universal value. Almost no reasonable person would want to suffer from violence. Therefore, peace is a legitimate aim of a society, whether the system is democratic or authoritarian. It is one of the few areas about which there is general assent.

To investigate peace as a universal value, however, we must have a genuinely universal picture of what it is. That means moving beyond stories that are, by their nature, partial. They are mostly told from one point of view: tales about goodies and baddies that depict grievances from one quarter without considering the grievances of the other quarter.

We need to redefine peace in more dispassionate terms, to create an Olympian view that is big enough to take into account varying cultural norms. That is what Positive Peace helps to provide. It may not be the totality of a new philosophy appropriate for our age, but it does provide the context and backdrop from which a new phase of thinking can arise and gain traction. It also provides an excellent starting point, which is practical and can be used today, both at the national level and also locally, even in a school.

When peace is accepted as a universal value, we can get a glimpse of what the new politics could be like. In the half-century up to the end of the Cold War, politics was defined by the competition between communism and capitalism: two opposed versions of materialism. It was a divide underpinned by the threat of extreme violence in the form of opposing nuclear arsenals. That divide has largely collapsed, with the break-up of the USSR and the rise of capitalism in Russia and China, leaving something of a vacuum that is quickly being filled by new forms of authoritarianism, national self-interest and a shift away from multilateralism. However, many of the tensions addressed by the old ideologies remain and we do not have the philosophical framework to capture what a new flourishing conceptualisation of humanity can be. One of the beauties of the terms 'left' and 'right' is that they were neutral terms, implicitly in balance. What is the new dialectic that will enable us to discuss the new challenges of a new age?

What will be the future fault lines for global issues? One of these dimensions is appearing. It's a fallback to past glories and values, nationalistically based with an 'us versus them' mentality. China wishes to erase the 100-year humiliation and again be the centre of the world, while the United States' mantra is 'Make America great again', and many of the new European political parties are emphasising national identity above all else, even at the expense of higher prosperity. In a resource-constrained world this competition will lead to national winners and losers, but most likely even the winners will be seriously worse off.

Systemic Positive Peace provides a way forward, one that creates the most likely avenues for adaptability in a resource-constrained world in need of management and connectivity. Without peace we will never be able to achieve the levels of trust, cooperation and inclusiveness necessary to solve our global challenges. Therefore, peace is a prerequisite for the survival of humanity as we know it: wars between nations will destroy infrastructure on an unparalleled scale, while nuclear weapons, even on a limited scale, will leave many parts of the world uninhabitable.

On the positive side, human beings have shown an ability to deal with disruptive change. Humanity has also exhibited a slow but steady ability to create greater, more peaceful conditions over millennia. The problem is not that we are faced with disruptive change, but that we are faced with waves of disruptive change on so many fronts, and that our ability to deal with it must be enhanced.

More importantly these changes are of our own making. Increasingly, we are bringing into existence these massive changes, even though the physical, environmental and political outcomes of our actions are frequently not what we intended. The law of unintended consequences often turns our dreams into nightmares. In these Anthropocene environments that we humans are creating, two aspects become critical – our capacity to deal with rapid change and our ability to manage the ecosystems of the planet.

Adaptability and resilience will be the key. Positive Peace is both the measure and the solution for these. It provides a mechanism to understand which countries are most at risk. These future shocks could be financial, biological, ecological or societal. Given the right severity of shock all countries will implode, but with an understanding of the likely shocks and levels of resilience, development can be better targeted. Through building up the Positive Peace factors a country's resilience can be enhanced, thereby improving its adaptability and responsiveness when shocks do occur. The examples of Haiti and Iceland illustrate the effects of high and low resilience and adaptability. Haiti after the earthquake received billions in aid with little effect; Iceland received IMF loans after the Global Financial Crisis, but it restructured its political system and five years later was thriving.

Systems thinking and the nation – new ways of conceptualising

The scale of the issues confronting humanity is truly daunting, and our current approaches are simply not working. The truth is that the complexity of many of these problems is beyond our ability to grasp. The most talked about problems of our era have been climate change and, more recently, pandemics. Many countries have impressive records in reducing emissions but these countries are in the minority. Most are still stuck, their systems unable to adapt to the threat even when the majority of their citizens believe it to be real. This is only one problem, there are many more.

Systems thinking does provide a solution, a new way of conceptualising our world, our societies and how politics should function. It circumvents the complexity by focusing on the flows and relationships within the system, rather than individual actions or events.

At the heart of this new view is that complexity cannot be understood by breaking problems down into ever smaller and smaller bite-size chunks. The application of systems thinking to societies is a recognition that the whole is greater than the sum of its parts, and that emergent phenomena like peace or climate change are irreducible. Positive Peace provides the vision of where to take the system. In terms of changing the system, small steps are needed, but they should be continuous and there should be many of them, thereby nudging the system into a virtuous cycle. Change needs to be gradual but constant, which reduces the risk of systemic failure. Large changes increase the risk of collapse or unforeseen consequences, particularly if the society starts from a base of low resilience.

To be able to achieve this reality we need new leaders, who are capable of grasping a positive future with an inspiring vision, who are not hamstrung by the politics of fear. These leaders will need to be brave and above all literate in a new language encompassing concepts such as Positive Peace, systems thinking, and the limits placed on humanity because of the Anthropocene.

The leaders of the future will need more empathy than the leaders of the past, because without it the stark choices of the future will only lead to more suffering. The secret to good leadership is more than one's skill level; it's one's commitment to the morals of leadership, especially empathy. With empathy, leaders will move beyond their own self-interest and think of the long-term best interests of the societies they are governing. Modern politics is mainly dominated by two types of government. Western-style democracies that are plagued by short-termism, or entrenched autocratic to semi-autocratic leaders who are obsessed with maintaining the status quo. Moving beyond these two modes will prove difficult, but for a sustainable future and a politics of flourishing it will be extremely important.

In writing this book I have aimed to build a compelling vision for the future, one that is based on fact, one that is positive, but above all one that is based on a profound understanding of the interdependencies between individuals, their societies, their relations with other societies and their utter dependency on the larger ecosystems that we partly inhabit. Positive Peace provides a mechanism to restructure our societies so that they have the capacity to adapt and modify to the changing environment of the Anthropocene. Change does not mean upending societies; it means continuously nudging a society in the desired direction. Small changes, but many of them, limit risk. Resilience will be important as societies struggle with the pace of rapid change. As we have read, Positive Peace is an excellent measure of resilience.

Peace can be a rallying cry. The desire for it is as old as society itself. It is a positive aspiration for many of the best qualities of human beings and lies at the heart of all major religions. But more importantly, we now have a much better understanding of how to achieve it and an approach that is actionable.

Index

Figures are indicated by page numbers followed by '*f*'.

D

E

F

O

P

Q

R